LEADING TEAMS

Tools and Techniques for Successful Team Leadership from the Sports World

Paolo Guenzi and Dino Ruta

A Wiley Brand

To Stefania, Sofia, and Elena: the team I love most. And to all of our fans!
Paolo Guenzi

To sport, a metaphor for life.
Dino Ruta

The authors have decided to donate their royalties from this book
to the charity La Gotita – www.lagotitaonlus.org

CONTENTS

CONTENTS

FOREWORD

Born in 1965 in Imola, Stefano Domenicali has been the team principal of the Ferrari Formula One racing team since January 1, 2008. He has played a major role in Ferrari's victories in the Formula One championships during the 2000s. After initially overseeing development of the Mugello Circuit, in 1995 he became head of personnel at Ferrari's sports department, also handling sponsorships. In late 1996 he took over as team manager. After serving as head of logistics, from 2002 until 2007 he became sports director, supervising every race and handling relations between the team and the racing authorities.

If, in the history of business, there is an emblematic case of the link between sports and business management, that case is no doubt Ferrari: a company born from a sporting spirit that has always closely connected competition with production. This connection is not only economic (production financed the races) but managerial and administrative as well.

This natural inclination in Ferrari by now has become the general *modus operandi* for two basic reasons. First, sports have a major social and economic impact, and, as a result, a series of elements are needed that are not only related to technical and sports specifications, but that are also based on people. These have to facilitate effectively the integration of people with a variety of backgrounds, often with different personality traits. This is particularly important when it comes to high-level sports, where it's not uncommon to find strong individuals who have to be guided according to a group rationale. Second, the evolution of business has given rise to organizations that increasingly require cross-functional work, where everyone is personally invested in reaching the final outcome.

In this book, there are testimonials from people in sports. If we substitute their names with those of top managers, this would be a perfect book for business management. Knowing how to motivate others, to take on responsibilities, to manage the group, to get the best out of talented people, to implement meritocracy: these are key concepts for modern firms where, tellingly, more and more often we hear references to coaching rather than managing people.

The current business model calls for people to have something more than know-how. Competencies are a given: it's about being able to analyze the details, make people emerge, share goals with collaborators and get them on board. These are all attributes that make a firm successful, not to mention continually searching for innovation, and—last but not least—effectively managing economic resources and contending with regulatory restrictions.

These processes are inborn at Ferrari, because the sport and the business grew up together. We've always worked with the restrictions set down in regulations; innovation has always been a prerequisite; and we've always had to contend with finite resources, obviously. The concepts that all the top coaches write about in this book are the norm for Ferrari, even though as sports teach us, you can never stop changing and learning from everyone. The companies or the teams who think they know everything because they win are destined to fail. Today's companies have to strive for improvement and innovation when they're at the top. It's easy to have to change when things are going wrong: you don't have any choice and it's a battle for survival. But it's hard to know how to change, and how to foresee the future when things are going well, when instinct tells you that if you've been successful working in a certain way, the safe thing to do is to keep on going in the same direction.

It's also important not to let obstacles stop you. A defeat has to be an opportunity to start again; you need to turn disappointment into positive energy. The desire to make a comeback, if properly channeled, can be an important driver for innovation. This is one of the many lessons from sports: don't ever think you've made it. Beyond this, on today's global market, with information circulating almost instantaneously, maintaining a competitive advantage is more and more challenging. The only way is to be ahead of the game, to come in first ahead of the others.

There are so many other things to say, including numerous interesting insights from the interviews collected in this book. For example, the importance of being consistent in how you treat your brand, the proper stance to take with the media, and so on. But to conclude, what I really want to emphasize has to do with customers and fans: any company or team that doesn't think about them will be shut out of the market. The offering is vast and there are a wide variety of options, so listening to your public doesn't simply mean collecting data; it's a strategic moment for growth. New media, the Internet above all, let you get immediate feedback on your actions. Listening and understanding the different backgrounds and the relative needs of your public is an opportunity for enrichment, not only from a managerial standpoint but on a personal level as well, whether this involves fans, consumers, or simple enthusiasts.

Stefano Domenicali

INTRODUCTION

Sport can certainly use some managerial know-how and, by the same token, managers have a lot to learn from the world of sport. These simple ideas are the guiding inspiration for our work. We set out to discover if team management models typically used in traditional businesses can be found in or transferred to sports teams, and vice versa. Simply put: what can business executives and sports coaches learn from one another?

To answer this question, we carried out an in-depth investigation of relevant research in both managerial and sports contexts. Then we analyzed the work of coaches, identifying similarities and differences between various sports, and comparing them to the business world. After completing this process, which lasted nearly four years, we selected 13 interviews with coaches from a variety of sports (soccer, basketball, volleyball, rugby, and tennis), and we used transcripts of interviews with 80 coaches in all.

We tried to strike the right balance, applying scientific rigor while avoiding a dull, dry approach to addressing a "light" yet germane topic such as team leadership. That's why our book stands out from all the others on this topic. Some are based on the experience of individual coaches — a useful and interesting approach to be sure, but with the fundamental limitation of offering the perspective of a single person. Other books relate a plethora of experiences, or simply offer a compendium of meaningful quotes from various coaches, but neglect to conduct any systematic analysis.

Both kinds of books provide ideas and insights, but they make no reference to the immense store of knowledge on leadership, team leadership, coaching, and management in general. Why waste this priceless patrimony? Our challenge was to merge the empirical/anecdotal viewpoint that springs from the experiences in (or we should say on!) the field by leaders in team sports with a more "scientific" perspective based on research carried out in academic and managerial contexts, and bring the issue at hand into clear focus.

And so we begin. In Chapter 1 we systematically compare and contrast the worlds of sport and business, to avert any inappropriate comparisons and highlight the conditions that enable us to make useful ones instead. Chapter 2 gives an overview of current thinking on leadership in general and team leadership in particular, to sum up what everyone who's interested in these topics should know. The aim here is to build a solid methodological foundation that can serve as a framework for interpreting our interviews with the coaches. In Chapter 3 we propose an original model that illustrates team leadership both for coaches and for executives. Our model places particular emphasis on credibility at four interdependent levels: individual motivation, team spirit, organizational synchronization, and reputation within the relevant context. Next, using applicable excerpts from interviews with our protagonists, Chapter 4 outlines the key functions and strategic behaviors of team leaders as managers, proposing an innovative perspective and a comprehensive, modern interpretation of leaders in professional sports clubs and in modern society. Chapter 5 is dedicated to team coaching, with special focus on the processes that team leaders implement to promote team motivation. Here, too, we offer dozens of salient citations and "food for thought" from our coaches, which we systematically organize in logical categories and classes of behaviors that have the power to impact team performance. In Chapter 6 we summarize the key passages from conversations with 13 professional coaches; each of them has an exceptional and unique personal story, replete with insight and inspiration. The entire book is interspersed with the words and witness of all 80 coaches, with examples and anecdotes that enrich the content and provide a powerful patrimony of real-life experience, a source that can be tapped by coaches and managers who want to shore up their team leadership skills.

Readers will find pertinent, practical ideas and incentives for proactively developing a more organized, responsible, meritocratic, and collaborative way to work together as a team.

Every book is the conclusion of an adventure and the beginning of a new path, one that we want to share with our readers most of all. So we extend an open invitation to those of you who want to give us your thoughts and reflections, and any ideas and suggestions that can help us gain a better understanding of the worlds of management and sport. Write to us at teamleadership@sdabocconi.it.

We want to express our gratitude to all the people who have contributed to the realization of this book. First and foremost are our colleagues at the SDA Bocconi School of Management and at Bocconi University, who encouraged us to use sports metaphors as a form of innovative learning, giving us the chance to develop a different way to teach management. Special thanks go to all the coaches we interviewed, who offered us their time, their skills, and their boundless passion for their work. And finally, thanks to Michele Martinelli for his brilliant, thought-provoking illustrations that have added so much to the presentation of the contents.

Enjoy the book!

Paolo Guenzi
Dino Ruta

CHAPTER 1

WHY SPORT AND MANAGEMENT?

SPORT AND THE FIRM: IS A MEANINGFUL METAPHOR POSSIBLE?

The sports context is often used as a powerful analogy for analyzing and interpreting phenomena such as teamwork, motivation, and leadership, with professional sports coaches held up as role models for managers. But it's not always advisable to take principles, models, and best practices from the world of sports and apply them to business. Managers often look to sports for inspiration and useful examples for working with a group—but they should be aware of the risks involved in transferring these models to a business setting. Any comparison with the world of sports, if applied inappropriately, can lead to mistakes and end up being ineffective or even counterproductive.

Managers often look to sports for inspiration and useful examples for working with a group—but they should be aware of the risks involved.

Countless books on sports and leadership are based on a premise that is profoundly simplistic: that firms and sports teams are very much alike. Some researchers[1] even assert that soccer represents the ideal management model for modern firms. But it's wrong to assume that parallels can always be drawn and, although business and sports share some similarities, they have deep differences from myriad perspectives.

To transfer ideas from sports to business and vice versa, first we need to clarify the key similarities and dissimilarities between the two.[2]

The main differences between sports and firms

The first thing that differentiates sports from business is the very concept of *performance*, and what makes it good or bad. Bill Parcells, one of the most successful coaches in the history of American football, sums it up well:

> *"This is not a business where we have quarterly reports, or earnings are up 10%. This is a black-and-white business: you either win or you lose. There isn't any gray area. There isn't any, 'Well, you kind of did okay.'"*[3]

In sports, two athletes or two teams may have nearly identical performances in the same competition, but have completely different results. In business, by contrast, a 1% difference in market share would not have a radical implication in terms of winning instead of losing. In sports, you can win or lose an Olympic medal by a few hundredths of a second, or make it to the next round of a tournament or be eliminated by a single point. Luck can often play a decisive role in the career of an athlete or a coach.

If we break this down into *type of performance*, firms primarily pursue profit. In sports, instead, the "bottom line" is competitive performance—not always and not only measured in terms of victories, but also in light of quality of play and ability to satisfy the fans' expectations. Sports clubs have to strike a balance between competitive, financial, cultural, and social results that involve the fans and the values of sportsmanship. Another point of divergence lies in the *determinants of performance* on an individual level, for managers and athletes. In a business context, *talent* is basically defined in terms of competencies and cognitive capability. In the sports arena, instead, talent encompasses both cognitive and mental skills as well as athletic, physical, and technical prowess.

In fact, because of the physical side of sports, the *career* of an athlete is often short lived, rarely lasting past 35–40 years of age. This compressed time horizon also gives rise to crucial differences for coaches, who have to deal with certain vital and unique needs of their athletes. In sports, playing just a few more minutes, or starting in a big game, can be life-changing moments for a player. *Age* is another differentiator of sports and business. Athletes peak at a younger age than managers. Just imagine playing in a soccer World Cup final at 18 or 20: this kind of responsibility calls for special psychological skills that older managers do not normally need. In longer professional business careers, it's the norm for managers to attain major responsibility after the age of 35.

As for *level of education*, in contrast to what happens in most businesses, sports coaches usually find themselves leading teams made up of very young members with little formal education, and dealing with all the related repercussions on team management.

Athletic performance is also subject to high *risk*, due in part to the fact that often only a limited number of major sporting events mark an athlete's career. During these competitions, luck can play a vital role. Injuries are another serious risk; consider the countless world-class athletes who've had to abruptly suspend or even end their careers following a serious injury.

Apart from all these differences, one thing sports and business share is the importance of learning, which takes the form of training in sports, and education and development in business. Both athletes and managers are expected to strive for self-improvement, continually learning new individual techniques and team formations or methodologies. Willpower, intellectual curiosity, the drive to do better, and a sense of commitment are critical success factors for individual performance common to both sports and business.

Given that when we compare sports and management, we usually refer to professional sports with high media impact, we need to take into account the sizeable gap in *level of remuneration*. Athletes can earn enormous sums at a young age, which for young managers would be unheard of. So the challenge that coaches face—managing a pool of players who often collectively earn millions—would be an exception to the rule in a business context.

The public visibility of professional sports gives rise to intense *environmental pressure* from myriad stakeholders, most often fans and the media. Business managers hardly ever experience this kind of pressure, except for top executives in organizations that are subject to institutional controls, such is the case with listed firms. Here is what a former president of Manchester City has to say on the subject:

> *"With football, it's like having at least 40 board meetings a year, where 40,000 shareholders show up, and they all want to have their say."*

This means that athletes, coaches, and sports managers are continually being critiqued by a vast audience, including fans, of course, but in a broader sense encompassing public opinion in general. These stakeholders are far more interested, engaged, and informed than those we'd find in most firms. All this is fueled by the media's habit of spontaneously spotlighting what goes on in professional sports clubs. What's more, everyone can check the sports scores in the paper at least once a week; they're a popular topic of conversation.[4]

Generally speaking, sports also have a more powerful *social impact* than business. While the most influential people in a firm are its shareholders, in the sports world the owners of a club or the organizers of an event often have to contend with a wide array of interests, and find a way to balance and satisfy them all. Players, agents, staff, owners, young athletes on feeder teams, as well as external stakeholders, such as the media, the fans, sponsors, sports regulators, the local community, and on and on—the club has to take into account all these interests, all at the same time. As we can see, with respect to firms, sports clubs have to strike a balance between the often-conflicting interests of wider, more diversified group of stakeholders.

Summing up, then, we've established that there are notable points of divergence between sports and management practices, some of which will never be aligned (see Table 1.1). That said, parallels

Table 1.1 The main differences between sports and business

Key factor	Business	Sports
Performance priority	Profit	Final score
Nature of results	Primarily absolute	Primarily relative to competitors
Interpretation of results	Often subjective, because results can be interpreted using various parameters	Almost always objective, immediate (win or lose)
Talent	Primarily mental–cognitive	Physical–athletic and mental–cognitive
Career	Typically long, protracted over time, normally peaking when managers are older	Typically short, concentrated; often players peak young
Remuneration	Variable, usually increasing with age	Often very high, even when players are young
Level of risk	Medium–low	Often high, e.g. linked to injury or performance in a single major event
Level of education	Medium–high	Low
Social impact	Variable	Often very high
Environmental pressures	Variable	Often very high

do exist that can become sources of reciprocal inspiration between sports and business. But before making any meaningful transposition from one context to the other, first we have to scrutinize both, and verify that substantial similarities actually do exist. To this end, in the following sections we present a number of interpretative models that identify the key factors to consider coming up with comparisons that are truly useful and appropriate.

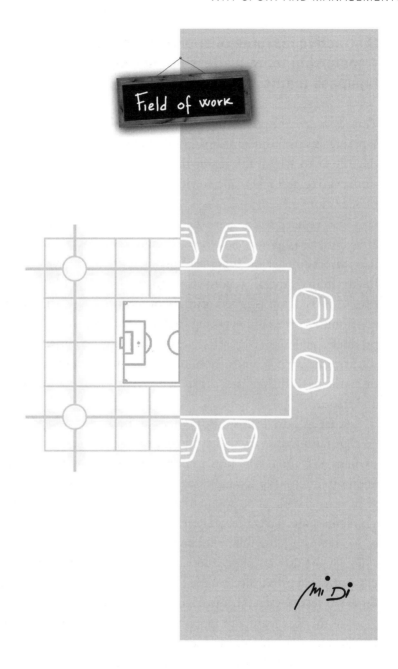

Distinctive features of sports teams to consider for transferring team leadership models and practices to business teams

Transposing concepts and managerial models from professional sports teams to business teams can and should be done, but only to the extent to which the teams in both contexts are alike, sharing similar goals and tasks, and having similar structures and methods of operation, etc.

First we need to compare the teams' *goals* and *tasks*. Sports teams are examples of *performance teams*. Members have a significant, visible, direct impact on organizational results; they have to possess innate ability, as well as motivation, to be successful. Many business teams, instead, are assigned primary or exclusive *tasks* that can vary enormously, for example taking strategic decisions, developing new products, generating creative ideas, planning activities linked to specific initiatives, commissions or complex projects, etc. Both types of teams need different competencies, rules of operation, timing, and resources.

As far as how teams are *structured* and how they *function*, team configurations can vary widely in, for example, terms of size (number of members) and interaction among members (how this takes place and how often). For example, *virtual teams* are often used in firms, with team members occasionally interfacing long distance, usually via technological channels. These teams have little in common with sports teams, whose members normally spend a great deal of time together and do a number of activities collectively. Typically there is close physical proximity and face-to-face interpersonal interaction on sports teams, virtually on a daily basis (for practices and matches).

Another key feature of sports teams is that they tend to be *permanent* groups. As such, they shouldn't be compared to temporary teams such as task forces, unless the time frame for the relative work lasts as long as a season or a sports project. There are noticeable differences in the structure and functioning of teams in business and sports, for example, companies often set up *self-managed* teams. These can't be readily compared to sports teams, which instead are hierarchies with a clearly delineated leadership and coordination role played by the coach.

When considering how teams *function*, sports teams alternate *matches* with *practice*. Obviously, these are two distinct models for team operations: when playing a match, the team's priority is performance, while with training the focus is learning. What's more, sports training takes up far more time than actual competitions. In the business world, we don't normally see such a clear-cut distinction, except for specific occasions dedicated to training, coaching, mentoring, and other initiatives for personal development. But in contrast to sports, as a rule these situations are very few and far between.

In sports teams we typically find both *competition* and *cooperation* among members. Often a priority for athletes is to maximize their personal performance and individual visibility—but this may have negative repercussions on cooperation, which is essential to team success. Similar mechanisms can emerge in the business world as well, depending on the values that are prized in a given organizational culture.

In sports teams we typically find both *competition* and *cooperation* among members.

Unlike most business contexts, sports coaches normally *interact* with members of the team almost on a daily basis. Coaches watch what players do during training and in matches, and get *clear and immediate feedback* on their coaching decisions (for example, the team wins or loses, plays well or badly, etc.). All this happens rarely with business teams.

Sports teams differ widely in terms of *interdependence* among the athletes.[5] The importance of teamwork and the best methods for optimizing it are highly contingent on the interdependence of the tasks that team members perform. This is true for both business and sports. In various team sports, the activities of team members are interdependent to different degrees.

Interdependence reflects how much the activities and performance of an athlete influence (and/or in turn are influenced by) the activities and performance of the other members of the team. Interdependence is the extent to which team performance is contingent on the ability of its members to work in an organized and coordinated fashion. Players are interdependent to the degree that their performance is impacted by their teammates' performance, and the final outcome essentially depends on the interaction between the athletes on the team.

This is true for football, rugby, volleyball, and basketball—all sports with a high degree of interdependence among players. Even though there are champion athletes who act as "game changers" in certain scenarios, individual performance is strongly impacted by the actions of all the other players. In some sports, by contrast, the performance of the team is basically the sum of the individual performance of its members. Examples are relay races in swimming, or the men's Davis Cup or women's Fed Cup in tennis. In sports with low interdependence, integrating and coordinating the activities of individual athletes are relatively inconsequential matters.

In individual sports such as skiing, although activities are not interdependent in the least (because athletes obviously compete on an individual level), there are other forms of interdependence. For example, on a psychological level, interdependence is what pushes athletes to emulate the performance of other competitors in a race, or to copy the commitment of teammates during training. Interdependence also ties into learning, for instance by enabling a skier to hone their skill by measuring themselves against their teammates. We can interpret these forms of interdependence as the influence that teammates have on an athlete by pushing themselves to do better, for example through processes of emulation or reciprocal moral obligation. Naturally, this interdependence is a very powerful motivator, because when an athlete sees their teammates work with intense determination in practice and achieve outstanding results in competition, this may spur them on to strive to do their best. It may also become a demotivator if behaviors not oriented to commitment and competition are adopted by some team members—see the example of social loafing, where athletes tend to make less of an effort if they realize that their teammates aren't doing their best.

Team sports are also very heterogeneous as far as *rules of play* are concerned. For example, a match can end with a draw in football, but not in basketball or volleyball. In some team sports players can continually rotate on and off the field of play during a single game, but in others, because of regulations on substitutions while the game is in progress, there's a clear distinction between first and second stringers. This makes the choice of the starting lineup critical, and allows limited maneuvering room for fine-tuning strategies and organizing athletes during a match. Such dissimilarities strongly shape the priorities and impact methods for managing the group, for example in terms of communication and motivation processes.

Different sports operate according to different models. Since not everything we learn from sports is transferable to the world of business, what's needed is a situational perspective. As a precondition for using sports as a meaningful analogy and a model for firms, first we have to identify the distinctive features of sports in general, and the unique traits of specific disciplines and individual clubs. Then we need to evaluate these contexts, select the ones with similar characteristics, and pinpoint the factors they have in common that we can learn from and transfer to our own business environment.

With this very aim, Keidel[6] analyzed three sports (American football, basketball, and baseball), and then associated each one with a specific business context. For example, considering the nature of the activities relating to each sport, Keidel points out that in baseball, focus primarily lies on individual players, who are highly autonomous in relation to their teammates. In football, on the other hand, planning activities in the different units takes higher priority. These units (e.g. offense and defense) are highly specialized and act

Table 1.2 Variables to consider when choosing the most appropriate sport for an organization to model

Variable	"Baseball" organization	"American football" organization	"Basketball" organization
General nature	Sum of soloists who are largely autonomous and independent	Planning complex but predictable activities carried out sequentially by groups of specialists	Flexibility based on the capacity for self-coordination, speed and autonomous decision-making by interconnected players who are capable of orchestrating organized reactions to unpredictable events
Dominant type of interdependence	Associative	Transactional sequential	Transactional reciprocal
Spatial concentration of team members	Low	Medium	High
Unit of reference	Individual	Group	Team
Main coordination mechanism	Rules of the game and responsibilities of individual roles	Planning and hierarchy	Reciprocal adaptation
Main managerial competency	Tactical	Strategic	Integrative

Focus of development	Individual	Individual and group	Individual and team
Importance of managerial continuity	Low	Medium to high	High
Ease of integration for team members	High	Medium	Low
Possibility of using incentives linked to group performance	Low	Medium, preferably at a group level	High
Need for auto-coordination by team members	Low	Medium	High
Need for team leader (coach) to coordinate team members	Low	High	Medium
Importance of aligning the individual and the organization	Low	Medium	High
Examples of organizations	Sales networks Franchises University researchers	Assembly lines Construction companies	Task force for inter-functional projects Consulting companies Creative agencies

Source: adapted from Keidel (1984)

sequentially but independently of one another during different stages of the game. Last, basketball players need a high level of flexibility and connection; they have to make rapid-fire decisions and real-time assessments to determine the best response to a game scenario that's in constant flux, where it's hard to predict what will happen next. Analyzing the interdependence among activities in these sports brings to light the fact that basketball has high reciprocal interdependence, football has a medium level of sequential interdependence, and baseball has low generic or associative interdependence.

Table 1.2 provides a complete summary of the main areas of focus and specific critical success factors for each sport (and the best match in terms of business models). This analysis is an indispensible prerequisite for linking a given sport to a corresponding business context, and consequently for effectively transferring concepts and experience from sports to management and vice versa. Keidel[7] recommends interpreting sports such as baseball as a model for sales networks, franchises, or university research teams. In these contexts, everyone works toward the same goal, but performance determinants are linked exclusively to the individual. By contrast, American football is the best fit for organizations such as construction companies or assembly lines, where the overall outcome is based on specialization and planning. Last, basketball is the proper metaphor for tightly connected, cohesive teams, like the ones we find in creative agencies and consulting companies, or on task forces for inter-functional projects.

The detailed observations and reflections emerging from our work have prompted us to analyze other sports as well, specifically soccer, road cycling, and volleyball. These three disciplines provide additional analogies we can apply to the multifaceted world of business organizations. For example, soccer is a sport with specialized positions, but at the same time players have to be extremely flexible and know how to organize themselves during the various phases of the game. In other words, every player covers several positions depending on whether the team is on defense or offense, during a play or a penalty kick. This organizational model looks a lot like the one used by small and medium-sized enterprises that deal with a limited number of products or services. These businesses count on their employees to have specific, advanced competencies, along with the capacity to cover a number of roles, given the company's size and its highly interdependent activities. We find similar models in organizations that operate on a project basis in the cultural sphere (festivals, exhibits, etc.). Here, too, employees follow planned processes in their work, but at the same time they have to take an evolving, adaptive approach in response to the needs of the project at hand.

Road cycling presents a different scenario. For this sport, individual performance is far more important than team performance, both in a single race or a leg of a race. Yet the support of the other team members is indispensible to individual success. Organizations that match this model may include large professional firms that employ "captains," i.e. roles with noteworthy competencies and reputations (e.g. lawyers and architects) who have a highly qualified team of "followers." The same analogy can apply to design and fashion companies headed by a designer or stylist who enjoys a prominent market profile and reputation.

Last, in the highly specialized sport of volleyball, activities are carried out in sequence in specific game scenarios within the framework of pre-established plays. The business analogy that best fits this sport is hospitals or emergency rooms, where specialized competencies and formalized processes and procedures have to be continually adapted on a case-by-case basis. Post-sale customer care companies, such as some call centers, also fit the bill. The customer support activities these organizations provide are based on formalized responsibilities and procedures. All the same, employees often find themselves facing scenarios that are new and different, and having to work to earn customer satisfaction while respecting roles and procedures. Table 1.3 summarizes other variables to complete our organizational analysis of these sports.

From the six sports described here, what emerges is the need for "organizational lenses" when analyzing sports. Only by looking through these lenses can we draw correct comparisons and parallels with the world of business.

The differences and similarities we've discussed (see Table 1.4 for a summary) profoundly impact the nature, structure, and functioning of teams, substantially shaping the priorities and the critical success factors of team management.

Consequently, successful leadership models in sports can be used in business contexts, keeping in mind that the greater the similarity between the specific sports and business teams, the more expedient this transposition will be. Managers who look to sports for useful tips to apply to their business should think carefully about which particular sport would best serve as their model.

Some studies on this topic even question whether it's appropriate to compare a business leader to a coach. Kellett[8] analyzed the use of leadership models by professional sports coaches and concluded that coaching in this context and leadership in business management are two fundamentally different things. In addition, Peterson and Little conducted research comparing sports and management, and came to this conclusion:

> **Managers who look to sports for useful tips to apply to their business should think carefully about which particular sport would best serve as their model.**

Table 1.3 Variables to consider when choosing the sport model that best matches an organization: analysis of on-road cycling, soccer, and volleyball

Variable	"On-road cycling" organization	"Soccer" organization	"Volleyball" organization
General nature	Autonomous, specialized soloists who coordinate their actions to achieve individual and team success	Specialized units simultaneously play several phases of the game; flexible, auto-coordinated, and able to adapt to any game scenario	Highly specialized by role (player), actions executed sequentially in specific situations, following pre-established patterns/plays
Dominant type of interdependence	Associative and reciprocal transactional	Reciprocal transactional	Sequential transactional
Spatial concentration among team members	Low	Medium	High
Unit of reference	Individual	Team	Team
Main coordination mechanism	Planning and hierarchy	Tactical modules and plays	Rules of the game and reciprocal adaptation to situations
Main managerial competency	Strategic	Tactical	Integrative
Focus of development	Individual and team	Team	Team

Importance of continuity in management	Medium	High	High
Ease of integration for new team members	High	Medium	Medium
Opportunity for incentives linked to group performance	Medium	High	High
Need for auto-coordination by team members	Low	Medium	High
Need for team leader (coach) to coordinate team members	High	High	Medium
Importance of aligning the individual and the organization	Medium	High	High
Examples of organizations	Professional firms Designers and stylists	Cultural projects: festivals, exhibits, etc. Small and medium-sized entrepreneurial initiatives	Hospitals, emergency rooms Customer care, call centers

Table 1.4 Some variables to consider in evaluating the differences and similarities between sports teams and businesses

Team objectives	• Number, type, compatibility
Tasks of team members	• Number and variety of tasks, nature of activities, level of training for specific roles
Team structure	• Size (number of members) • Team stability over time • Spatial concentration of members • Level of competency (including managerial) • Leadership and hierarchical levels • Time dedicated to training and development
Team functioning	• Level of interdependence among team members • Balancing competition and cooperation • Coordination mechanisms • Frequency and methods for interaction (e.g. communication, feedback) among team members • Ease of integration for new members • Principles for motivation (individual or collective)
Rules of play/ work	• Timing (play time, break time) of sports event • Substitutions

"Certain principles drawn from sports coaching are useful in managerial coaching but the necessary skills and models are fundamentally different."[9]

We believe that we can draw parallels between the roles of coach and manager/business leader, but only when there are similarities among the variables described above.

WHAT MAKES A SUCCESSFUL COACH? HOW SPORTS CAN LEARN FROM MANAGEMENT

We actually know very little about the traits that typify a successful coach: research on this topic has arrived at contradictory conclusions. Research on coaches in US Major League Baseball[10] found that the impact of their skills and competencies (measured in terms of age, years as head of current team, total number of years as a professional Major League coach, career total of teams coached, career percentage of wins, playing experience, and career total of dismissals) on the relative number of team wins is only around 1%, in contrast with players who impact final scores by 67%.

A study carried out on the English Football Association concluded that a soccer team's success depends for the most part on the quality of the players, measured in terms of their estimated market value.[11] Analogous investigation found a strong correlation between players' salaries (as a measure of talent) and team performance. Research estimates that the contribution of a coach impacts approximately 2%, while the amount spent on players' wages accounts for 92% of team performance.[12]

Another study[13] on English soccer demonstrated that, on average, around 80% of sports performance depends on investments made in highly skilled players and technical staff. But this research also shows that, even when investments are equal, there are substantial dissimilarities in team results. Likewise, some teams achieve very similar results to their competitors, on average, although relatively speaking they have invested far fewer resources. The explanation for these differences essentially lies in how the resources in question are employed, a decision that rests largely with the coach.

Research on various English Football Association leagues seems to suggest that the managerial efficiency of a coach (measured by number of wins or points), depends mostly on his prior experience as a player, even more than the total wages paid to players. Specifically, what counts is the coach's prior affiliation with the club he's leading and the international recognition he won as a player, more so than previous coaching experience. We can hypothesize that this previous playing experience equates with deeper technical and tactical knowledge and sharper skill at reading and interpreting complex situations before and during a match. Also, professional players are more willing to listen to a former player/coach, thanks to enhanced credibility and greater trust.

According to a study conducted on coaches in the US National Football League, managerial skill can be measured as the percentage of career wins, the number of years as coach, the number of games as coach, the number of wins in the regular season, coach of the year awards, division titles, league titles, and all-pro players (best player of the season in a given position). The study shows that skill (quantified as above) explains a team's positive performance on offense and defense, and that the lower the quality of players, the more critical the role of the coach's managerial skill. Furthermore, this skill also impacts team performance, thanks to the ability to create an optimal combination of available resources. In short, this study shows that the role of coaches (read managers) in generating value is just as critical as that of available resources (players).

A coach's impact on team performance is also contingent on numerous managerial decisions made by the club, for example how long the coach is allowed to lead the team. A study investigated the longevity of the head coaches of major national football teams over a 13-year period.[14] Findings show that teams tend to perform better when they play for the same coach for an extended period of time.

Summing up, then, it's hard to say if, how, or how much a coach influences a team's track record. Empirical research has attempted to quantify the effect a coach has on team performance in sports, revealing that with few exceptions this influence is very low. The inherent limitation of these studies, however, is that they take a range of personal traits of the coach, and measure the *direct* impact of these variables on performance parameters such as the team's percentage of wins, points scored, or ranking. But the chief influence that coaches have on team performance is actually *indirect*, springing from their capacity to enhance players' performance, which in turn affects competitive results. This influence mainly involves the ability to motivate athletes and hone their skills (technical, tactical, physical, etc.). But even research based on more complex statistical models fails to capture this phenomenon. In short, we argue that if one wants to understand the impact that sports team leaders have on performance, what coaches do is more important than how coaches are. This is why in this book we investigate coaches' behaviors more than their characteristics and attributes.

A point of interest here is a study carried out on the Bundesliga (Germany's professional soccer league),[15] which found that the average number of points tallied up by a coach during his career does not significantly factor into his salary. Similarly, research on Major League Baseball (MLB) revealed that coaches are not paid according to results, but based on their experience measured as age, number of teams on their coaching record, years of experience in the Major League, and number of Coach of the Year awards. This suggests that clubs pay more for experience than for performance outcomes in competitions. From this finding, we can infer that when choosing coaches, sports clubs take into account factors other than a winning record: these may include the coach's public image, media approval rating, quality of play, and alignment with the club's technical/tactical project and its values.

From a managerial standpoint, it actually makes sense for sports clubs to use a variety of parameters in assessing a coach. Beyond wins, they should also consider the coach's ability to raise the bar for the athletes and the team as a whole in terms of performance, and to realize players' maximum potential. Other considerations include profits generated by the team, and the relationship that the coach builds with the community and with the fans. Findings from a study on the Spanish soccer championship[16] show that when coaches decide who to field in a game, the economic value of the player outweighs past performance. A player's game time, in terms of number of minutes played during the season, enhances his value as a resource of the club, because if an athlete doesn't play, the risk is his value will decrease. This tells us that coaches are very much aware of the economic value of their club. There may be a number of explanations for this, including pressure from the club, the media, and the fans, or the weight of a player's reputation, which ties back in to their market value.

We argue that a multiplicity of factors constitute pertinent parameters for assessing coaching performance. Coaches should possess a complex and articulated set of managerial competencies to effectively deal with the complexity of the sports business. Indeed, the rise in business volume in sports is triggering an increase in the organizational complexity needed to improve performance on the field, to win the game, to put on a show, and to satisfy the needs of the athletes, owners, media, fans, sponsors, etc. As an example, a study run for the *Wall Street Journal* by the Boston Consulting Group, on behalf of the NFL, found that to make the Super Bowl (which the New Orleans Saints won in 2010), across 18 games it takes 514,000 hours of work by 53 players, around 20 coaches, 12 scouts, in addition to the managerial support staff.

That's eight times as many hours to get to the Super Bowl than to conceive, construct, and launch Apple's iPod (granted with all the limitations that such a comparison entails). Moreover, in financial terms, even the least virtuous sports club generates higher revenues per employee than Apple, Google, and Goldman Sachs. The business volume of the sports industry is proof of the organizational complexity of this context; complexity which is more and more difficult to deal with because of the rising technical level, the growing expectations of athletes and fans, the number of stakeholders involved, and the extreme environmental pressure. All this underscores the need for a club to hire a coach who has the necessary competencies to deal with all these challenges, either personally or with the support of specialized managers.

TRANSFERRING IDEAS, METHODS, AND PRACTICES FROM SPORTS TO MANAGEMENT: SOME GENERAL GUIDELINES

The fundamental job of the person who takes the helm of a team is to make the team's performance superior to the simple sum of the performances of each team member. To succeed, a coach needs to know how to create the necessary contextual conditions; use appropriate criteria in selecting team members; and organize and manage work so that each member is willing and able to fully realize their potential, and knows how to go about it. The sports context, just like the business world, shows us that it's not enough to have the best human resources that the organization can afford; instead, the true source of success is the ability to hit on the optimal combination for these resources. This depends a great deal on the characteristics, decisions, and actions of the person in charge of the team.

There is a growing propensity among companies to manage processes, to set up inter-functional teams, and to use team-based evaluation and remuneration systems. All this makes it increasingly critical for managers to be able to create team spirit that facilitates and supports inter- and intra-functional integration. The foundations for this integration are, essentially, interaction (i.e. managing communication and information exchange) and a climate of collaboration.[17] People who lead teams can foster integration by acting on values, structures, processes, and people.[18] The number, complexity, and multi-faceted nature of these variables suggests that we should investigate team building and team management processes in their original context, i.e. team sports, from which managerial studies borrowed most of these ideas.

People who lead teams can foster integration by acting on values, structures, processes, and people.

For many managers, the biggest challenge is to incentivize their collaborators in ways that don't involve money, instead focusing on other motivational levers. In the sports world, that's exactly one of the problems that coaches face, because they're not the ones who decide how much to pay athletes. So coaches make an interesting case study for exploring how to motivate collaborators without using monetary compensation; indeed, the lessons learned on this topic from sports can be invaluable to business managers.

Coaches and managers have important things in common. Both roles have a more pressing need for clarity on leadership issues than

WHAT CHARACTERISTICS OF A BUSINESS TEAM MAKE IT MOST COMPARABLE TO A SPORTS TEAM?

1 The team has a clear, visible, direct, and often quantifiable impact on organizational performance.
2 Team members need innate ability, in addition to powerful motivation, to achieve a positive performance outcome.
3 The team is subject to intense pressure regarding its short-term (even weekly) performance, in addition to pressure generated by long-term results (for example, linked to a project or a season).
4 Team members are in direct competition for more resources and greater visibility, although they have to cooperate and collaborate to succeed.
5 Positive and negative results have a powerful effect on the team "climate."
6 The team is perceived as a separate entity from the rest of the organization because of the different way it functions, its responsibilities, and the powerful impact that it has on results.
7 The team has strong bargaining power with respect to its parent organization.
8 Non-monetary incentives are a major necessity for team members.

ever before, in light of the strategic and organizational complexity that sports and firms find themselves contending with.

Given the above, there are several aspects to consider when comparing sports and business teams: goals, structures, rules of operation, timing, and resources. The more similar these variables are, the more it makes sense to draw parallels between the two worlds; otherwise any comparison proves potentially superficial, ineffective, or even misleading.

OUR RESEARCH

Our objective in conducting the research presented in this book is as follows: to identify the competencies that coaches of sports teams use to manage a successful sports project; to frame these competencies in relation to models and theories developed for business; and finally, to evaluate the transferability of these competencies to business contexts.

Below are the analytical path and the expository framework we used for this book.

First, we take a look at the literature on teamworking, leadership, and team leadership, since these topics apply to business as well as sports (Chapter 2, "Management Models of Team Leadership"). From this review, we provide a summary of the current thinking on these topics.

Next, using a qualitative approach, we identify and analyze the main behaviors that coaches adopt to be effective and win games. Our perspective is theoretical modeling through field observation (grounded theory).[19] We collected data by interviewing coaches of team sports, and by exploring secondary sources as well (published books and interviews with the same research objective).

We did semi-structured interviews with current and former professional sports coaches from premier league sports teams or national teams (mostly soccer, basketball, or volleyball). Generally speaking, we asked our interviewees to outline the main behaviors they adopt(ed) to improve team performance. By analyzing their responses, we pinpoint the variables that a coach can leverage to shape team reactions and in turn team performance. We focus specifically on factors that can directly or indirectly enhance motivation, knowledge, skills and behaviors of the team as a whole and individual team members. Moreover, we take an organizational perspective, highlighting factors that can alleviate the pressure from external stakeholders, growing the quality of available resources and information to engender more effective decision-making processes.

Secondary sources include transcripts of numerous interviews with professional coaches published in books and articles. By analyzing this material, we were able to add further examples that slot into categories and theoretical concepts delineated in the literature and identified in the interviews.[20] The words of the coaches exemplify how they behave in relation to many of the areas we explore here, and express their ideas and opinions on how to properly handle specific circumstances.

The material we collected and organized by logical categories/content provides a rich source of anecdotes, examples, and specific real-life references, which we use to introduce, discuss, and comment on the theoretical models and conceptual frameworks developed in the literature.

What emerges from analyzing our findings is a series of key behaviors that we have summarized in an original team leadership model[21] (Chapter 3). Our model offers a framework of reference for coaches and managers who want to learn from each other's experience. This model suggests two main classes of macro-areas of action for coaches:

- Managerial processes for handling relationships with stakeholders outside the organization (e.g. media, fans, etc.) or with people who belong to the organization but are not members of the team (illustrated in Chapter 4, "The Team Leader as Manager").

- Motivational coaching with regard to team members under direct supervision of the coach—in other words, players (discussed in Chapter 5, "The Team Leader as Coach").

In Chapter 4 we detail behaviors that coaches adopt toward various stakeholders outside the team in order to increase available resources, handle external pressure, and generate positive energy within the team. In fact, by effectively managing relationships with key stakeholders (owners, fans, media, staff, etc.), coaches can create a team environment that serves to improve team performance. Examples of ways to do this include leveraging their influence on decisions regarding buying and selling players, on planning team and staff activities, and on the climate created through press releases, obligations toward sponsors, and so forth.

In terms of motivational coaching (Chapter 5), we observe what coaches do when they manage their teams that have a positive influence on team performance, in particular in terms of impact on individual and collective motivation. Beyond pointing out the key functions of *motivational coaching,* we dedicate special attention to managing interdependence and encouraging reciprocal social support among team members. We focus primarily on communication processes between the coach and the players.

Last, in Chapter 6, "Team Leadership: A Word from the Coaches," we pick out some of the more insightful passages from our interviews with coaches that best illustrate the key behaviors we discuss in this book.

SPORT AND MANAGEMENT: KEY MESSAGES

1 Sports and firms have some significant similarities, but also deep differences in terms of:
   • Priority performance goals.
   • Nature and interpretation of results.
   • Key determinants of performance.
   • Success factors.
   • Social visibility of activities.
   • Environmental pressures.
2 These differences directly impact the nature, functioning and critical success factors of leadership in the two contexts.
3 Different sports use different organizational models: managers have to identify the sports and teams that most resemble their own businesses.
4 Management concepts, models and practices of team leadership and coaching can be transferred from sports to business and vice versa, keeping in mind that the more closely the teams in question resemble one another, the more expedient this transfer will be. Similarities involve:
   • Goals.
   • Tasks.
   • Structure.
   • Functioning.
5 There is much that managers in the business world can learn from the sports context, especially regarding ideas and tools that optimize teamwork and motivate members through non-monetary incentives.
6 By adopting methods and tools used in the business context, clubs in the sports world can improve decision-making in many critical areas, for example: recruitment, remuneration, managerial style, and dismissal of a coach.

NOTES

1 Brady, C., Bolchover, D. and Sturgess, B. (2008) "Managing in the Talent Economy: The Football Model for Business," *California Management Review*, 50, 4 (Summer), pp. 54–73.

2 Wolfe, R.A., Weick, K.E., Usher, J.M., Terborg, J.R., Poppo, L., Murrell, A.J., Dukerich, J.M., Core, D.C., Dickson, K.E. and Jourdan, J.S. (2005) "Sport and Organizational Studies—Exploring Synergy," *Journal of Management Inquiry*, 14, 2, pp. 185–210.

3 Fagenson-Eland, E. (2001) "The National Football League's Bill Parcells on Winning, Leading, and Turning Around Teams," *Academy of Management Executive*, 15, 3, pp. 48–55.

4 Devine, K. and Foster, W.M. (2006) "Off-the-Ice Action in the National Hockey League," *Journal of Management Inquiry*, 15, 3, pp. 290–98.

5 Keidel, R.W. (1984) "Baseball, Football and Basketball: Models for Business," *Organizational Dynamics*, Winter, pp. 5–18.

6 Ibid.

7 Keidel, op. cit.

8 Kellet, P. (1999) "Organizational Leadership: Lessons from Professional Coaches," *Sport Management Review*, 2, pp. 150–71.

9 Peterson, D.B. and Little, B. (2005) "Invited Reaction: Development and Initial Validation of an Instrument Measuring Managerial Coaching Skills," *Human Resource Development Quarterly*, 16, 2, p. 180.

10 Smart, D.L. and Wolfe, R.A. (2000) "Examining Sustainable Competitive Advantage in Intercollegiate Athletics: A Resource-Based View," *Journal of Sport Management*, 14, 2, pp. 133–53.

11 Gerrard, B. (2000) *Football, Fans and Finance: Understanding the Business of Professional Football*, Edinburgh, UK: Mainstream Publishers.

12 Szymanski, S. (1998) "Why Money Talks Louder Than Managers," *The Observer*, 22 February.

13 Brady et al., op. cit.

14 Nikolychuk, L. and Sturgess, B. (2007) "Managerial Performance and Contract Instability in the Market for National Football Coaches," *World Economics*, 8, 3, pp. 147–70.

15 Frick, B. and Simmons, R. (2008) "The Impact of Managerial Quality on Organizational Performance: Evidence from German Soccer," *Managerial & Decision Economics*, 29, 7 (October), pp. 593–600.

16 Garcia-del-Barrio, P. and Pujol, F. (2009) "The Rationality of Under-Employing the Best-Performing Soccer Players," *Labour*, 23, 3, pp. 397–419.

17 Kahn, K.B. (1996) "Interdepartmental Integration: A Definition with Implications for Product Development Performance," *Journal of Product Innovation Management*, 13, 2, pp. 137–51.

18 Rouziès, D., Anderson, E., Kohli, A.K., Michaels, R.E., Weitz, B.A. and Zoltners, A.A. (2005) "Sales and Marketing Integration: A Proposed Framework," *Journal of Personal Selling & Sales Management*, 25, 2, pp. 113–22.

19 Glaser, B. and Strauss, A. (1967) *The Discovery of Grounded Theory: Strategies for Qualitative Research*, Chicago, IL: Aldine.

20 Eisenhardt, K. (1989) "Building Theories from Case Study Research," *Academic Management Review*, 14, 4, pp. 532–50.

21 Miles, M. and Huberma, A. (1984) *Qualitative Data Analysis*, Beverly Hills, CA: Sage Publishing.

CHAPTER 2

MANAGEMENT MODELS OF TEAM LEADERSHIP

THE EVOLUTION OF THE CONCEPT OF LEADERSHIP

There are countless leadership models and studies—but as some observers claim, "there is no other topic on which so much has been written but so little said."[1] Scholars and practitioners offer a variety of interpretations and definitions of leadership. The Global Leadership and Organizational Behavior Effectiveness (GLOBE) project proposes this one:

> *"The ability of individuals to influence, motivate, and enable others to contribute toward the success of the organization of which they are members."*[2]

So we can say that leadership has to do with a person's influence on the cognitive, motivational, affective, and behavioral responses of others (followers), who in turn have to make their own decisions and take action. The ultimate aim is to raise the level of both individual and collective performance. But what kind of influence should a leader have? Over whom and what? Why? How?

For leaders, it's imperative to shape the *behaviors* that impact the individual and group performance of an organization. Since group members' behaviors (what they do and how they do it) spring from their competencies (skills and knowledge) and their motivation, the leader can and must leverage these variables in several ways. In this book, after introducing general leadership concepts and models, we turn our attention to team leadership. Our aim is to dispel any misleading interpretations of leadership, what leadership is *not*, to disassociate this concept from some common connotations.

For leaders, it's imperative to shape the *behaviors* that impact the individual and group performance of an organization.

Authority and power are often prerequisites for exercising certain forms of leadership, yet many researchers question whether authority and power are actually distinctive features of leadership. For example, it's not unusual to find people in charge who wield coercive, legitimate, or reward-contingent power—but they aren't necessarily seen as leaders. By the same token, some people are often looked up to in organizations as leaders even though they don't hold a hierarchical position of power or authority. These two factors, consequently, are linked to the context of the organization and how it functions. Leadership, by contrast, is based on an individual's ability to exert some form of influence in interpersonal relationships. Simply put, leadership is about what you do and what you obtain, more than the role and responsibilities you have.

Now we provide an overview of the major streams in leadership studies, later moving on to explore the emerging theme of team leadership.

Leadership as personality, skills, behavior, and functions

Below is a summary of the basic concepts and models in the literature on leadership that are most relevant to our aims.

Personality

The first perspective in this research stream holds that leadership is an innate *personality trait*[3] and, as such, isn't something that can easily be learnt or developed. Although some traits are more commonly associated with effective leaders (e.g. self-confidence, emotional stability, energy, a spirit of initiative, a high tolerance for stress), research on this topic has failed to demonstrate that successful leaders always necessarily possess certain personal characteristics.

Skills

The same conclusions emerge in studies on essential *skill sets* of effective leaders, i.e. combinations of innate personality traits and past experience.[4] In general, this view distinguishes three main classes of skills that are indispensable for successful leaders:

- *Technical skills* needed to actually perform the job in question.
- *Interpersonal skills*, i.e. the ability to communicate, the sensitivity to be able to perceive and interpret feelings and emotional states of others, empathy, etc.
- *Conceptual skills*, i.e. analytical aptitude, creativity, the ability to understand complex phenomena, attention to details, a capacity for critical thinking.

Functions and behaviors

A third perspective relates to studies that take a functional or behavioral approach. Instead of considering the characteristics and competencies that typify a leader, both these approaches focus on which roles leaders actually play, and what activities they

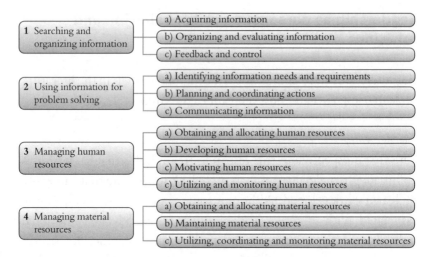

Figure 2.1 Compilation of leader behaviors
Source: adapted from Fleishman et al. (1991)

have to do—and urge their followers to do—for the sake of team performance.[5]

The problem with the behavioral approach lies in the number and variety of behaviors we need to consider as "typical" of a leader. The most often cited taxonomy uses 65 categorization schemas for leader behaviors proposed in the literature, offering the compilation shown in Figure 2.1.[6]

Leadership styles: situational and personalized leadership

Another stream in leadership studies holds that combinations of personal characteristics, skills, and specific behaviors of leaders give rise to different *leadership styles*.[7]

Following this logic, the *Leadership Grid*[8] identifies relevant styles based on a combination of behaviors oriented toward tasks on one hand, and people on the other. These two parameters constitute the axes of a matrix where four different leader profiles can be positioned:

- *Country club manager*, who focuses on people, but not tasks.
- *Task manager*, who concentrates on task productivity, but neglects people.
- *Middle-of-the-roader*, who uses a mixed approach, with a mid-range ranking on both variables.
- *Team manager*, who ranks high on both axes.

Charismatic leadership

Charismatic leaders are sensitive to the environment and to the needs of their collaborators; they can articulate a strategic vision; they have a propensity for risk-taking and a flair for acting unconventionally.[9] Yet basing action on charisma can sometimes have negative repercussions for this type of leader, dampening the creative contribution of collaborators, and inhibiting criticism and dialogue between the leader and collaborators. Charismatic leaders may also become overly confident and risk underestimating problems. What's more, they tend to create followers and enemies. Finally, the organization may become excessively dependent on the charismatic leader and fail to find and groom a successor.

Transactional leadership

The literature on leadership styles draws a noteworthy distinction between *transactional* and *transformational* leadership.[10] The first centers on rewarding or punishing followers according to how they carry out their tasks and what performance level they achieve. So transactional leadership follows a "give and take" approach that centers on realizing immediate efficiency instead of envisioning and developing future orientations.

Transformational leadership[11]

Leaders who adopt a *transformational style* try to project a compelling vision of the future to their collaborators, providing appropriate models, encouraging everyone to embrace group objectives, setting the bar high for performance expectations, supporting their subordinates on an individual level, and offering intellectual stimuli.[12] Essentially, the aim of transformational leaders—as the label suggests—is to transform their followers by fostering growth both in competencies and ambitions. The key here is the capacity to create a challenging and motivating vision of the future, and then actually make it materialize. Four pillars underpin transformational leadership:

- *Individualized consideration*: Paying attention to the needs of individual team members, accepting and enhancing unique personality traits, and communicating in a personalized way.
- *Intellectual stimulation*: Fostering the desire and the ability to put forward new ideas, suggest creative solutions, and work innovatively.
- *Inspirational inspiration*: Setting future targets that are challenging and compelling, and which often give greater meaning and motivational content to the team's activities.
- *Idealized influence*: Followers perceive the leader as a model to aspire to or emulate.

Transactional and transformational leadership styles are not diametrically opposed. In fact, a leader's ability to influence followers' performance in a positive way often comes about by successfully combining both approaches.

Servant leadership

This concept,[13] as the name suggests, envisages a leader as someone who serves the organization and the people who belong to it. The basic skills required for this leadership style involve listening and helping collaborators realize their maximum potential, as well as an aptitude for persuasion, vision, and guidance.

Situational view

Although some attempts have been made to come up with general models representing an ideal, universal leadership style, most studies on this topic adopt a *situational view*—specifically, by striving to match the most appropriate leadership styles with each specific set of circumstances.[14] According to this perspective, leaders must first correctly interpret their work context, and then adopt the most congruent behaviors and leadership style.

Goleman[15] offers a noteworthy example of the situational perspective with his six leadership styles. This author's contribution is particularly enlightening for our understanding of leadership, because it places a strong emphasis on "emotional intelligence." The term refers to leaders' capacity to be sensitive to their own emotions and those of their collaborators, and to recognize and appreciate those feelings as a source of energy, influence, and connection among people. Goleman identifies five capabilities that constitute emotional intelligence: *self-awareness, self-management, motivation, empathy,* and *social skill*. These are the building blocks of six different combinations of leadership styles, which are more or less appropriate depending on specific contexts and circumstances:

- *Coercive style*: In other words, laying down the law, which may be appropriate in the face of emergency contingencies when the leader needs to set a clear path and get immediate results. In other situations, this style can be demotivating.
- *Authoritative style*: Striving to mobilize people toward a vision, yet letting collaborators choose the most appropriate methods for realizing this vision. This style is effective when the team needs a clear plan of action; it might not be very effective when the group has more expertise than the leader.
- *Affiliative style*: Placing people at the center of every action at all times. This style facilitates interpersonal connections and building relationships among collaborators, and proves particularly useful in situations that call for team spirit. However, the affiliative style may sacrifice performance orientation.
- *Democratic style*: Encouraging group participation in decision-making, with the aim of generating consensus, fostering a sense of

responsibility, and eliciting new ideas. This style can be practical when the group is more expert than the leader, but it runs the risk of weighing down decision-making processes and creating confusion about who's in charge.

- *Pacesetting style, oriented toward excellence*: This style sets extremely challenging goals and high personal performance standards, and works exceptionally well with motivated, competent groups; but it can trigger demotivation when collaborators can't keep up with the pace.

- *Coaching style*: Focusing more on personal growth than the tasks at hand, this style can be very constructive when group members recognize their limitations and they want to improve and learn. But a coaching style may be inappropriate when working under urgent deadlines, increasing the need for collaborators' patience and tolerance for errors; it can also cause problems when the group shows resistance to change.

According to the situational view, the better the leader is at analyzing the situation and choosing the leadership style best suited to it, the more successful that leader will be. What this implies is that leaders need to adopt different styles depending on the specific circumstances they find themselves facing. However, because of the enormous number and heterogeneity of situational factors, it's extremely complicated to establish an optimal level of conformity between a specific situation and the leadership style that provides the best fit.

Relational leadership

One of the key messages of the situational view is that the leadership style should be consistent with the maturity, competency, and motivation[16] of followers. The relationship between leader and follower is the nexus of a relationship-based leadership approach.[17] Leadership is seen as a two-way influence relationship between a leader and a follower oriented to reaching common goals: individuals in different levels align with one another to accomplish mutual and organizational goals. Graen and Uhl-Bien[18] point out a taxonomy that refers principally to the three domains: leader, follower, relationship. Leadership is a multi-faced construct involving aspects of the leader, the follower, and the relationship between the two.

The first relevant relationship-based theory is the *leader–member exchange (LMX)*. It attempts to encompass the nature, determinants, and consequences of the dyadic relationship between leader and follower, and advocates *individualized leadership*. According to this view, successful leaders shouldn't treat all their followers the same way; instead, leaders should build individualized, personal relationships with every subordinate or collaborator, in keeping with each one's unique characteristics such as their personal needs and motivations. LMX focuses on personalized attention to collaborators' needs, which can serve as a motivator. But when there's not enough time or resources to dedicate this attention to every single person, LMX recommends building solid relationships with an exclusive inner circle of "trusted lieutenants" as an effective and efficient alternative. This "in" group could act on the leader's behalf, following specific guidelines when interacting with the rest of the team.

The relationship between leader and follower is the nexus of a relationship-based leadership approach.

The focus can be on the interpersonal relationships among leader–member exchanges, but also between a leader and a group. This interpretation of the LMX is related to its extension of dyadic partnership to group and network levels. The LMX theory is a particularly interesting one when exploring team leadership because of one of its logical consequences: the team leader establishes heterogeneous relationships with different team members. This phenomenon—so-called *LMX differentiation*—can elicit negative reactions from group members who may feel they are being treated unfairly. Clearly this could lead to potentially destructive group dynamics; consequently, dyadic relationships between the leader and followers impact the wider context of lateral relationships among team members, which are in turn influenced by this context.

A recent relationship-based approach is the relational bureaucracy theory.[19] A hybrid organizational form, relational bureaucracy is distinguished by its ability to use formalization to embed reciprocal relationships between worker–worker (relational coordination), worker–manager (relational control), and worker–client (relational coproduction) into work roles themselves by showing participants how they connect with the whole. Finally, the relational bureaucracy approach's dynamic integration of these three types of relationships makes up for the gaps in terms of effectiveness found in the classic relational leadership theories and provides the foundation for organizations that are sensitive, responsive, high-performing, reproductive, and sustainable.

DETERMINANTS OF MOTIVATION

The ability to motivate lies at the very heart of leadership; indeed, "the conceptualizations of motivation and leadership are closely interrelated."[20] We can interpret *motivation* in light of three dimensions with regard to a given task: the activation of the effort required (i.e. the decision to carry out a certain activity), the intensity of the effort expended to execute the task, and the persistence of that effort (in the face of possible failures). There is a vast and varied array of forms of motivation that differ from person to person, or even for the same person at different times of their life. In light of this variety, it's only logical that there is also a wide range of motivational processes and tools that we can utilize.

In this regard, the distinction between *extrinsic* and *intrinsic* motivation is worth noting. People who respond better to extrinsic motivation thrive on recognition from colleagues and superiors, and the rewards that ensue. Yet monetary compensation alone is not always enough to engender high motivation—particularly when salaries and bonuses are already substantial (for example in showbusiness, cinema, television, sports, etc.). In work situations, in fact, people are often motivated by intrinsic factors—for example:

- When they are interested in the activities at hand.
- When they have a predisposition for their work.
- When they can see their skills improve.
- When the work climate is positive.

So motivation in this sense essentially springs from satisfying personal needs, such as honing individual skills or realizing personal aspirations.

A systematic survey of motivation models and studies would take us beyond the scope of this book, but we should mention certain key concepts and theories, the latter which primarily focus on *reducing uncertainty*.[21]

According to the *goal-setting*[22] and *path-goal*[23] theories, the major source of motivation for followers is information that minimizes *uncertainty* pertaining to credibility, validity, and attainability of the goals set by the leader. The most important implication here for team leaders is that they need to spend time and resources setting goals, both at an individual and team level. Then they have to get team members to accept, share, and embrace these goals. There are a number of ways to make this happen: leaders can use objective analysis and data to identify the most appropriate goals, and if team members have a voice in the goal-setting process, they will more readily accept and share goals.

A useful technique to get the group to assimilate very demanding goals is to break them down into partial sub-goals that are more accessible. Unlike the final goal, the team can glimpse these intermediary milestones not too far down the road. What's more, reaching these sub-goals can boost self-confidence and reinforce the conviction that the final goal actually is attainable. Naturally, the success of this approach depends a great deal on the team's actual ability to achieve these intermediate objectives.

Beyond investing in the goal-setting process, a second valuable piece of advice for team leaders is that they need to reduce *uncertainty* among team members by clearly and convincingly explaining exactly *how* to achieve the goals in question. This calls for a precise project, detailed plans, and an organization that gives the impression that the path ahead is clearly mapped out and the necessary resources are available. Team leaders have to decide where they want to go with their teams, and how they intend to get there. This doesn't simply involve leaders selecting an appealing destination, but instead demonstrating their planning ability and attention to detail, which would instill confidence in their teams. Another essential element in this process is the leader's capacity to minimize role ambiguity for every member of the team; in other words, any uncertainty as to what they have to do, how they should do it, and the relative importance of team activities.

According to the *self-efficacy theory*,[24] people are motivated by information that reduces their *uncertainty* concerning their own abilities. Put another way, the source of motivation lies in the conviction that you have what it takes—a conviction that leaders should know how to cultivate in every follower.

The *equity theory*[25] holds that people are highly motivated by all the information that reduces *uncertainty* as to fair treatment with respect to their co-workers. The basic assumption here is that, in an organization, people don't assess their situations in absolute terms, but by comparing themselves with others. To illustrate this theory, receiving a reward might not motivate a team member in the least if they think that another employee is getting the same reward but doesn't deserve it. Fairness can be measured in terms of assigning resources and offering opportunities (*distributive fairness*), as well as performance assessments and consequent compensation (*procedural fairness*).

Fairness is based on the premise that the compensation people receive is proportional to the effort they expend, and to the extent that their input contributes to reaching a specific objective. If team members are convinced they're being discriminated against or their leader is behaving arbitrarily, they'll feel dissatisfied and may become demotivated. This explains why it's often crucial to establish and enforce a clear set of rules, along with sanctions for relative infractions, to ensure that the team functions effectively. Another essential way to convey a sense of fairness is to invest time and resources in the vital process of performance evaluation for all team members.[26]

Team leaders can boost team motivation via a series of actions that directly or indirectly provide team members with information that can reduce their *uncertainty* about various aspects of their job and, more generally, their life. Myriad variables impact motivation by reducing uncertainty through the quantity, quality, and type of information given to team members. This makes the communication skills of the team leader particularly important.

In addition to the points discussed above, there are also other ways to motivate people. Some models emphasize the importance of giving meaning to the work of team members—leaders can do this by helping their team realize that they play a key role in achieving useful and interesting organizational goals. Other models stress that interpersonal relationships are essential to motivation, along with a sense of belonging to a social group in which members feel emotionally invested.

Motivational communication by team leaders can take the following forms:[27]

- Modeling success, both by identifying people and examples of excellence to emulate, and by personally acting as a role model through exemplary behavior in terms of professionalism, enthusiasm, and energy.
- Paying personalized attention; for example, by offering constant encouragement and helping team members solve personal problems.
- Creating a work climate centered on a positive attitude, fun, and friendship.
- Delegating responsibility.

As we can see, communication skills are an indispensible resource for team leaders, who are called on to be excellent listeners and observers, to ask exhaustive questions, to provide detailed feedback, and to offer personalized advice.[28]

Summing up, then, we need to remember that motivation is a determinant of individual performance, together with competencies and organizational context. What's more, these factors are not independent; on the contrary, they tend to influence each other, both negatively and positively. Studies on team leadership have to take all these variables into account in order to come to an understanding of the link between motivation and individual or team performance.

TEAM LEADERSHIP

A team-based approach to organizing work has become standard practice in many organizations.[29] Recent studies with the participation of high-profile managers confirm this trend: 91% of respondents claimed that "teams are vital to organizational success."[30]

Although leadership can play a key role in shaping the individual and organizational performance of a team, research underscores the fact that "we know surprisingly little about how leaders create and handle effective teams."[31] Generally speaking, team performance often depends a great deal on the ability of team leaders to manage interdependencies; in other words, to successfully integrate, coordinate, and synchronize individual contributions to team processes.

Teams are groups whose members have a clear sense of *belonging*, and who *share responsibility* for accomplishing tasks.

Teams are groups whose members have a clear sense of *belonging*, and who *share responsibility* for accomplishing tasks. These tasks have a certain level of *interdependence*, and serve to reach *common objectives*. All teams are groups, but not all groups are teams. In fact, a number of conditions have to be in place for groups to become teams: disciplined action, often guided and coordinated by a leader, which leads to setting collective goals; coming to a consensus on these goals; finding a common work method; and assigning differentiated roles for doing specialized tasks. Also, every member of the team has a responsibility toward all the others for team results.

The main factors that typically distinguish a team, as compared to a group, are the following:

- Interdependency of tasks (members of a team depend on one another to accomplish tasks and reach objectives).
- Collective responsibility.
- Shared information, resources, competencies, and rewards.

Finally, interpersonal trust is often more important for a team than for a generic group.

Leadership, team-activated processes, and team results impact one another reciprocally. For example, the characteristics, competencies, and behaviors of the leader shape team processes that, in turn, influence performance. Vice versa, attaining positive results prompts the team to work harder and better; likewise if leaders see team processes functioning more efficiently and team performance improving, this reinforces their conviction and self-esteem, which is basically what they need to lead.[32] Figure 2.2 summarizes this reciprocal influence.

To assess team performance we can apply a variety of parameters that are often interdependent. These are the most important:

- How far the team succeeds in achieving goals.
- Quality of team processes.
- Learning.
- Psycho-social processes that underpin relationships among team members.

Goal attainment corresponds to the capacity to achieve results that are in line with expectations. Beyond the congruency of outcomes to goals, we can also measure team performance in terms of the quality of team processes. For example, disregarding whether teams win or lose, they can play skillfully and put on a great show by making the best of available resources: time, competencies, energy, trust, collaboration, etc.

Figure 2.2 The links between team leader, team processes and team results

Learning, on the other hand, can be considered both a prerequisite for reaching goals and an outcome in itself. In fact, learning enables a team to deepen their store of competencies, laying the groundwork for reaching future targets.

Team performance can be affected by *psycho-social states*, such as a sense of belonging, a low level of conflict (or none at all), and the ability to settle disputes and controversies among team members. Conflict, a critical consideration for teams, arises from inconsistency in individual values, goals, and convictions, which can translate into tension among team members with negative repercussions that can impair team effectiveness.

The potential impact of psycho-social relationships on team performance is particularly significant when the tasks that team members perform are highly interdependent. In these circumstances, social cohesion and a positive team climate usually enhance intra-team interaction because members come to share values, interests, and convictions, all of which often exert a powerful influence on collective results.

Regarding team processes (i.e. activities carried out by team members), management literature draws a basic distinction between the following behaviors:

- *Behaviors focused on tasks* that are essential for an organization's activities to run smoothly; each organizational role is normally assigned specific tasks.
- *Contextual behaviors* that serve to support task-focused behaviors, creating the psycho-social conditions that make it possible to perform tasks effectively and efficiently. Key contextual behaviors include *organizational citizenship behaviors*—in other words, discretional behaviors adapted by personnel that go above and beyond formal requirements of individual organizational roles, and that are not directly or explicitly compensated by the company in any

formal way.[33] One of the most widely accepted classifications gives four categories of organizational citizenship behaviors:

- *Conscientiousness*: commitment and dedication that goes beyond role requirements; an example is willingness to work overtime.
- *Civic virtue*: active participation in all aspects of the life of an organization, and taking the initiative to speak up and make suggestions for improving business processes.
- *Sportsmanship*: willingness to accept less-than-ideal working situations; for example, when a substituted player on a sports team willingly leaves the field without complaining, accepting the coach's decision.
- *Altruism*: a natural inclination to help co-workers.

A good team leader has to make sure that team members perform their role-specific task behaviors to the best of their abilities, while at the same time encouraging contextual behaviors that can generate positive results for the team and individual members. In this book, we focus primarily on contextual behaviors for a number of reasons.[34] Several empirical studies on this topic[35] demonstrate that contextual behaviors have a significant positive impact on individual and organizational performance.

Leaders can foster both the willingness to adopt contextual behaviors and the skills needed to do so. They can do this in part by acting on individual followers, and in part by creating a psycho-social climate and building lateral relationships among team members. All this paves the way for enacting contextual behaviors.

To evaluate, understand, and improve team performance, the first thing we have to consider is that individual performance depends on knowledge and skill, level of motivation, and the organizational context. In a team, however, the collective performance has to be more than simply the sum of individual performances of team members. In light of this, leaders play a key role both in creating a team and in planning and managing team processes.

The functions of a team leader

Many different models illustrate the major functions that typify team leadership. Research on this topic indicates the following functions as determinants for team success:[36]

- *To formalize roles* in order to clarify responsibilities, minimize confusion and ambiguity, and underscore the interdependencies among team members.
- *To structure* decision-making processes related to critical team activities in a disciplined and methodical way.
- *To encourage a reciprocal sense of responsibility* so that every member of the team "owns" outcomes and feels morally obligated to do their best to reach the goals set for the team and for individual teammates.
- *To establish and share group goals* that take priority over the individual goals of team members. The aim here is to promote interpersonal cooperation and reduce conflicts deriving from contrasting individual objectives.

The model illustrated in Figure 2.3 sums up the relevant variables proposed in the most rigorous and prominent studies on the issue.[37] As we can see, team leaders basically have to make a series of decisions and perform various functions, as described below:

- *To obtain and use information* that minimizes the risk of errors in decision-making. This calls for an ability to select the quantity and quality of information that's actually necessary and appropriate, to identify the most valuable information sources, and to structure information and use it effectively.
- *To specify a compelling purpose* for the team that is clear and concrete, directs the team toward a reasonable common goal, and maps out a path they can believe in and contribute to.

- *To draw clear boundaries for the team* so every member knows who's on the team and who's not; the tasks, roles, and responsibilities of each member; and the relationships that link everyone on the team, e.g. in terms of authority and hierarchy. This means the leader has to carefully analyze and design the team's work.

- *To acquire the necessary resources* (personnel and material) for optimal team functioning, with the aim of maximizing the probability of achieving goals effectively and efficiently, while working according to plan in terms of timing and methods. Here the most crucial skill for leaders involves negotiating for resources with the external stakeholders who can supply them. Leaders may also have to substitute resources (typically personnel) that are inconsistent or incompatible with the goals and processes of the team.

- *To build an enabling structure* by implementing the optimal team size, and clearly designing and explaining work methods and core norms of conduct for the group. All this serves to ensure that the team works effectively to achieve its goals.

- *To make every effort to secure the best possible support for the team* from the rest of the organization. This includes reasonable deadlines for achieving goals, rewards for team members, access to information systems for decision-making, training opportunities, etc.

- *To provide coaching*, engaging in activities that serve to motivate team members and help them grow.

Figure 2.3 shows that these functions influence team members' different responses—cognitive (awareness of goals, roles, responsibilities, etc.), affective (sense of belonging, cohesion, etc.), and behavioral—all of which impact team performance. This last type of response can be interpreted not only in terms of goal attainment, but also learning (deriving from cognitive responses) and the quality of interpersonal relationships (psycho-social responses at an affective level).

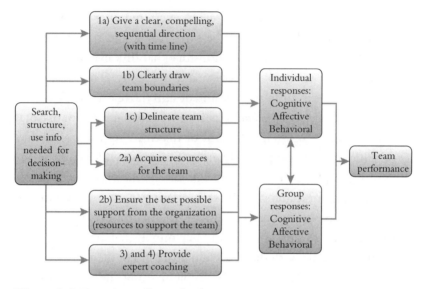

Figure 2.3 Functions of team leaders
Source: adapted from Burke et al. (2006)

Condensing the model even further, we can assert that team leaders typically play four main roles:[38]

- Structuring the team and setting team goals (phases 1a, 1b, and 1c in Figure 2.3).
- Acquiring all necessary resources and eliminating any organizational obstacles that hinder team efficiency (phases 2a and 2b).
- Providing coaching to each team member personally to enhance individual contributions to the team (phase 3).
- Offering team coaching, working with the whole team to help tap into collective resources as effectively as possible in order to achieve team goals (phase 4).

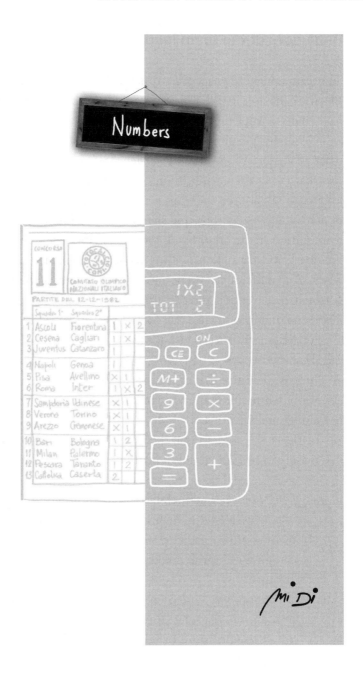

Behaviors of the team leader

The team leader can enact every function by combining a wide array of specific behaviors in different ways. So what exactly does a team leader have to do to implement the functions described above effectively?

Generally speaking, we can classify team leader behaviors into two macro-categories: *collective* and *individualized*. The first refers to behaviors that target the entire group or a sub-group. For instance, team leaders usually address the team as a whole when they convey standards of behavior, expectations, and shared values with the aim of creating team spirit. On the other hand, some behaviors center on single team members, for example providing feedback. This needs to be taken down to an individual level because every member of the group needs personalized attention and communication. In fact, "people who feel heard and understood are easier to motivate and influence."[39]

A particularly critical task for the team leader involves reconciling these two types of behaviors in the most appropriate way. The aim here is to ensure that everyone gets personalized treatment and attention, while simultaneously maintaining consistency and equity in managing the team as a whole.

Burke et al.[40] suggest that the immense inventory of team leader behaviors can be broken down into two main categories.

- *Task-focused behaviors*, which fall into the following classes:
  - *Transactional behaviors* such as dispensing rewards, compensation, and punishments for team members who adopt behaviors that align with or run counter to expectations of the leader and the team.
  - *Initiating structure*, which entails clearly defining the roles and responsibilities of each team member, either with the leader directing these decisions or with team members providing some level of input as well. In practice, this translates into organizing group activities, assigning tasks and goals, and specifying how work needs to be done.

- *Boundary spanning*, which refers to expanding resources available to the team (materials, information, etc.). To do so, prerequisites are skills in negotiating and collaborating with anyone outside the team who may be in a position to supply these resources.
- *Person-focused behaviors*, which can be divided into the following classes:
  - Behaviors associated with *transformational leadership*, which serve to create a compelling vision for the group's project and its members, inspiring hearts and minds.
  - *Personal consideration and individualized attention* based on building interpersonal relationships and creating strong group cohesion (e.g. a common purpose, shared views of phenomena that impact the team, collaborative behavior, a natural inclination to help one another, etc.). Leaders typically enact this behavior by using two-way communication; investing in growing respect, esteem, and interpersonal trust; and taking into consideration the individual needs of every team member.
  - *Empowerment* by encouraging team members to work autonomously and by promoting self-management, typically using a participative leadership style structured around delegating responsibilities.
  - *Motivation* of team members, spurring them on to do their best—especially in the face of adversity.

Management studies on team leadership indicate that people-centric behaviors have a more powerful impact on team performance compared to task-centric behaviors. What's more, the work of Burke et al. shows that the greater the interdependence of team tasks, the more powerful the impact of the team leader's behavior, be it task- or person-focused. Naturally, as interdependence increases, so does the team's need for coordination and guidance; this means that the leader has to adopt behavior centering simultaneously on both tasks and people.

How the team leader can influence processes and performance

The characteristics, competencies, and behaviors of the team leader influence team performance to the extent that these factors impact team processes (i.e. what team members do and how they work). In light of this, Zaccaro et al. have developed a model that analyzes processes by which team leaders can shape team performance.[41] The model in Figure 2.4 identifies *cognitive, motivational, affective,* and *coordination* processes, described below.

According to the model in Figure 2.4, there are three key *cognitive processes* for a team:

- *Collective information processing*: This calls for sharing information and comparing opinions to understand team problems; setting goals; coming up with possible solutions; building consensus on a plan of action; and implementing chosen solutions and monitoring consequences.
- *Developing shared mental models*: These pertain to the strategies, roles, and required behaviors of each team member, and interpersonal interaction patterns that serve to optimize the collective action of the team. The team needs to arrive at a shared view that is as precise as possible of who has to do what, how, when, and why.
- *Growing collective metacognition*: This means that team members reflect, both individually and collectively, on the sources of the team's problems, appraising the solutions they've tried and the results they've obtained. The team sets a vital learning process in motion by contemplating the cause–effect links of team experiences. In concrete terms, collective metacognition can materialize through specific behaviors by team members, such as giving one another feedback on work methods, being open to criticism from others, and proposing possible solutions to teammates.

Team leaders can attempt to stimulate cognitive processes in the team. Here are the best ways to go about this:

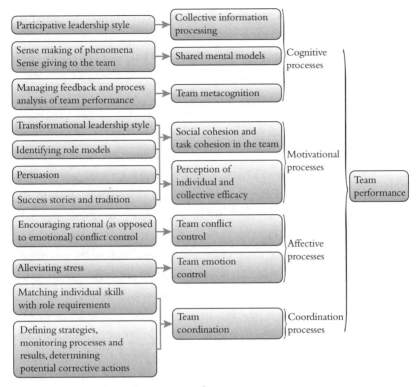

Figure 2.4 Functional processes of a team
Source: adapted from Zaccaro et al. (2001)

- *Use a participative leadership style*: Get team members involved in decision-making processes and encourage them to do things like pinpointing and diagnosing problems, brainstorming, and selecting possible solutions.
- *Sense making of phenomena*: This entails carefully analyzing problems, solutions, and results, and coming up with credible interpretations of phenomena that impact the group. *Sense giving* is the ability to convincingly convey to team members the roles, responsibilities, and behaviors expected from each one of them to solve team problems and successfully implement the best solutions.
- *Handling feedback*: The key here is that the leader has to be able and willing to be self-critical; to accept criticism and input from others;

to focus feedback on specific task-related behaviors rather than personal traits of team members; to offer detailed, constructive advice; and, during meetings, to encourage active participation of all team members and set aside time especially for discussing group work.

The model in Figure 2.4 also highlights two key *motivational team processes*:

- *Creating group cohesion*: This can be seen from a social perspective, in terms of the number and intensity of friendships among the people on the team. Group cohesion also refers to tasks and goals, when team members offer their collaboration and commitment to the group because they sincerely believe that if they want to achieve their individual goals, they must attain collective goals.
- *Developing a sense of collective efficacy*: This relates to the individual and group conviction that by working together, the team can be successful. Confidence in individual and team capabilities spurs members to work harder, to persist in the face of adversity, to accept tough challenges, and to make any personal sacrifice needed to reach the goals in question.

Leaders can activate motivational processes by:

- *Adopting a transformational leadership style* that can inspire team members to direct their efforts toward more ambitious, challenging goals.
- *Identifying and proposing role models*, and exploiting emblematic examples of ideal behavior that can lead to success.
- *Using persuasion* to enhance the team's self-esteem and self-confidence.
- *Enacting* any behaviors that increase self-esteem and self-confidence *indirectly*, building a successful track record and a winning tradition for the team.

Regarding *affective processes*, the key here is to prevent or control conflicts and negative emotional states. To do so, team leaders should strive to alleviate stress, encourage team members to have self-control on an emotional level, and look for rational and constructive solutions to problems and conflicts.

Finally, *coordination processes* pertaining to team members' activities primarily correspond to task-focused behaviors. To implement these processes, **The team leader needs** the team leader has to establish in no un- **to offer well-defined** certain terms what has to be done by whom **strategies, plan work** and how. Specifically, this means assigning **meticulously, moni-** clear-cut roles and responsibilities to team **tor team processes** members that are compatible with their **scrupulously, provide** skills and competencies. What's more, the **detailed feedback, and** team leader needs to offer well-defined **recalibrate actions and** strategies, plan work meticulously, moni- **roles when need be.** tor team processes scrupulously, provide detailed feedback, and recalibrate actions and roles when need be.

The model most often cited to explain the complex interaction between coaches and athletes is the *revised sport leadership model* developed by Zhang et al.[42] This model, based on the *multidimensional model of leadership*,[43] examines five categories of variables that are contingent on the situation and level of maturity of team members:

- The *training and instruction* variable encapsulates the coach's ability to develop and transfer skills and knowledge to team members.
- *Democratic behaviors* serve to elicit team involvement in decision-making.
- In contrast, *autocratic behaviors* are adopted by coaches who prefer to make decisions autonomously, and leverage their authority when interacting with athletes.
- *Social support* comes about by building and fostering interpersonal relationships both between the coach and the team, and among the team members themselves.
- Last of all, *positive feedback* means playing up the team's strong points and putting a positive, constructive spin on their weaknesses.

A coach, just like a business manager, has to effectively enact a broad set of behaviors that focus on tasks and people (both personalized and collectively); these may be directed toward athletes or other people in the organization, and the ultimate goal is of improving team performance. The purpose of our research is to develop a team leadership model, starting with the most recent and exhaustive investigations of this topic[44] and integrating these findings with the results of our empirical study of sports coaches. In the following chapters, we present our empirical evidence, summarized in an original team leadership model.

MANAGEMENT MODELS OF TEAM LEADERSHIP: KEY MESSAGES

1 "Group" and "team" are two different concepts. Distinctive features of a team are:
   - Action coordinated by a leader.
   - Common objective.
   - Shared work method.
   - Success largely dependent on managing interdependencies among team members.
2 Team performance can be measured in terms of:
   - Results with respect to pre-set goals.
   - Learning.
   - Quality of team processes.
   - Psycho-social outcomes that shape relationships among members.
3 Team performance is determined by team processes, which are shaped largely by the team leader's characteristics, competencies, and behaviors. These factors in turn impact the team's cognitive, motivational, affective, and coordination processes.

4 Leadership has been interpreted as a personality trait, or a set of skills, functions, or behaviors centered on tasks or people.

5 Leadership styles (authoritarian, democratic, charismatic, transactional, transformational, and servant) are combinations of personal characteristics, skills, and specific behaviors of leaders.

6 According to the contingent (situational) view of leadership, the leader has to adopt different styles depending on contexts and circumstances.

7 The *leader–member exchange theory* (LMX) focuses special attention on the leader–follower relationship, and proposes personalized and differentiated leadership styles in dealing with different followers.

8 Team leadership centers on:
- The relationship between the leader and the team as a whole.
- Relationships among team members.
- Interdependence and reciprocal social support among team members.
- Organizational structure needed to generate resources and information that serve to make decisions.

9 Team leaders have to balance relationships with team members and with the team as a whole in order to impact performance in a positive way. Leaders need to leverage team members' motivation and their perception of distributive, procedural, and relational fairness.

10 In sports, team leadership suggests that coaches should:
- Create a supportive climate for continuous learning and improvement.
- Organize and delegate responsibilities.
- Manage communication.
- Plan.

NOTES

1 House, R., Javidan, M., Hanges, P. and Dorfman, P. (2002) "Understanding Cultures and Implicit Leadership Theories across the GLOBE: An Introduction to Project GLOBE (Global Leadership and Organizational Behavior Effectiveness)," *Journal of World Business*, 37, 1, p. 5.

2 Ibid.

3 Stogdill, R.M. (1948) "Personal Factors Associated with Leadership: A Survey of the Literature," *Journal of Psychology*, 25, pp. 35–71.

4 Mumford, T.V., Campion, M.A. and Morgeson F.P. (2007) "The Leadership Skills Strataplex: Leadership Skill Requirements Across Organizational Levels," *The Leadership Quarterly*, 18, pp. 154–66.

5 Hackman, J.R. and Walton, R.E. (1986) "Leading Groups in Organizations," in Goodman, P.S. (ed.) *Designing Effective Work Groups*, San Francisco, CA: Jossey-Bass, pp. 72–119.

6 Fleishman, E.A., Mumford, M.D., Zaccaro, S.J., Levin, K.Y., Korotkin, A.L. and Hein M.B. (1991) "Taxonomic Efforts in the Description of Leader Behavior: A Synthesis and Functional Interpretation," *The Leadership Quarterly*, 4, pp. 245–87.

7 In particular, see: Tannenbaum, A.S. and Schmitt, W.H. (1958) "How to Choose a Leadership Pattern," *Harvard Business Review*, 36, March–April, pp. 95–101; Likert, R. (1961) *New Patterns of Management*, New York, NY: McGraw-Hill; Blake, R.R. and Mouton, J.S. (1964) *The Managerial Grid*, Houston, TX: Gulf Publishing.

8 Blake and Mouton, op. cit.

9 Weber, M. (1922) *Wirtschaft und Gesellschaft, Tubingen* (translation: (1980) *Economia e Società*, translated by Rossi, P., Milano, Italy: Edizioni di Comunità; Yukl, G. (1998) *Leadership in Organizations*, Englewood Cliffs, NJ: Prentice-Hall.

10 Bass, B.M. (1985) *Leadership and Performance Beyond Expectations*, New York, NY: Free Press; Bass, B.M. (1990) *Bass & Stogdill's Handbook of Leadership*, New York, NY: Free Press.

11 Bass, B.M. (1990) "From Transactional to Transformational Leadership: Learning to Share the Vision," *Organizational Dynamics*, 18, 3, pp. 19–31.

12 Burns, J.M. (1978) *Leadership*, New York, NY: Harper and Row; Bass (1985), op. cit.

13 Greenleaf, R.K. (1977) *Servant Leadership: A Journey into the Nature of Legitimate Power and Greatness*, New York, NY: Paulist Press.

14 In particular, see: Fiedler, F.E. (1967) *A Theory of Leadership Effectiveness*, New York, NY: McGraw-Hill; Hersey, P. and Blanchard, K. (1982) *Management of Organizational Behavior*, Englewood Cliffs, NJ: Prentice-Hall.

15 Goleman, D. (2000) "Leadership that Gets Results," *Harvard Business Review*, 78, 2, pp. 78–90.

16 Butler, J.K. and Reese, R.M. (1991) "Leadership Style and Sales Performance: A Test of the Situational Leadership Model," *Journal of Personal Selling and Sales Management*, 15, 3, pp. 37–46.

17 Uhl-Bien, M. (2006) "Relational Leadership Theory: Exploring the Social Processes of Leadership and Organizing," *The Leadership Quarterly*, 17, pp. 654–76.

18 Graen, G. and Uhl-Bien, M. (1995) "Relationship-based Approach to Leadership: Development of Leader–Member Exchange (LMX) Theory of Leadership over 25 Years: Applying a Multi-level Multi-domain Perspective," *The Leadership Quarterly*, 6, 2, pp. 219–47.

19 Gittell, J.H. and Douglass, A. (2012) "Relational Bureaucracy: Structuring Reciprocal Relationships into Roles," *Academy of Management Review*, 37, 4, pp. 709–33.

20 Zorn, T.E., Jr. and Ruccio, S.E. (1998) "The Use of Communication to Motivate College Sales Teams," *Journal of Business Communication*, 35, 4, pp. 486–92.

21 Sullivan, J.J. (1988) "Three Roles of Language in Motivation Theory," *Academy of Management Review*, 13, 1 (January), pp. 104–15.

22 Locke, E.A. and Latham, G.P. (1990) *A Theory of Goal-setting and Task Performance*, Englewood Cliffs, NJ: Prentice-Hall.

23 House, R.J. (1971) "A Path-Goal Theory of Leader Effectiveness," *Administrative Science Quarterly*, 16, pp. 321–38.

24 Bandura, A. (1982) "Self-efficacy Mechanism in Human Agency," *American Psychologist*, 37, pp. 122–47.

25 Adams, J.S. (1965) "Inequity in Social Exchange," in Berkowitz, L. (ed.) *Advances in Experimental Social Psychology*, vol. 2, pp. 267–300, New York, NY: Academic Press.

26 Graham, S., Wedman, J.F. and Garvin-Kester B. (1993) "Manager Coaching Skills: Development and Application," *Performance Improvement Quarterly*, 6, 1, pp. 2–13.

27 Zorn and Ruccio, op. cit.

28 Lowe, P. (1995) *Coaching and Counseling Skills*, New York, NY: McGraw-Hill.

29 In particular, see: Hills, H. (2007) *Team-based Learning*, Burlington, VT: Gower; Lawler, E.E., Mohrman, S.A. and Ledford, G.E. (1995) *Creating High Performance Organizations: Practices and Results of Employee Involvement and Total Quality Management in Fortune 1000 Companies*, San Francisco, CA: Jossey-Bass.

30 Martin, A. and Bal, V. (2006) *The State of Teams: CCL Research Report*, Greensboro, NC: Center for Creative Leadership.

31 Zaccaro, S.J., Rittman, A.L. and Marks M.A. (2001) "Team Leadership," *The Leadership Quarterly*, 12, p. 452.

32 Day, D.V., Gronn, P. and Salas, E. (2004) "Leadership Capacity in Teams," *The Leadership Quarterly*, 15, pp. 857–80.

33 Netemeyer, R.G., Boles, J.S., McKee, D.O. and McMurrian R. (1997) "An Investigation into the Antecedents of Organizational Citizenship Behaviors in a Personal Selling Context," *Journal of Marketing*, 61, July, pp. 85–98.

34 Borman, W.C. and Motowidlo S.J. (1997) "Task Performance and Contextual Performance: The Meaning for Personnel Selection Research," *Human Performance*, 10, 2, pp. 99–109.

35 For example, see Podsakoff, N.P., Whiting, S.W., Podsakoff, P.M. and Blume B.D. (2009) "Individual- and Organizational-level Consequences of Organizational Citizenship Behaviors: A Meta-analysis,"

Journal of Applied Psychology, 94, 1 (January), pp. 122–41; Nielsen, T.M., Hrivnak, G.A. and Shaw, M. (2009) "Organizational Citizenship Behavior and Performance: A Meta-analysis of Group-level Research," *Small Group Research*, 40, 5 (October), pp. 555–77.

36 Holland, S., Gaston, K. and Gomes, J. (2000) "Critical Success Factors for Cross-functional Teamwork in New Product Development," *International Journal of Management Reviews*, 2, 3, pp. 231–60.

37 In particular: Burke et al., op. cit.; Wageman, R., Fisher, C.M. and Hackman, J.R. (2009) "Leading Teams when the Time is Right: Finding the Best Moments to Act," *Organizational Dynamics*, 38, 3(July – September), pp. 192–203.

38 Hackman and Wageman, op. cit.

39 Kets De Vries, M.F.R. (2005) "Leadership Group Coaching in Action: The Zen of Creating High Performance Teams," *Academy of Management Executive*, 19, 1, pp. 61–76.

40 Burke et al., op. cit.

41 Zaccaro, S.J., Rittman, A.L. and Marks, M.A. (2001) "Team Leadership," *The Leadership Quarterly*, 12, pp. 451–83.

42 Zhang, J.J., Jensen, B.E. and Mann, B.L. (1997) "Modification and Revision of the Leadership Scale for Sport," *Journal of Sport Behavior*, 20, 1, pp. 105–22.

43 Chelladurai, P. (1990) "Leadership in Sports: A Review," *International Journal of Sport Psychology*, 21, pp. 328–54; Chelladurai, P. and Carron A.V. (1983) "Athletic Maturity and Preferred Leadership," *Journal of Sport Psychology*, 5, pp. 371–80; Chelladurai, P. and Riemer, H.A. (1998) "Measurement of Leadership in Sport," in Duda, J.L. (ed.) *Advances in Sport and Exercise Psychology Measurement*, Morgantown, WV: Fitness Information Technology, Inc., pp. 227–53.

44 Burke et al., op. cit.; Mathieu, J.E., Maynard, M.T., Rapp, T. and Gilson, L. (2008) "Team Effectiveness 1997–2007: A Review of Recent Advancements and a Glimpse into the Future," *Journal of Management*, 34, pp. 410–76; Zaccaro et al., op. cit.; Morgeson et al., op. cit.

CHAPTER 3

A NEW TEAM LEADERSHIP MODEL

INTRODUCTION

The following chapters give an overview of the most relevant ideas and examples that emerged from our interviews with coaches of professional sports teams. We've taken quotes and anecdotes from these coaches to illustrate each variable that we discuss.

The aim of our interviews was to find answers to the following key questions:

- What functions do professional sports coaches carry out to impact team performance?
- Which specific practices and behaviors do coaches enact and how do they do so for the specific purpose of enhancing individual and team motivation?
- Can we draw parallels between these functions and practices, and the models developed in the business world? Can we transfer these functions and practices to firms? How?

The indications we gleaned in the interviews have enabled us to come up with an outline of *which* functions coaches perform, *how* they do so, and *who* is targeted—all with the aim of improving team performance.

In this chapter, we sum up the main conclusions of our research, and present an original model of team leadership. This model represents the summary of our work and serves as a frame of reference for coaches and executives who want to learn from one another's experiences. In keeping with the relational view of leadership (see Chapter 2), the new team leadership model in Figure 3.1 shows that the capacity of team leaders to impact team performance in a positive way depends primarily on their credibility. Coaches must build credibility with multiple stakeholders at different levels, from micro (typically the players on the team and the technical staff) to macro (other members of the organization and external actors). This refers specifically to:

- Individual team members (athletes).
- The team as a whole (including technical staff).
- The organization as a whole (including non-athletes who work for the sports club).
- All relevant actors outside the club (media, fans, etc.).

These four levels of action are interdependent. For example, a coach who is a successful team leader on an individual and group level is usually also credible in the eyes of the club's other stakeholders. By the same token, the legitimacy derived from these stakeholders typically gives the coach more credibility with the team as a whole and with individual team members.

Team leaders, in turn, need to motivate individual athletes, build team spirit, synchronize organizational resources, and construct a positive reputation within their sphere. Their ability to achieve all this depends on what they do (their behaviors) and how they do it. We break down these behaviors into two macro-classes—managerial

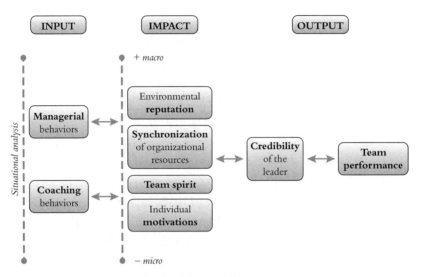

Figure 3.1 A new team leadership model

behaviors and coaching behaviors—that we explore more fully in the following chapters. Lastly, to determine the effectiveness of these behaviors and how they are put into practice, we have to consider a number of circumstances. In other words, whether or not these behaviors are appropriate depends on how consistent they are with specific situational variables, as our model shows. The following statements support this assertion:

"In my career I've often heard players say things like, 'That coach was credible because he took us to the training camp two days before the game,' and others talk about the same coach saying, 'He wasn't credible because he took us to the training camp two days before the game.' Being credible in the eyes of everyone all the time is unthinkable." (Serse Cosmi)

"Coaching a club team and a national team are two completely different jobs. You can be great at one and have a hard time doing the other, because you need different skills. With a national team you have very little time to practice on the pitch, and less chance to get to know the players as people, and as

athletes. The big event is the key motivator for a national team: participating in the Olympics or a European Championship is a source of motivation in itself. What's more, the coach can hand-pick the players for the national team who are best suited to the type of strategy he has in mind. Instead, with a club, the coach usually finds a team that's already been built, for the most part anyway. For a coach, it's important to understand errors and try to figure out why mistakes were made, and then to correct them. On club teams it's easier to do this and to teach your players, because they're under your control 24/7, 365 days a year. On the national team, on the other hand, there's not much time to understand and intervene when you're playing in a tournament with lots of games back to back. What's more, when you train athletes with different backgrounds, it's essential to be flexible." (Sandro Gamba)

The model we describe in the following sections is based on the theories illustrated in Chapter 2. In particular, our model contributes to the team leadership literature, highlighting the relevance of the impacts of team leaders' behaviors and, as a consequence, its focus on multiple relationships rather than other elements such as leaders' attributes, team leaders' behaviors and functions, and one-directional relations between the leader and the follower. We see organizations as elaborate relational networks of changing persons, moving forward together through space and time, in a complex interplay of effects between individual organizational members and the system into which they enter. As a consequence, team leaders' relationships must be considered inside and outside the organization, at different levels (individual, team, organization, and environment, from micro to macro).

Team leaders become more effective when they are able to establish multiple relationships with target actors that are instrumental in generating team members' motivation.

Team leaders become more effective when they are able to establish multiple relationships with target actors that are instrumental in generating team members' motivation. Relations in a team leader's network tend to influence each other. The number and the quality of relationships needed depend on the situational and social complexity that the team requites. To integrate and fine-tune this model, we also took into account the indications and recommendations of the managers and coaches that we interviewed. In the following chapters we detail the two macro-categories of behaviors that designate two areas of action for team leaders. Specifically, in Chapter 4 we discuss "The Team Leader as Manager" and in Chapter 5 "The Team Leader as Coach."

CREDIBILITY AND TEAM PERFORMANCE

Coaches do not tend to perceive themselves as leaders; in fact, this word rarely comes up in our interviews. But everyone realizes that coaches contribute to shaping individual responses, team processes, and team results. The following statement exemplifies this rationale:

"The coach is considered a leader when he manages to make his players do things they would never have thought they could do." (Gian Paolo Montali)[1]

"I think the most important thing about coaching is that you have to have a sense of confidence about what you're doing. You have to be a salesman and you have to get your players, particularly your leaders, to believe in what you're trying to accomplish on the basketball floor." (Phil Jackson)

A coach's ability to influence team members largely depends on certain personal characteristics and actions that ultimately drive personal credibility. In fact, coaches almost always cite their personal credibility as the key to their success in leading teams and winning team trust. Credibility is about how leaders win the confidence of their constituents. It's about what people demand of their leaders, before they are willing to dedicate their hearts and minds to a common cause. And it's about the actions leaders must take in order to intensify their constituents' commitment.[2]

In our research, we find that this credibility derives from several attributes. Every coach has a personal notion of what it means to be credible and how to act, in concrete terms, to be seen as credible. Yet, despite these subjective interpretations of the concept of credibility, certain components emerge time and time again. In general, credibility is the outcome of countless actions. It is the result of the combination of *what* team leaders do (i.e. their behaviors) and *how* they do it (their attitudes); in other words, how they work and interact with several key actors, not only the team members (players and staff, in our case).

As for the "what," our research has identified two macro areas of conceptually separate yet interdependent behaviors: managerial and coaching behaviors. The latter are targeted to team members, whereas the former mainly address other actors, both inside and outside the sports organization.

Credibility derives from several perceptions that followers develop toward the team leader. The most frequently cited perceptions are:

- *Technical competency*, which is normally seen as essential, but not sufficient in itself, to be considered credible.
- *Energy*, often associated with the outcome of both enthusiasm and passion.
- *Fairness*, which can be seen as a combination of sincerity, spontaneity, and good ethics.
- *Consistency* of actions and underlying principles across time and situations.

The first dimension of credibility derives from the perception of technical competency. This is attributed to the team leader, not only by team members (athletes, in the sports context), but also by various other key actors identified in our model—for a sports club, these other actors would be the staff, owners, managers, fans, media, etc.). Technical competency is essential, as reflected in the following statement:

"Knowledge, clarity, intuition, and training capability matter, since without these qualities it is difficult to gain the players' respect and trust." (Arrigo Sacchi)

If coaches were once great athletes themselves, this can contribute even more to legitimizing them from the viewpoint of technical competency. However, some coaches point out that being a former star athlete also has a negative side-effect—namely, it's hard to fully comprehend certain issues that may arise when dealing with individual athletes or managing the team. One typical example is the fact that coaches who were once champions often have served no bench time; they've never been left on the sidelines.

Importantly, coaches can't be credible if all they have are technical competencies. In fact, although these competencies are necessary, they aren't enough for a team leader to earn adequate legitimization. Credibility also encompasses the ability to engender trust and to manage relationships not only with the team and with individual members, but with external actors as well.

This is a key consideration within the framework of our research. In any given professional field, in fact, a precondition for team leadership is based on a minimal level of specialized technical competencies. But precisely because they are specialized, these competencies do not equate to credibility in any other context. Just as a successful basketball coach can't be considered credible if they switch to volleyball, a highly competent production manager can't be credible if they take over the leadership of a sales team.

Seeing as the aim of our work is to facilitate the transfer of competencies and best practices across different contexts (sports organizations and business firms), we'll focus on factors that generate credibility regardless of technical competencies—or, better still, in additional to these competencies.

In light of this, we can assert the following:

- Since technical competencies are necessarily specialized competencies, they differ between a sports coach and a business manager, and even between managers in different departments. So, for the purposes of our work, suffice it to say that good team leaders have to have specialized technical competencies to perform their tasks. But we should point out that these competencies are almost always simply preconditions—necessary, but not sufficient for building credibility. What's more, by definition, these competencies can't be transferred between teams that perform different tasks.
- Relational competencies and meta-competencies, however, are more universal in nature. That means that they are generalizable and transferable to different contexts, in particular from sports to business. Our research pinpoints certain fundamental concepts here: energy (basically a mix of enthusiasm and passion), fairness (spontaneity and ethics), and consistency.

With regard to the first point, especially in terms of impact on individual and team motivation, the coach's personal enthusiasm and passion play important roles as sources of energy:

"The most important quality that a coach has to have is energy." (Dan Peterson)

As for enthusiasm, a recurring theme is that coaches need to be motivated themselves in order to motivate their athletes. As one coach succinctly put it, his decision to quit coaching was due to:

"The fact that I no longer have enthusiasm, so I can't pass it on to the players." (Arrigo Sacchi)

More generally speaking, in our interviews, passion often came up as the essential characteristic of a good coach. Recalling his own coach, a former player/coach said:

"[Giovanni] Trapattoni has a unique passion for his work and the player senses it. … He has contagious, extraordinary enthusiasm" (Walter Zenga)

Fairness is another indispensible precondition that allows a team leader to win credibility by earning followers' trust. In particular, spontaneity often emerges from our interviews as a key driver of personal credibility: many coaches point out the need to "be themselves," "behave like they normally would," and to act naturally, showing their strengths and weaknesses. Another essential element of fairness related to personal credibility is the need always to act ethically, which means adopting moral principles to guide one's decisions and actions. Indeed, even if coaches effectively manage and motivate their teams, they lose credibility if their conduct is unsporting—exchanging favors on the pitch or encouraging players to use performance-enhancing drugs, for example.

An additional key driver of credibility is consistency: both of the coach's behavior over time, and between the coach's "style" and the club's project. Consistency minimizes uncertainty and insecurity. Numerous coaches emphasize the need to feel part of a clear, well-defined, realistic project designed by the club. Specifically, the project, the club's consequent expectations, and the coach's own ideas have to be aligned, both as far as tactics and group management. If everyone is "on the same page," it's easier to handle relationships with the public (the fans and the media in particular), and avoid the risk of delegitimization. This can happen if, for example, team players choose to go to club management to solve their problems with the coach, instead of confronting the coach directly.

In the following section, we'll discuss the main aspects of team leadership effectiveness at the four levels outlined above. Then in the next two chapters we'll describe the specific behaviors needed to be effective at these four levels: managerial behaviors (Chapter 4) and coaching behaviors (Chapter 5). These can serve as useful guidelines for any team leader, in sports and business alike.

IMPACT ON THE INDIVIDUAL: MOTIVATION

Leadership processes revolve around the ability of leaders to influence motivation among individuals in a team. Motivation is a psychological process that affects the mental state of team members; in sports, a key concept is that coaches can get the most out of an athlete in terms of competitive performance when they can bring them into a psychological state of "flow." In a nutshell, the flow theory states that the "optimal experience" for people performing an activity (whether it involves sports or work) is when they feel that it challenges them to the limits of their abilities, but not beyond—in other words, when they possess the skills they need to overcome these challenges.

The state of flow is a subjective psychological state in which people feel a sense of total "immersion" in the work at hand. They become so deeply and intensely focused on what they're doing that they even lose track of time. They feel pleasure and satisfaction in performing the activity itself, regardless of the outcome. We can compare this with what's commonly called "being in the zone." Flow is facilitated by certain conditions such as clear goals, immediate and objective feedback on performance, and the feeling of being in control.[3]

As illustrated in Figure 3.2, the flow theory postulates that people work at their full potential under two basic conditions:

- When they believe that their skills and abilities consistently align with the nature of the task they're assigned (in terms of how important the activity is, the opportunities it offers and challenges it entails).
- When they face ambitious targets that push them to their personal limits.

Summing up, the motivational role of a team leader chiefly involves avoiding or minimizing the perception of imbalance (which can

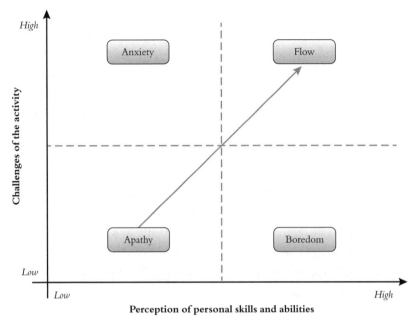

Figure 3.2 The flow model
Source: adapted from Csikszentmihalyi (1997)

generate anxiety when people don't feel up to the task at hand) or boredom, the opposite extreme when they don't feel challenged.

Similarly, good coaches should try to raise the level of ambitions and abilities of their athletes. Low levels of both—even if ambition and ability do align—aren't enough to create an optimal state of flow and instead lead to apathy.

Good coaches should try to raise the level of ambitions and abilities of their athletes.

All this is consistent with what some coaches say about how important it is to prevent players from feeling apathy, anxiety, or boredom, as well as indifference or fear:

> "A good coach has to ... show his player wider horizons and work on his dreams, snap him out of boredom, help him to realize the potential that he didn't imagine he had, drive him to overcome his limitations ...

It's up to the leader to monitor [players] daily; it's his job to break free of routine and indifference, and motivate all of his players. We're all born warm-blooded, but boredom, indifference, lack of self-esteem tend to cool us down. … We need strong commitment by the coach to instill passion in those who lose it …, to strive to find new ideas. A good coach has to help players overcome fear, to make them feel responsible by scratching the veneer of indifference that … hinders any growth." (Gian Paolo Montali)[4]

The specific team coaching functions and activities we discuss in Chapter 5 represent concrete ways that coaches can limit states of psychological disequilibrium, ranging from anxiety and fear to complacency and overconfidence. We also outline how coaches can raise the bar in terms of challenges (by providing new incentives, increasing responsibility, etc.) and perceived capabilities (e.g. through educational coaching).

IMPACT ON THE GROUP: TEAM SPIRIT

In addition to motivating individual team members, ideally leading them as far as possible towards a state of flow, the team leader should optimize intra-team interactions. This involves managing the interdependent activities assigned to various team members. To do so requires relevant technical and tactical expertise that may be difficult to transfer from the sports arena to business world. In addition, team literature places great importance on social cohesion and shared goals among team members.

In keeping with this, our research unequivocally demonstrates that one of the fundamental tasks of a coach is to create and continuously nurture "team spirit." But what is this, exactly?

Team spirit encompasses a number of elements, and different interviewees give us a variety of definitions and interpretations of the concept. It ultimately embodies many of the cognitive, affective, and behavioral responses of the team members that a coach can and should try to shape, with the support of the staff and the club. Here are the responses from our interviews and in the literature that are worthy of note.

First, team spirit is a combination of unity of purpose, shared aims and concurrence on how to achieve them, consistent and integrated actions, willingness to sacrifice personal goals (at least partially) by integrating them with a common overarching goal, solidarity and reciprocity, shared mental models, respect, esteem, mutual trust, and a collective desire to improve.

The following excerpts from our interviews give some idea of the variety of ways coaches interpret the basic ingredients of team spirit:

"The team is here to help individual players to do their best. ... All players go through hard times, so when a teammate plays badly, if the team is pursuing a common goal all the other members will help him. But if everyone is playing to look good, it becomes impossible to play together and sometimes even to train." (Cesare Prandelli)

"[It exists if I see] individual players learning to accept decisions in favor of a teammate with equanimity, despite being in competition." (Luigi Delneri)

"It is the group that enhances the quality of the individual ... if everyone gets the ball more or less the same number of times, participates in the game and feels involved, they improve and, from this, group cohesion also emerges." (Mino Favini)

"The hardest thing is not working on the pitch, but giving the team a common philosophy and idea." (Gianni De Biasi)

"There are many groups, but few teams. This is because people who are part of a group don't feel the joy of being together, they don't feel a sense

of belonging, they think differently. That's why it's so important to find people who have an affinity for each other." (Arrigo Sacchi)

"For me, the greatest satisfaction was seeing the group emerge and grow in self-esteem as well as in technical and tactical learning skills." (Gianni De Biasi)

"A good coach makes the group handle the hard times, and helps the team work through them. Otherwise the players delegate all problem-solving to the coach and that isn't feasible." (Serse Cosmi)

These team results are crucial, together with the impact of individual team members on knowledge, skills, motivation, and behavior. Coaches, with their personality, decisions, and actions, have the ability—and even the responsibility—to influence all these factors.

All this tells us that creating and nurturing team spirit is a fundamental process for team leaders—one that can and should be shaped by the many functions and actions they perform.

IMPACT ON THE ORGANIZATION: SYNCHRONIZATION OF RESOURCES

Individual motivation and team spirit typically relate to the role of the team leader-coach, who works primarily with athletes in the locker room and on the pitch (see Chapter 5). We can integrate this view with that of the team leader-manager who focuses on the organization and functioning of the club, and the resulting benefits for the technical project (see Chapter 4). From the interviews we conducted, the issue of synchronizing resources clearly emerges as the focus of managerial behaviors. The technical project centers on the coach, but so do corporate dynamics. This means that the coach is called to play a proactive role in striking a balance between the needs and pressures of the owners and the players. In this regard, one coach told us:

"A team is like a pyramid: at the top is the club, in the middle the coach, and on the bottom the players. During a match, the pyramid turns upside down: the players are at the top, the club at the bottom. But the coach is always in the middle." (Zoran Mustur)[5]

Synchronizing means rather more than "organizing" and "managing." A team leader who has good organizational skills knows how to divide the work among the various roles, assign responsibilities, allocate skills, and design coordination mechanisms for pertinent activities. Organizing work effectively can increase the club's productivity, but the coach must also worry about synchronizing the various managerial processes inside and outside the club.[6] This involves integrating and balancing interdependent activities to ensure a continuous alignment between team goals and individual performance.[7] The coach commits to building a technical project by integrating expertise, resources, and actors, combining them in a unique way to generate valuable performances and results. This entails making decisions based on the scarce resources that are available, and choosing between incompatible alternatives—often under difficult conditions. Synchronizing, therefore, means more than just optimizing individual functions or units, such as the youth sector, logistics, physical training, and so forth; it means planning internal and external processes that are useful to the team, combining and integrating the performance of various actors.

In doing so, the coach doesn't have hierarchical responsibility for all the activities that need to be synchronized. But as the head of the technical project, the coach's opinions count, and can help integrate the work of actors with different skills, needs, and perspectives. So a team leader who knows how to synchronize these resources is someone with the ability to play the role of orchestrator, catalyst of resources and energy, collector of internal needs, and proponent of organizational solutions. Here we're painting a picture of a coach who can manage relations with a number of internal and external parties that handle various activities. This leader also has to build consensus with other club managers to create the organizational conditions that foster the success of the technical project, as illustrated by the following statement:

"I talk to the president, and then I also interface with the sports director and team manager. Mutual harmony is essential for a successful program. We have to make sure that everything that revolves around the team conveys a sense of efficiency. Players can't have any excuses—everything has to be perfect for them, even the small things. Because if anything is neglected, I lose my footing with the team, and I can't expect them to have the right attitude." (Simone Pianigiani)

From this we can see that coaches may find themselves explaining to sponsors the reasons behind decisions regarding exposure of the players and the team, or summer exhibition games or international tours, or about which players to buy, how to perform certain medical procedures, or how to prepare for away games. Although coaches are not always directly responsible for these activities, they have to know how to present their own needs, make themselves heard, and monitor the processes involved to ensure everything runs smoothly. These activities determine the season's scheduling, the athletes' energy management, and the quality of services available week by week to support the team, and so on. This does not mean that there should not be a general manager role in the club, or that this role should be taken on by the coach—indeed, our research suggests that the role of club general manager is key—but it is up to the coach to state what they need for the technical project, spurring the organization to adapt accordingly.

In conclusion: in highly competitive and challenging environments, the coach must be able to synchronize a number of complex activities that, in turn, are handled by competent and specialized people, leveraging skills and knowledge pertaining to managing and improving relationships in the organization.

IMPACT ON THE ENVIRONMENT: REPUTATION

In addition to the team and the organization, the coach's actions also have an outward focus toward anyone who interacts with the club—the media, fans, sponsors, referees, agents, etc. We call these people *key actors*. Adopting this external focus is one of the most important messages of our work, which emerges from the description of managerial behaviors oriented toward dealing with key actors and relationships (as described in Chapter 5).

We can frame this outward orientation with the concept of "reputation," something that coaches must earn and preserve in their competitive arenas. By *reputation* we refer to an opinion that is often more of a social pronouncement rather than a technical evaluation. This opinion is expressed by a group of key actors towards a person, group, or organization, on a certain topic and according to criteria shared within the context of reference.[8] Reputation builds on what a person says and does, and what others say about that person. It's a complex concept, based on the impression that key actors have developed over time by observing and analyzing important factors. Reputation in part can be attributed to the subject in question, and in part to anyone who expresses an opinion or judgment regarding that person.

Reputation builds on what a person says and does, and what others say about that person.

Reputation is most relevant in situations of high social impact, as in the case of sports. The identity of a sports club is rooted in its social context, and based on cultivating and transferring the positive, fundamental values of sport. It follows that a sports club is an open system that is heavily influenced by other actors and other institutions.

Our interviews with coaches reveal that reputation is a critical issue for sports clubs—but it is especially so for coaches because, in their role as technical project managers, they answer to the club and to key stakeholders. In line with this interpretation, the reputation of CEOs in management literature is linked to their power and their relationships across organizations.[9]

For coaches, acquiring and managing their reputation is an intricate process. To fully understand it, we have to examine the causes and the consequences of reputation. The *causes* relate to the experiences of various key actors in their interactions with the coach. We can see reputation as based on daily activities and interactions with other actors and the effectiveness of these exchanges. We find the *consequences* of reputation in the willingness of various actors to collaborate with the coach. In fact, a positive reputation fosters co-operation, trust, and encouragement, which help the team overcome hard times that they may have to face during the season. Often, the coach's reputation alleviates pressure on the team, creating a less stressful work environment that fosters better results. A coach's reputation is also reflected in their ability to act as a manager, which is an indispensable element for heading complex technical projects and attracting talented people, sponsors, volunteers, employees, sup-pliers, and partners. The following quote clarifies these concepts:

> *"When I had my first coaching position, one of my old coaches called me and said if you want to win, you always have to keep five things under control: (1) the owner, (2) the fans, (3) the press, (4) staff, (5) the players and the technical preparation of the team. If you want to succeed on the court you have to earn your reputation with the others." (Sasha Djordjevic)*

Reputation is decisive for collecting resources internally (by the owner) and on the market (think of the players), for handling ex-ternal pressures (from journalists and the media), and for heading a technical project. Reputation is not only linked to victories and trophies; it's the consequence of a number of different actions and a crucial source of legitimization in the eyes of the players. Coaches can ruin their reputations in any number of ways: adopting aggressive or unprofessional behavior towards journalists, making technical decisions in their own self-interest instead of striving to enhance the value of the team, establishing self-serving relationships with other stakeholders, falling short of expected results based on the technical endowment available, being inconsistent in their choices, failing in their career to build a consistent and winning track record, behaving unethically, and so forth.

The coach's reputation differs from the club's reputation. Although often the two go hand in hand, in some cases there may be a mismatch. A coach in good standing can be hired to improve the processes and practices of a club and, over time, enhance its reputation. Conversely, a club with an excellent reputation for ethics, values, and behaviors can hire a coach who hasn't established a reputation in the sports context—or even someone who has a bad reputation. In this case, key actors will keep a close eye on the club's new addition.

A coach with a poor reputation is more susceptible to attacks by supporters, journalists, referees, critics, and everyone else who can influence their work. Our study shows that, because of this, coaches need to be better at identifying the people who are most essential to their project, and activate listening and management mechanisms towards these actors to build consensus through collaboration and integration, rather than conflict and negotiation. To do this, coaches need the support of the team, the coordination of the staff, and the full backup of the entire organization.

THE SITUATIONAL PERSPECTIVE

Our team leadership model ties into the principles and considerations set out in Chapter 1: the more similarities between specific business and sport contexts, the more opportunities there are to transfer ideas and best practices from one to the other. Managers who want to find useful ideas and inspiration from sports coaches should identify the sport and the teams that compare most closely with their business environment. This means adopting a situational perspective.

This perspective is also appropriate to interpret our model. By this we mean that the relative importance of the functions we identify, and the best way for the coach to enact them, are often situation-specific. In other words, an effective practice in one context is not necessarily a guarantee of success in another.

One of the most important management skills is the ability to interpret situations at different levels and to make choices that are most consistent with the context in question. This is a key parameter for measuring the success of coaches and managers. In fact, credibility—and, ultimately, better team performance—can be achieved by working more on either a micro or a macro level (individual, team, organization, and environment), as well as adopting more managerial or coaching behaviors (see Chapters 4 and 5).

Which option to choose depends on a number of situational factors and circumstances; there are myriad situational variables that we can take into consideration. Table 3.1 summarizes some of the most important ones for each of the four team leadership levels that we previously identified. The best coaches are highly skilled in self-analysis, emotional control, and maintaining mental clarity. This is what enables them to stay focused when emotions run high, and to modify their behaviors in light of the emotional state of the team and the underlying causes of this state, which may be external or internal. Therefore, the ability to evaluate, comprehend, and deal with specific situations—adapting managerial or coaching behaviors accordingly—is an additional competency that team leaders have to hone to reinforce their credibility at various levels: the individual, the team, the organization, and the environment.

Table 3.1 The main situational variables relevant to team leadership

Variable	Structural characteristics	Functional characteristics	Results characteristics
Individual	• Demographic characteristics (e.g. age) • Knowledge • Capacity • Motivation • Clarity of roles	• Number and type of activities to be performed • Programmability of tasks	• Number and type of individual targets • Measurability of individual results • Ability to analyze and understand the causes of individual results
Team	• Size (number of members) • Composition (e.g. homogeneity on an individual level) • Specialization and differentiation of roles • Decision-making structure (e.g. hierarchy) • Duration (temporary or permanent)	• Quantity, type, and quality of interactions between team members • Degree of interdependence • Type of interdependence (objectives, tasks, rewards, social) • Balance between competition and cooperation among team members	• Amount and type of team objectives • Measurability of team results • Ability to analyze and understand the causes of team results • Ability to identify individual contributions to group performance • Time lag between actions and team results • Orientation time of team objectives (short or long term)

(Continued.)

Table 3.1 (*Continued.*)

Variable	Structural characteristics	Functional characteristics	Results characteristics
Organization	• Nature of activities (organizational boundaries) • Complexity of activities (skills and specialization needed) • Complexity of objectives • Resources available • People's skill level	• Criteria for division of labor and coordination mechanisms • Organizational design of information flow for decision-making • Managerial and leadership style (hierarchical or democratic) • Formal and/or informal processes	• Economic, sports, and social results • Integration of these results and sustainability over time • Organizational efficiency and effectiveness • Quality of internal services • Synchronization of activities and resources (internal and external)
Environment	• Number of key actors • Interests of the club's external actors (divergent or convergent) • External pressure exerted on the team	• Mapping and knowledge of key actors • Organizational awareness of the environment and its key actors • Relationships among external actors and between them and the club	• Reputation in the context of reference • Quality of relationships with key actors • Support (or conflict) of the key actors (media, fans, etc.).

A NEW TEAM LEADERSHIP MODEL: KEY MESSAGES

1 Team leaders' success in positively impacting team performance depends primarily on their credibility. They must build credibility with multiple stakeholders at different, interdependent levels: individual team members (athletes, in the case of sport), the team as a whole (including technical staff), the organization as a whole (including non-athletes who work for the sports club), and all relevant actors outside the club (media, fans, etc.).

2 At these four levels, team leaders build credibility mainly by (respectively): motivating individual athletes, building team spirit, synchronizing organizational resources, and constructing a positive reputation.

3 Their ability to achieve all this depends on what they do (their behaviours) and how they do it. The key drivers of a team leader's credibility are coaching and managerial behaviors, and the perceptions that followers develop toward the team leader. These include: technical competencies (i.e. specialized competencies needed to perform their tasks), energy (a mix of enthusiasm and passion), fairness (spontaneity and ethics), and consistency.

4 The best team leaders are highly skilled in self-analysis, emotional control, and maintaining mental clarity: all this increases their ability to evaluate, comprehend, and deal with specific situations, adapting managerial or coaching behaviors accordingly.

5 The extent to which these behaviours are appropriate depends on how consistent they are with specific situational variables.

NOTES

1 Montali, G.P. (2008) *Scoiattoli e tacchini—Come vincere in azienda con il gioco di squadra*, Milano, Italy: Rizzoli.

2 Kouzes, J.M. and Posner, B.Z. (2011) *Credibility: How Leaders Gain and Lose it, Why People Demand It*, 2nd edn, Jossey-Bass, p. xi.

3 Csikszentmihalyi, M. (1990) *Flow: The Psychology of Optimal Experience*, New York, NY: Harper and Row.

4 Montali, op. cit.

5 Di Lenna, A. (2008) *Time out management: Citazioni dal mondo dello sport per manager appassionati e vincenti*, Milano, Italy: Il Sole 24 Ore.

6 Sirmon, D.G., Hitt, M.A. and Ireland, R.D. (2007) "Managing Firm Resources in Dynamic Environments to Create Value: Looking Inside the Black Box," *Academy of Management Review*, 32, 1, pp. 273–92.

7 Siggelkow, N. (2001) "Change in the Presence of Fit: The Rise, the Fall, and the Renaissance of Liz Claiborne," *Academy of Management Journal*, 44, 4, pp. 838–57.

8 Jackson, K.T. (2004) *Building Reputational Capital: Strategies for Integrity and Fair Play that Improve the Bottom Line*, New York, NY: Oxford University Press; Klewes, J. and Wreschniok, R. (eds) (2010) *Reputation Capital: Building and Maintaining Trust in the 21st Century*, Heidelberg, Germany: Springer-Verlag.

9 Zajac, E.J. and Westphal, J.D. (1996) "Director Reputation, CEO-Board Power and the Dynamics of Board Interlocks," *Administrative Science Quarterly*, 41, pp. 507–29.

CHAPTER 4

THE TEAM LEADER AS MANAGER

DEALING WITH COMPLEXITY TO ENSURE SUSTAINABILITY

In this chapter we turn our attention to the emerging role in the sports world of the team leader as manager. Executives are responsible for setting goals for their project or firm, organizing available resources (material and human, tangible and intangible), making decisions aligned with strategic orientation, and vouching for results. This job description refers to a coach who doesn't deal exclusively with technical concerns, but also has a voice in strategic decisions and takes direct responsibility for activities that impact the team project.

This role first emerged in the English Premier League, where soccer coaches began taking charge of long-term technical projects. A case in point is Sir Alex Ferguson, who has led Manchester United since November 1986 and is a likely record-holder for the longest tenure on the same bench. Other examples are Rafael Benítez, José Mourinho, Arsène Wenger, and Gérard Houllier. The team leader as manager is a role that encompasses every facet of the life of a club, from the field to the office. This all-round coach has a hand in technique and vision, tactics and market, and answers for the quality of the project to the players, the fans, the owners, and the media. But it's up to the organization to create the conditions that enable the team leader to act effectively. It's no coincidence that the English League coaches we mentioned above have succeeded in realizing their roles in progressive sports contexts such as Liverpool, Chelsea, and Arsenal. These teams have owners who trust their team leaders to execute their club's technical project. The team leader is most likely to be found where complexity is high, resources are limited and valuable, and pressure to perform is extreme.

In recent years we've witnessed a rise in complexity in sports, and the dawn of the sports business. This new era is marked by the growing business volume generated by sports associations, clubs, leagues, and federations, and increased investments and returns for companies offering sports products and services. Riding high on this wave are media firms, high-tech sportswear companies, and event organizers such as ESPN, Eurosport, Sky, Adidas, Nike, Reebok, and IMG, to name a few.[1,2] But this business boom is not always a good thing for the sports system, fans, or athletes:

"I once loved this game. But after being traded four times, I realized that it's nothing but a business. I treat my horses better than the owner treats us." (Dick Allen)[3]

Sports differ from traditional businesses because of the major cultural impact on local communities and society at large. The aim of every professional sports organization in the strict sense (clubs, leagues, and federations) is to generate economic sustainability or eventually also profits. A prerequisite for the survival and growth of a sports organization is the integration of sporting results (related to athletes), cultural results, and economic results, as shown in Figure 4.1.

Sports differ from traditional businesses because of the major cultural impact on local communities and society at large.

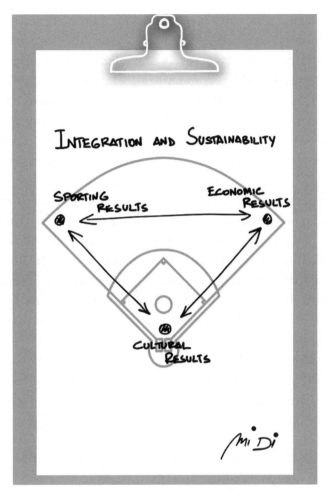

Figure 4.1 Prerequisites for integration and sustainability in a sports organization

Sporting results clearly encompass everything associated with winning: success in competitions, individual and team trophies, new records, and first-time achievements. Examples of cultural results are the messages that athletes and team leaders transmit to their fans and to the community at large; the ethical and moral behavior of athletes and coaches on and off the field; the quality of their relationship with the host community; the number of fans who participate in sporting events and initiatives; the opportunities for interacting and learning; and the values promoted by the organization. Values associated with sports include competition, excellence, solidarity, tolerance, respect, responsibility, friendship, commitment, team spirit, a sense of belonging, respect for individuals and adversaries, loyalty, honesty, courage, determination, support and collaboration, and friendship and trust. Finally, economic results enable the team to find a constructive balance between costs and revenues, with satisfactory returns for investors. Clearly, if sports organizations fail to secure even one of these three types of results, this could potentially damage the other two.

The sports business warrants a combined approach to balancing the needs of various stakeholders and institutions, with competencies that differ from the ones we find in the business world. It's not simply a question of marketing or finance: sports managers have to start with the technical side of the game and then combine the managerial side to enhance the value of the project. But what's the connection between business volume, spectators, recruitment, results, and the role of the coach?

With the advent of the sports business, coaches find themselves engulfed in greater organizational complexity that is more similar to a corporate business context due to an increase in many relevant factors:

- Technical level of players, acquired through multi-million market transactions.
- Expectations of athletes in terms of services and resources.
- Expectations of fans and often of owners as well (the team has to win and keep entertainment value high).
- Number of stakeholders who affect the club's choices, and who have different agendas (e.g. sponsors, suppliers, players, families, technical staff, sports institutions, etc.).
- Environmental pressure.
- Difficulty of balancing and integrating sporting results (on the field), social results (positive values for fans and the community), and economic results.

In organizational terms, the coach plays a central role as the "go-to" person for the sports project, answering to a variety of interlocutors who revolve around the club. Coaches can shape the rules, the behaviors, and the culture of the team and the club as a whole. Because of this, they often find themselves juggling the expectations and emotions of various actors inside and outside the locker room. The choices that coaches make are vital in light of the different kinds of results we've described above and the ensuing need to integrate them all.

Clearly, coaches impact sporting results with their technical and tactical decisions. They influence cultural results by their public statements and the relationships they establish with sports institutions, the media, and the fans, and through the values they promote in their athletes, which represent the image of the whole team. As for economic results, coaches are not only in a position to enhance the value of athletes and select good coordinators, but they can also attract businesses and sponsors who are compatible with the sports project they're trying to build. Finally, technical choices more and more often resemble managerial decisions. So we can see how for a sports team[4] the coach plays a strategic role with major influence over the three types of results we've identified.

When we use the terms "manager" or "management" with reference to a coach, we're accentuating activities and behaviors linked to running a team; as opposed to the more traditional technical/ tactical role, also encompassing locker room morale. By analyzing the interviews we conducted with coaches and then drawing comparisons between their input and other experts in the field, we've come to a clearer understanding of five managerial functions and related behaviors, which we'll detail in the following sections:

- Setting goals, planning, and executing the season.
- Negotiating resources, role, and autonomy with owners and their interlocutors.
- Organizing staff activities.

- Selecting athletes and enabling them to realize their full potential.
- Managing relations with stakeholders.

SETTING GOALS, PLANNING, AND EXECUTING THE SEASON

Setting goals means determining what results the team intends to achieve during a set period of time.[5] The basic assumption is that clearly defined goals regulate human behavior in a direct and immediate way far better than simply saying, "Do your best," or "Give it your all."[6] The team leader must first set goals that are attainable, understandable, specific, and challenging, and communicate them effectively. Every member of the group should then accept and embrace these goals. This ensures that all group members have a clear idea of what they are striving to attain, and how they can personally contribute (motivation). This engenders a sense of belonging to a community working together to create something that will benefit everyone (satisfaction).[7] One coach provided a clear description of this process:

> "I believe in setting goals, but goals should be realistic, not idealistic or simplistic. Idealistic goals become counterproductive. When goals are set unrealistically high, it soon becomes apparent that they are not going to be met. This stifles initiative. On the other hand, if a goal is too simple then it is achieved too easily. Without a stretch there is little reward." (John Wooden)[8]

When discussing goals in a sports context, there are two dynamics to consider: *designing a sports project* and *planning the season*. The timeline for a sports project often coincides with the duration of the season, but it can be longer, for example in anticipation of upcoming national or international championships such as the Olympics. As far as goal-setting is concerned, the coach is the person in the best position to evaluate the technical assets of the team and the potential for the project. Specifically, the coach sets short-, medium-, and long-term goals, ensuring that they are backed by the club and aligned with the individual goals of the athletes. Then the coach communicates these goals to the key interlocutors inside and outside the club, plans relevant activities and creates the conditions to ensure that everything goes according to plan, monitors progress, and gives feedback on results.

The coach sets *short-term goals* (e.g. for a single season) that are compatible with the club's available resources, and deals with the expectations of the owners, the media, the fans, and the players themselves. Although the coach works with management to verify team resources, they alone are the one who decides whether goals are appropriate, and when and how they can be achieved. All this rarely happens in a coordinated way, as the experience of this coach illustrates:

"I came to Roma after a long line of different coaches; I had to produce results right away. What's more, the club had made some public statements that I didn't see as realistic. With Roma I had to give them results and hold up a high standard right from the start. All this caused so many more problems." (Luigi Delneri)

The coach needs to establish a relationship with management and the owners that is transparent and, more importantly, congruent and conflict-free:

"It's crucial to set the club's goals immediately, expressing your opinions on the actual chances of reaching these goals. ... Here is where initial conflicts sometimes emerge between the coach and the management." (Luigi De Canio)

"The club always gives you input, goals to pursue. For example: 'Get into the top six in the rankings and let the young players realize their potential.' Often the mistake we coaches make is to say yes just to sign

the contract. Instead, the most common mistake that clubs make is to only communicate strategy: it's not enough to come up with a strategy, you have to work together to put it into action." (Serse Cosmi)

"It's a good idea to set down a few rules, to set reasonable goals and to avoid excessively pressuring the players." (Dan Peterson)

Some goals are highly challenging and extremely difficult to achieve, especially in sports where the possibilities for winning victories or trophies are few and far between. We should understand the relevance of the goal, but with all due caution, as the following quotes suggest:

Some goals are highly challenging and extremely difficult to achieve, especially in sports where the possibilities for winning victories or trophies are few and far between.	*"When you're playing for the national championship, it's not a matter of life or death. It's more important than that." (Duffy Daugherty)*[9] *"If you make every game a life and death proposition, you're going to have problems. For one thing, you'll be dead a lot." (Dean Smith)*[10]

Although wins and losses generate very different levels of energy and enthusiasm for players, coaches can't let the outcome of a single game sway their decisions. Instead they have to take a comprehensive view of the project, and work to manage time and motivation:

"People think the coach is happy when the team wins and upset when the team loses. Yet most coaches are generally process-driven, and coaching really goes much deeper than the simple results of a single game. The outcomes are felt deeply, yet the everyday mentality keeps the coach very much in the moment with the team and staff." (Joanne P. McCallie)[11]

In fact, the coach is responsible for designing a project and setting pertinent *medium- to long-term goals.* A season-long project has to fit into the bigger picture of a four- to five-year time horizon. Within this framework, the coach has time to build the team, acquire new resources year by year, focus on winning something substantial, and stay consistent and sustainable over time. When the team wins in the championship almost by accident, and victories aren't followed up or supported by an adequate medium- to long-term project, this calls for revolutionizing the team and its work methods. Winning teams and clubs have a meticulous approach to planning, as the following quotes confirm:

> *"Siena in these years has become the top Italian basketball club and team. There's no doubt about it. Because Siena succeeded in drawing up a long-term plan that started years ago. Management did right by not wanting to rush into things. The staff has always studied wins to see if they were the result of the plan or accidental factors, as is sometimes the case in sports. The club managed to move forward with the plan independently of people and improvised events."* (Carlo Recalcati)[12]

> *"The winner takes advantage of a lucky break; the winning team builds day by day, with method and practice."* (Pasquale Gravina)[13]

In these cases the coach has to design the technical project, but more importantly the club has to back it. Club, team, and coach—all three work together:

> *"The greatest victory for a coach (and for a team) is to start out in Serie C [the third tier of Italian soccer] and make it to Serie A with nearly the same group of players. This means you've done a good job building a valuable project."* (Serse Cosmi)

Establishing a medium- to long-term timeframe also means having a club that puts the conditions in place for realizing ambitious projects.

But when coaches work under constant threat of being let go, they're driven by insecurity and often the fear of failure as well. This distorts the natural role of the coach as a leader. Here are the words of some coaches who corroborate this concept:

"Long-term planning isn't always feasible. I have to listen to the coach of the youth team who tells me he has the best 14-year-old, but sometimes I think, 'What good does that do me right now?' It's hard to believe that I'll still be around when he makes his debut. It's better not to get too involved with promoting young players, because they won't make you win anything."(Graham Barrow)[14]

"When a coach is hired, he's fired. The date just hasn't been filled in yet." (C.M. Newton)[15]

"Every coach is in the last year of his contract. Some just don't know it." (Dan Henning)[16]

So, the organizational conditions created by management are what give coaches what they need to be their most effective. Yet these conditions can be negotiated and created by the coaches themselves when they bring their leadership skills into play.

Another key point pertaining to goals is that they have to be *communicated inside and outside the club.* Often managers or owners promise that the team will win or perform beyond their abilities, sometimes without even conferring with the coach. The aim in so doing is to stir up interest in the project, gain visibility and bring the media on board to sell sponsorship, season passes, and tickets. But what happens when the team is on a losing streak, or when performance doesn't live up to promises? In these cases, fans and media usually act like disappointed friends showing little understanding of the obstacles that the team faces or support for the club when times get tough. In situations like these, coaches recommend an open approach:

"I'd rather be sincere and honest about our expectations, even if they're different from what the fans expect, and to explain what path we intend to take to reach our goals." (Gianni De Biasi)

Identifying and communicating goals that align with the team's values: these steps are essential to winning consensus from the fans and earning credibility with the media. The main ingredient in being credible is setting and communicating goals in a professional fashion. But what can occasionally happen is that goals set pre-season are changed *by the owners during the season*, driving the team to reach higher targets. In some cases, this escalates the pressure, especially on young players. So it's important for the team to set attainable goals, for the sake of the players more than other external stakeholders.

Goals that challenge the team too much or too little can have a negative impact on motivation and consequently on performance, especially if these goals are not shared. When goals are extremely challenging, they generate expectations for outstanding performance. In some cases, making these goals public can motivate a team, and testify to their potential if they have yet to build a winning reputation, reinforcing the relationship of trust between the coach and the team. Although communicating with outsiders might be considered risky, some coaches often reiterate their faith in their team, as do these two greats of professional coaching:

"My players are the best in the world—first the players at Porto, then Chelsea, and now Inter." (José Mourinho)[17]

"I've never been in a losing team in my life, and I don't think I'll start now." (Vince Lombardi)[18]

The key here is sharing, especially with the athletes. Team goals have to integrate with *individual objectives*. Often in sports, though, we hear that team spirit and goals have to be placed above everything else, as this coach said:

"Team has to come first. You have to care about each other more than you care about yourself. If you care about the guy to your left and the guy to your right more than you care about yourself, you know who's going to get taken care of? The guy in the middle." (Sam Mitchell)[19]

But this is true only if individual players believe in the team, and think that by believing they can reach their personal objectives. People always tend to fulfill their own needs, even if they may be generous and considerate of others. One coach talked about his conception of cooperation and group goals:

"Cooperation is working with others for the benefit of all. It is not sacrificing for someone else's benefit. If what you are doing doesn't help everyone involved, then it is something other than cooperation, perhaps you would call it ministry, service, or selfishness." (John Wooden)[20]

Balancing individual expectations of visibility or success and the collective desire to win is part of the coach's job:

"Every player, especially in the first few days of training, checks out the others and tries to figure out if this group will be able to win. If someone starts having doubts, that's when the really hard part begins for me." (Ettore Messina)

Sharing players' individual objectives can often lead the coach and other teammates to gain a better understanding of what kind of contribution they can expect from one another. More importantly, this process reveals the most effective mechanisms to activate on the field of play to ensure that team goals and individual goals will clearly align. Implementing a formal process can help, as one coach suggests:

"One of the things I like to do at the beginning is to give a piece of paper to each group member (not only players, but the general manager, the doctor, the physiotherapists) where they write down their thoughts and

ambitions, their motivations and expectations from the club. At the end of the year, I always compare them with the actual results we attained, to take stock of the season.

"I had the good luck of coaching Danilo Gallinari in Milan when he was 18. Today he plays for the NBA with the Denver Nuggets. Danilo wrote, 'Earn the respect of the others on the court.' Back then I'd already realized that a talented player was emerging." (Sasha Djordjević)

Another phase that ties into goal-setting is *planning*. Planning the season means channeling energy, dealing with possible lapses in concentration, and knowing when the athletes need a break or when different players should work on specific exercises during pre-game training sessions. Thanks to a good working relationship with their staff, coaches can anticipate all these scenarios as much as possible—observing even the smallest detail, as the following statement confirms:

"During our meetings, I also provided a staff organization plan for 2009. It consisted of more than 200 points of concern, but the plan also was littered with famous quotes and parables that were important to me. The plan included a team slogan—'It's not about me! It's about us!'" (Bobby Bowden)[21]

Failing to prepare properly for a match, or making mistakes in planning activities and workloads, may result in losses for the team. Planning begins when the coach has the season schedule in hand, which may work to the team's advantage or disadvantage. For some key games the dates are set, but the opponents are question marks. For the national championship, the coach can study the game sequence to see which games are home or away, at the start or end of the season, before or after international engagements, and when there are breaks due to national team engagements, and so on. Planning means predicting every possible scenario, weighing up the risks and

Planning means predicting every possible scenario, weighing up the risks and opportunities.

opportunities. The schedule also allows the coach to set partial goals (which shouldn't always be shared with the team) regarding how the team should execute game plays, how players should move, how fluid play should be, etc. Here's what one coach had to say:

"You can't always manage a season 100%, so you also have to plan so you can let players know the times when they need to give extra energy. At the beginning of the season I figure out the identity the team has to have, and plan the technical objectives, decide how we have to play during the championship, and the intermediate milestones that we have to hit from a technical, physical, and emotional viewpoint. I share some of these things with the players, whatever I can. I give them credible technical individual and team goals." (Simone Pianigiani)

Many coaches only plan week by week, or from one event to the next, sometimes even changing the plan for the season in progress. But this gives the players the impression that the team is disorganized; instead, having a definite training schedule with personalized interventions based on what happens during the season is a plus for the athletes. However, a single well-executed practice isn't the answer, as this coach says:

"One day of practice is like one day of clean living. It doesn't do you any good." (Abe Lemons)[22]

The success of a project depends largely on the ability to create an organization that functions effectively, striving to support the sports project. Building the *organizational capability* of a team calls for clear goals, knowing what it takes to become a winner. In the words of José Mourinho:

"When I take over a club I might stay there 10 years or 20, or even one year or one month. Because everything is possible in football. But when you become the manager of a club, you have to think in terms of staying

there for 50 years, you mustn't work for tomorrow but for the future of the club. For example, Felipe Scolari took over at Chelsea a month ago and said he'd never seen such a well-organized club, with a fantastic training structure: to me this is worth as much as winning a title, because I worked to create that structure." (José Mourinho)[23]

Unfortunately, coaches who dedicate all their time to goal-setting and planning but lack a concrete sense of execution will not be effective. In fact, most managerial problems are linked to *doing things* and effectively *getting others to do things,* rather than formulating and formalizing plans. Coaches and managers often have a hard time living up to their commitments, following timetables and respecting deadlines, and realizing when and how to control and monitor what others do:

"In leading others, action is what matters. Action is the catalyst. Thinking about something is fine. Talking about it is nice. But only through action will one of two things happen. You will fail or you will succeed. Either way, you win." (Bill Yoast)[24]

Coaches who have a sense of execution are sharply focused on seeing that the job gets done down to the smallest detail, even if they aren't directly responsible for the tasks in question. This approach is usually very time-consuming, but it guarantees coaches the chance to use advanced, innovative work methods, as these words affirm:

"Perfection lies in the details. I'm intransigent: I won't excuse mediocrity and stupidity. I'm a perfectionist, which ruins the life of the people around me, and mine most of all." (Jean Todt)[25]

"When I coached basketball at UCLA, I believed that if we were going to succeed, we needed to be industrious. One way I accomplished this was with proper planning. I spent two hours with my staff planning each practice. Each drill was calculated to the minute. Every aspect of the

session was choreographed, including where the practice balls would be placed." (John Wooden)[26]

So, in their vision of the project, coaches mustn't lose sight of the operational details. In fact, in the set of skills of the successful coach, two are inseparable: the ability to see the project as a whole with all the potential changes it may undergo, and the ability to formulate a minutely detailed operational plan. This dual sensitivity/ability makes the coach's job an extremely complex one, but it's also a unique trait of any manager who keeps hands-on contact with the project in progress, increasing the chances for success. The combination of goal-setting, execution, and feedback leads to better results, especially when complex activities and objectives are involved,[27] as these coaches succinctly put it:

"When I have to evaluate the performance of a player, I always give him the statistics and the images showing his athletic performance, but what makes the difference is always my conversation with him." (Ferdinando De Giorgi)

"The most important thing in coaching is to criticize the performance, never the performer." (Lou Holz)[28]

One final reflection relates to the negative side-effects of goals. One risk in setting goals in stone, for example, is that they become an end rather than a means. This can give rise to opportunistic behaviors, or the inability to react to unexpected events,[29] as this coach explains:

"We can plan a road trip down to the last detail, but the unexpected will always arise. When the unexpected happens, we must adapt. If the airplane arrives late or it is snowing, we must adapt our schedule. If, when we arrive at our hotel, other guests are making noise, we must adapt our routine. If the only restaurant open serves burgers and fries, we must adapt our diet. If we do not adapt, we will get left behind!" (John Wooden)[30]

KEY BEHAVIORS FOR SETTING GOALS AND PLANNING THE SEASON

Here's what coaches recommend for goal-setting and season planning:

- Set goals based on available technical resources.
- Design the sports project over a short- and medium- to long-term horizon.
- Set goals based on objective criteria as far as possible (e.g. economic and technical value of athletes).
- Get owners and managers involved in the process of goal-setting.
- Set team goals in light of individual objectives and expectations.
- Share goals with managers and owners to coordinate communication with the fans, the media, and other stakeholders.
- Plan the season based on the game calendar and the team's sports goals.
- Make changes to the plan during the season based on results (wins and losses), workloads, and the team's energy level.
- Share all partial performance targets with the staff and the club—but not always with the players, to avoid affecting their commitment.
- Follow the plan, i.e. monitor every detail of the operational progress of the project.
- Build a stimulating organization that encourages learning and improvement.
- Avoid centering coaching activities exclusively on individual and team goals.

Successful coaches use goals as a guide and focus on creating an environment that encourages work, commitment, and the drive to improve. By the same token, it's important to be open to discussing and revising goals, without letting the team lose the ambition to rise to the sport challenge.[31]

NEGOTIATE RESOURCES, ROLES, AND AUTONOMY WITH THE CLUB AND ITS INTERLOCUTORS

Negotiation is an interactive process in which two or more parties try to reach a mutually acceptable outcome,[32] usually where there is a divergence or conflict of interest.[33] The effectiveness of negotiations is highly contingent on the preparation and study that takes place beforehand. Knowing how to negotiate means framing this process as an opportunity for exchanging opinions, seeking consensus by discovering the reasons behind the other party's position, and coming up with innovative alternatives that are compatible with the preferences of everyone involved. Good negotiators set out to convince the other party that their proposal is the best solution.[34] Estimates show that around 20% of a manager's job involves negotiating,[35] so it makes sense to try to find an approach that works in a variety of negotiation scenarios.

Negotiations can have a *distributive* or *integrative* structure:

- With *distributive negotiations*,[36] the team leader or coach sees negotiating for resources as a zero-sum game: each resource gained for the team is lost from somewhere else, or for the rest of the organization.
- *Integrative negotiations*, on the other hand, are when the parties can identify effective exchange options while adopting a cooperative approach; in this case, the utilities of both parties improve. The team leader or coach who wants to adopt this type of negotiation

strategy needs great listening skills, a deep understanding of the context, and a generous dose of creativity and persuasion.[37]

The ability to persuade others in order to reach an agreement is based on personal credibility, the search for common and complementary interests, and a transparent approach backed by supporting evidence—all with an empathetic style.[38]

When a coach takes the helm of a team, there are many different resources and an array of conditions that are open to negotiation. First and foremost is the coach's *role* in terms of responsibilities and human resources. One of the top negotiation priorities is the *range of responsibilities*, which often equates to a role we call the team leader or manager. Control and/or autonomy over an annual budget, on the players' market, in the youth sector, and in planning activities—all these points can be clarified during contract negotiations. Generally speaking, the more competitive the club and the more efficient the structure, the more likely the coach will be asked to take on technical and managerial responsibilities for the team and the sports project, as an integral part of club management. One coach we interviewed gave this example:

> *"[Sir Alex] Ferguson with Manchester United ... has total control of the club, and he gets a budget from the owners that he handles entirely on his own."* (Carlo Ancelotti)

The view of the coaching role as a managerial one is not always seen in a positive light in the sports world. In fact, the risk is that coaches become detached from the team's technical project and from the locker room. Controversy also revolves around the question of instituting the role of Head Coach, who would have a number of specialized assistants for different phases of the game (offense, defense, etc.), as is the case in the US National Football League. One coach had this to say:

"We're talking about a sport project that is under public and market scrutiny every week, or even twice a week. You also need strategy in these 90 minutes of soccer, or that hour and a half of basketball, and it's only right that [the strategy] is formulated by the coach. He might turn to his collaborators for help, that's fine, but if he deals with other things and the game is run by his assistants, I think that's a mistake."
(Zare Markovski)

Once the contract is signed, a continual process of negotiations begins between the coach and the owners in order to get the team to perform at its best. The coach is part of the team and becomes the team's advocate when interfacing with the club, external interlocutors and, most importantly, the players themselves. The coach has to negotiate with the club for the good of the team, as this coach tells us:

The coach is part of the team and becomes the team's advocate when interfacing with the club, external interlocutors and, most importantly, the players themselves.

"The important thing is to negotiate for the team and not for the club. When the players realize that you're with the club and no longer with the team, it's over. Once I defended a decision the club made on a delicate matter, thinking I wouldn't be hurting anyone, but I lost the locker room." (Serse Cosmi)

Coaches are often proud of their bargaining power, which they can leverage both when they buy new players and when asking the club for the resources they need to empower their athletes to work and play their best. Some examples are coaches who insist on getting heated training facilities as soon as they arrive, or having the field returfed just before the end of the season—things that are clearly beneficial for the entire team. Although this type of intervention is expensive for the club, for the coach it sends a clear message to the team: I'm paying attention to details, and these are some of the resources I want my players to have access to.

"I had to give the impression of a high level of professionalism right from the start. For our training sessions we had a gym built that covered 600 square meters. Actually, we would only use 15–20% of that space, but the structure gave a strong sense of organization, work, and commitment. This was important because Juventus hadn't won anything for ten years and lacked self-esteem, and the team had to start believing in themselves again." (Marcello Lippi)

For a coach, one of the most critical factors is the recruitment campaign or transfer market in terms of the available budget, and the choice of specific athletes that the coach can acquire from the club or directly from the market. Items on the bargaining table include financial resources, autonomy in deciding who to buy and sell, determining players' contract terms and setting prices on transfers, making contact with agents and with other clubs, etc. It's very rare for coaches to handle all these processes alone, but there's no doubt that they carry a lot of weight in determining the success of the transfer market. Some coaches have negotiating skills and bargaining power that they leverage on the market with agents and athletes, so they can build the team they want and create optimal conditions to achieve outstanding performance:

"There are some coaches who aren't good at coaching, but they're good at getting [the club] to buy the players they want. It takes a lot more to buy them than to find them." (Daniele Ricci)

In any case, a coach who is active on the players' market, with an annual budget or the entire player portfolio in hand, is hard to find. In fact, we can easily imagine that total freedom in this process would also be extremely time-consuming for a coach, and a weighty responsibility. A better approach would be for the coach to play a central part in deciding on buying and selling players, supported by other roles in the club.

So the point is to balance the coach's "wish list" with what the club can afford and what the market has to offer—as English coach Gary Megson explains:

"Managing is about doing what you can, not what you would like to do. ... As regards management, I think that you come in with all these great ideals of 'This is how I'm going to get the team to play' and 'This is what I'm going to insist on'; your team has to be capable of doing those things, and I think you've got to look at what you've got, have a look at the scope and manage within that." (Gary Megson)[39]

All of these points of debate lay the groundwork for the relationship between the coach and the owners. In fact, the success of a coach depends largely on their ability to negotiate with the owners, earning esteem and respect by continually balancing interests and preferences, as this coach says:

"It's hard to go against the club, but if the club takes a line that's damaging to the team, or that isn't valid from a technical standpoint, you need to make that clear." (Serse Cosmi)

"My experience with one club ended when the president came into conflict with me. The strange thing was that it was never an open disagreement, only rumors. A few years have gone by and, in hindsight, my mistake was that I didn't try to clarify matters, because actually neither of us wanted to undermine the team or the desire to win. Even though the players defended me to the end, this lack of trust culminated in a total rupture, because it was unsustainable for everyone involved." (Alberto Zaccheroni)

"Management must speak with one voice. The chain of command must run from players to coach, from coach to manager, from manager to owner. When it doesn't, management itself becomes a peripheral opponent to the team's mission." (Pat Riley)[40]

Summing up, then, negotiation is a complex process that develops in different ways depending on who is sitting at the table: owners, management, agents, sponsors, etc. It's always best to focus on integrative mechanisms (win-win), especially when negotiating inside the club. The coach is the person directly invested in the main negotiation process (with the help of other club roles), in particular with external parties. In fact, the coach brings personal credibility to the table to identify what each party wants, come up with innovative solutions, and convince others that these solutions will be effective—fully exploiting their powers of persuasion.[41]

KEY BEHAVIORS TO NEGOTIATE ROLE, RESOURCES, AND AUTONOMY WITH THE CLUB AND ITS STAKEHOLDERS

Here's what coaches recommend in terms of content and approach to negotiations, whether internal (with the club and with various levels of ownership) or external (with agents and athletes that the club wants to sign):

- The role of the coach, clearly detailing responsibilities, the sphere of autonomy, and governance within the organization.
- The people on the coaching staff.
- The resources available to the team (time, infrastructure, technological resources, etc.) so the team can work to the best of its abilities.
- Financial resources for buying the best athletes, reinforcing the technical skill level of the team and increasing the chances for team success.
- Establishing a relationship built on respect and trust, which over time means laying the foundations for a long-lasting relationship based on dialogue.
- Always adopting an integrative approach that can enhance the benefits to all parties.

ORGANIZING STAFF ACTIVITIES

Organizing is the process of allocating the scarce resources available to interdependent actors in the organization effectively, efficiently, and fairly in order to carry out activities and achieve valuable goals. Organizing the work of staff members involves aligning all the behaviors that the team leader adopts to the activities performed by various roles to support the team, and to ensure that all effort is directed toward the final collective goal. The principles of organization are founded on various criteria pertaining to specialization, division of labor, types of interdependency, and forms of coordination—all factors that contribute to rational decision-making with regard to the most appropriate form of organization.

If we observe a sports club through an organizational lens, we see a coach who is responsible for the technical project, with the support of other specialized collaborators. The people in all these roles strive for excellence because they realize that the only way to achieve team results is through continual integration. The collaborators closest to the coach are the technical staff who undertake a number of activities to support the team. Here is one coach's description:

> *"After scrutinizing all the weaknesses of the previous game and the characteristics of the upcoming one, [my technical staff and I] analyze what the team needs right now and we create specific supplementary exercises that help us meet those needs. I can let the players out of watching the videos, but of course my staff and I can't avoid it, and analysis and discussion with the entire group is just as crucial. This is also a way to make the group start to communicate and feel engaged, to promote the development of the group."* (José Mourinho)[42]

In our study, we use the term "staff" in the broadest sense to include various coaching positions: assistant coaches, fitness coaches, coaches specialized in offense, defense, goalkeeping, pre-match training, tactics, etc., as well as sporting director, performance manager, technical director, team manager, the head of the junior team, the head of the medical team, the sports psychologist, the head of the press office, equipment managers, massage therapists, physical therapists, nutritionists, scouts, and the team captain. The player who fills this last position can provide a vital channel of communication for the coach, conveying the climate and the energy in the locker room.

The coach also works with those in other roles and functions of the organization, such as marketing and logistics. Although they are not part of the coaching staff, their activities are highly interdependent with the work and the agenda of the first team. It's important for a coach to be thoroughly familiar with all the roles in the organization in order to make collaboration easier and to get a different perspective of the team and the work being done. The following examples are emblematic:

It's important for a coach to be thoroughly familiar with all the roles in the organization in order to make collaboration easier and to get a different perspective of the team and the work being done.

"The first thing a good coach should worry about is to make friends with the custodian at the gym." (Dan Peterson)

"Even a pat on the back from the equipment manager builds the group, or the care and concern of the massage therapist. There's no doubt that the right kind of attention enhances the motivation and self-confidence of the player." (Claudio Gentile)

Some coaches hope that a new role of manager will emerge. In addition to coordinating the work of other roles and functions, this position would be supported by coaches specialized in technical training, tactics, defense or offense, etc. That way, in order to improve the team while keeping the project on track and avoiding any major upheavals, the club could simply replace the assistant coaches without substituting the head coach (manager). Having several assistants can also be a learning tool, a way to exchange ideas and opinions to find the best options and technical/tactical solutions. Here is what some coaches have to say about this idea:

"Another way to learn from other people is to surround yourself with highly competent collaborators. I've always had two or three assistants who are better than me in certain specific competencies. For example, one was an expert in offense, one in defense, and one was a genius in unusual or unpredictable situations, like the last kick of the game." (Sandro Gamba)

"I don't hire anybody not brighter than I am. If they're not brighter than I am, I don't need them." (Paul "Bear" Bryant)[43]

"The more popular the sport, the more the coach has to build his credibility at different levels, and the greater the complexity he has to deal with. In these cases, the coach has to be supported by an organizational staff, for example the team manager and the press agent, because the coach can't handle everything alone. Today's coaches, especially in challenging sports and contexts, are often expected to do too many things. You don't have to know how to do them all, but you should have the competency to understand, to coordinate, and to have your collaborators carry out certain activities in a specific way, creating the conditions around you to achieve success. But often leaders want to stand alone, so they don't know how to play on a team. For example, they don't want to be contradicted." (Julio Velasco)

"I derive my strength from my strong infrastructure. I have a team behind me that's been there for a long time and when I say something, they will be open about what they think we should do, and tell me before we take action if there are pitfalls. That's the reinforcement I need." (Mike Krzyzewski)[44]

So the higher the technical level of the athletes, the greater the need for information and services for the team. If this is the case, the coach will have to coordinate these resources carefully, taking on the role of governing and guiding the group, something like a prime minister. As this coach puts it:

"I always say that the coach has to be the prime minister of the club's government, where the assistants and staff members are 'specialized ministers' who need to be coordinated. And, like in politics, the president/ owner has to delegate and mandate the prime minister to guarantee that the club functions." (Zare Markowski)

Often the coach is not *formally responsible* for all these other roles on the organizational chart, but access to the information they have is vital in order to structure the team's work to maximum effect, orchestrating all relevant activities. For this reason the coach tries to influence the work of the staff to get the information they need to optimize operations. This information may pertain to rehabilitation for injured players, pre-game and post-game press statements, integration between the first team and the youth sector, market strategies aligned and shared with the team managers, informal statements made by players and other staff members, travel arrangements for away games, and so forth.

Every role is specialized in a clearly defined task. The coach is kept informed on everything that happens, and becomes the liaison between the club and the team. Specialization also brings up the topic of *delegation*, which entails assigning tasks and goals, attributing responsibilities and monitoring results. To delegate means to dedicate time to meetings, as this coach told us:

"I dedicate 50% of my time to the team, and 30% to the technical staff and the fitness coaches. The coach ... has to be informed about every aspect, because in the end he's the one who makes certain decisions. ... I trust my collaborators completely, but I always need to know what they're doing. The relationship ... with the doctors for example is more detached, and with them I delegate 100%. The rest of the time ... I spend dealing with the commercial side and the club management." (Carlo Ancelotti)

People in all roles have to be made to feel responsible, and aware of the collective goal: to prepare the team to face different competitions, knowing they can count on the best possible input from doctors, tacticians, etc. This is summed up in the following quote:

"You have to make your collaborators responsible, so that directives reach the targeted audience clearly and effectively." (Marcello Lippi)

Even with coaches who enjoy great respect and credibility, if there are any coordination glitches that affect the staff or the club, the team notices immediately. The athletes interact with all these roles in various ways and at different times, and the flow of information is a rapid one. This means that the staff are expected to make a considerable effort in terms of coordination, as the following example illustrates:

"Players are very observant, they understand perfectly well when a coach has the situation under control and he's on the same page with the other sectors and with the club. This keeps [the players] in line and allows them to work worry-free. Sometimes, most often with the medical staff, we don't exactly see eye to eye. When this happens, the player loses his bearings and the organization loses a bit of its credibility." (Carlo Ancelotti)

Beyond assigning roles and responsibilities and coordinating staff members, the coach also deals with their motivation, workload, and performance support. In other words, the coach has to manage the staff like a team that works for the main team (the athletes). Performance support calls for work evaluation, but often coaches don't have the technical expertise that allows them to do so (when it comes to the press office or the medical team, for example). What coaches can do, though, is assess the effectiveness and utility for their sports project. It's no coincidence that the best coaches have collaborators who work well together, and who move from one team to the next as a group to enhance their collective effectiveness. Here is one coach's experience:

"The medical side of things is the most delicate one, because often competencies are not easy to determine, since there are many types of injuries and recovery plans. On one hand the player should be looked after, and always have access to the best specialist. On the other the coach wants him back on the field right away. But then the club doesn't want to spend too much money, and last of all the physical therapist is offended if you go to someone else. This is a cause of continual conflict; sometimes the player goes on his own, but that instantly triggers disciplinary measures." *(Andrea Giani)*

Managing personnel begins with a thorough knowledge of the potential and the interests of each individual. This excerpt is emblematic:

"You have to respect roles—you can't demand that one of your assistants does more than he's supposed to. You have to respect the diversity of your employees and collaborators: never overload people, but always try to understand who you're dealing with and then give him appropriate tasks." *(Zare Markowski)*

The coach supervises the work of staff members by holding frequent meetings at regularly scheduled intervals, as this coach told us:

"My assistant coaches were expected to adhere to an even stricter set of standards than my players. I wanted strong, God-fearing men leading my boys. I expected my coaches to lead by example and serve as role models for the boys." *(Bobby Bowden)*[45]

Specifically, the assistant coach often serves as a filter in the relationship between the group and the head coach:

"The assistant coach has to know how to 'take the temperature' of the team, to give the head coach the pertinent details and mediate with the boys, making them understand certain decisions." *(Claudio Gentile)*

To further corroborate verbal interaction, the coach may also request written reports and memos to get an up-to-date, comprehensive picture of the activities carried out by the group or by individual athletes. In light of all the substitutions and transfers in a season, an essential part of tracking activities is formalizing decisions in writing—as this quote confirms:

> *"My method was to write everything down: 'Don't think it, but ink it!' I learned from the Americans and it's the best way to learn, and to be able to verify … what worked and what went wrong. I still have all of the notes I drew up to present to the players for every single game." (Sandro Gamba)*

Clearly, the coach can't hear, read, or know about everything that goes on in the locker room. A staff that works well together learns over time to filter out the salient information to pass on to the coach. Usually this process also goes through a phase of legitimization by the coach in relation to assistants and collaborators. The athletes have to respect every person on the staff as if they were the coach, and each staff member is always a spokesperson for the coach's work:

> *"We discuss [things] every time, but at this point, after two years, they are very autonomous. At the beginning, I monitored everything they did, every day, but now they can do it themselves. As for responsibilities, I believe that the players pick up on how important the assistants are based on the importance that the head coach gives them. For me it's important that they're able to run a practice session, and they get the utmost respect from the players. This is how we work with the staff, in total equality." (Simone Pianigiani)*

> *"As far as staff members, my relationship with them is simpler. The staff are very important, members have to have a good relationship with the team, and the players have to respect them and see them as people who are likable, people they can trust. A player might not directly confide in the coach very much, but he may do so indirectly by talking to the fitness*

coach, the massage therapist, or the assistant coach. These people have to serve as filters, passing necessary information on to the coach in a positive and constructive way." (Carlo Ancelotti)

One reason assistants are a valuable resource for a coach is that they can gather and analyze information that is extremely useful from a technical standpoint. For example, a number of scouts work for professional teams before, during, and after games. They represent sources of information for the coach, both for structuring training sessions and for activities that target the growth of individual athletes. With more specialized roles and more open access to data, a greater number of informed decisions can be made. One coach told us about his experience:

"Data are important, but you have to know how to read them. You show the numbers to the players not to say, 'You're doing poorly' but to make them see where they can improve." (Ferdinando De Giorgi)

When coaches want to reinforce their decision-making with as much objective input as possible, gathering and analyzing data are two key phases in the process. Setting aside impressions, perceptions, and intuitions is a way of making a conscious choice to take a rational approach to sports. One of the key tasks of a manager is to make decisions that impact the organization and the people in it under difficult circumstances, and often without all the necessary information to hand. Here is one coach's comment:

One of the key tasks of a manager is to make decisions that impact the organization and the people in it under difficult circumstances, and often without all the necessary information to hand.

"The biggest difference between a number one and a number two is decision-making. You have a thousand decisions to make in a day as a

number one, whereas as a number two you can give a thousand opinions on what should be the right thing or the right decision to make. As a number one [who] sat in the seat—you have to make that decision." (Steve McClaren)[46]

The ability to organize is one of the key characteristics of team leaders who act as managers; this translates into dedicating more time to co-ordinating staff members, which inevitably cuts into time spent with the athletes. The distance between the coach and the athletes grows, but for many this distance is essential for managing the team without taking locker room dynamics into consideration. In other words, "The coach should never shower with the players," as the saying goes.

"As coach you're in the dressing room and you're having a cup of tea with [the players] and you join in all the craic and the laugh; as a manager you can't do that—to a certain extent you have to distance yourself. The most difficult part of the job, I suppose, is going through the transition: stepping away from the players and having that distance, and just not having the closeness with them and the craic on the field that you used to have. You're looked at differently and you have to act differently." (Steve McClaren)[47]

The relationship between the coach and the team strikes a delicate balance between distance and familiarity, praise and criticism. A recurring theme among coaches is the alibi, and how important it is to make sure players never have one (for example when an event isn't organized well, or an episode isn't handled properly, etc.) But it's also essential to have players who don't live off of alibis to justify themselves or to make less of an effort. On the contrary, athletes should adopt a positive, collaborative approach to sports competitions and club events. This comment on artificial turf expresses the fear that the players can use anything as an alibi:

"It will revolutionize baseball. It will open a whole new area of alibis for the players." (Gabe Paul)[48]

"In life, like in sports, don't accept alibis." (John Kirwan)[49]

Organizing staff functions allows the team access to a greater number of higher-quality resources. Given the complexity of the role, the coach is no longer simply a technical coordinator; instead, they are a project leader responsible for myriad roles that revolve around the team. The team leader ensures that the organizational roles are well-defined and that relative objectives of each one do not conflict. What's more, this figure orchestrates and coordinates the contributions of team specialists who are all indispensible, especially in ambitious contexts. To sum up, adopting a managerial style for a coach means knowing how to delegate, taking a proactive approach to organizational life, refusing to accept alibis, and successfully applying a modern situational approach when dealing with different people in the organization.

In conclusion, organizing the staff's work is a process that involves designing roles and responsibilities that support the team, as well as removing possible organizational obstacles. All this coincides with what we find in the literature on team leadership.[50] In some less organized (and in some ways less mature) sports clubs, a community model is still common, which is often the outcome of the very nature of the activity: a team game. But with the competitions, matches, and events that make up a season for a sports team, a well-structured organization is needed that can function more like an assembly line than a research and development lab. Players work well when they can form a united group that works in harmony with the other people on the staff, as long as there is a support system characterized by discipline, respect for the rules, and planning.

We should also point out that sports organizations tend to go through two major phases: the first is linked to planning the season (transfer market, athletic training, etc.), which is a collective phase; the second, which can last even longer, involves preparing for and playing the actual matches, which is more mechanical (bureaucratic).

So, as head of the technical project, the coach orchestrates roles and synchronizes various activities inside and outside the club, gauging them to fit the various work phases and the characteristics of the people involved.[51]

KEY BEHAVIORS TO ORGANIZE THE STAFF'S WORK

Here's what coaches recommend for organizing the work of staff members:
- Identify (staff) roles that are useful for the sports project.
- Coordinate with the club's executives which members of staff are hierarchically responsible for roles that do not answer directly to the coach.
- Orchestrate and synchronize various roles.
- Adopt the approach of specialized roles, delegating tasks, and assigning clear responsibilities.
- Monitor and support the work of the staff; ascertain performance and competencies.
- Identify the most appropriate coordination mechanisms: formalization, written communication, periodic meetings, one-on-one meetings, etc.
- Gather information from various staff members to make effective decisions.
- Adopt decision-making models based on data and information that is as objective as possible.
- Organize activities to neutralize possible alibis among collaborators.
- Legitimize collaborators in front of the team.
- Differentiate managerial style for various roles in the club.

SELECTING ATHLETES AND ENHANCING THEIR VALUE

Choosing athletes and helping them fully realize their potential is a function of leaders who focus on discovering and growing talent in their teams. The leaders pick the players who have the right skill sets for the team and make sure that their talent fully emerges and serves the needs of the group. Similar activities are components of organizational processes that aim to manage human resources fairly and effectively.[52]

In a sports club, it is the athletes who are the key to achieving results (in economic, cultural, and sporting terms). Yet athletic performance doesn't depend solely on technical or tactical factors that come into play on the field; organizational factors such as design and function are critical as well.[53] It follows that in the context of sports teams, behavioral aspects and group orientation are just as important as technical considerations.[54]

Applying theories on human resource development to the context of team sports, we can see that potential is an even more relevant question when we're talking about athletes with special physical, cognitive, or emotional skills. This quote reflects as much:

"Every player who signs a professional contract has a level of talent that is special enough to create a chance to play Major League Baseball. But the percentage of signed players who actually reach the majors is relatively small. Sometimes the explanation for failing is an injury or a circumstance that could not be overcome. In most cases, though, having mental toughness defines those players who make it—and a lack of it dooms the ones who don't." (Tony La Russa)[55]

Player selection and team composition are key variables in explaining performance, as these coaches can attest:

"Recruiting is a true test of will, discipline, and character, yet it is also the most vital component of building a winning team, no matter what the sport or gender. A coach can know all the Xs and Os and be the best motivator around, but if she doesn't have the right group of players, all of the coaching in the world is not going to turn them into a championship team." (Joanne P. McCallie)[56]

"In sports it's become axiomatic: commitment beats talent every time. At NC State we won a number of football games when we weren't the most talented or athletic team on the field. We won because from the athletic director's office to the redshirt freshman on the sidelines, every person involved in that program committed himself to making the team a success." (Lou Holz)[57]

We should point out here that there is a significant difference between coaching players that other people have picked and coaching a team you built yourself through direct involvement in recruitment. In some cases, coaches take over a team that's already in place, or club policy dictates certain decisions with little room for debate due to limited financial resources or a restricted pool of available athletes. Without a doubt, taking over a pre-existing team is harder for the coach. Here's one coach's experience:

"Just because you were not the coach who recruited a particular player does not mean you cannot develop a good relationship with that individual. When I have changed jobs, I have inherited many players on my teams whom I did not recruit and, even though it took extra work, I was able to establish a positive rapport with almost all of those players." (Joanne P. McCallie)[58]

In any case, many people think that player selection (i.e. buying and selling athletes) is strategic, and if the process isn't handled properly it may even compromise the season. This is especially true when the behavioral style and the expectations of individual players clearly contrast with team and club goals. So the strategy to adopt should center on team-building; it's not enough to have players who look good on paper, based on personal statistics. Some strategies can be simple, like the ones described below. Others might be more complex, based on various player attributes taken together (emotional, physical, technical, etc.).

"The secret is to have eight great players, and four others who will cheer like crazy." (Jerry Tarkanian)[59]

"The main ingredient of stardom is the rest of the team." (John Wooden)[60]

A key aspect of selecting players is verifying their compatibility with the goals and expectations of the club.

A key aspect of selecting players is verifying their compatibility with the goals and expectations of the club. You don't pick players solely based on their on-the-field experience. When an athlete is good, that's a starting point. But to complete a player profile other information is needed with regard to family, friends, mistakes, strengths and weaknesses, etc. These are things that statistics or performance on the field won't reveal:

"In America they hire four secret agents to find out everything there is to know about the athlete they want to buy. Statistics aren't enough. Also, everyone sees and knows the stats, but what's important to understand is the style and personality of the athlete." (Sasha Djordjevic)

"A person of character works better with others—with teammates, for example—day to day, game to game. Such a person is more polite, more courteous, more in tune. And most of all, he or she is most eager to do what's best for the team. I repeat: eager to do what's best for the team." (John Wooden)[61]

"In my business, togetherness is not just a nice concept that you can take or leave according to taste. If you don't have it, you are nothing.

Selfishness, factionalism, clique-ishness are all death to a football team. As a manager in football, I have never been interested in simply sending out a collection of brilliant individuals. There is no substitute for talent but, on the field, talent without unity of purpose is a hopelessly devalued currency." (Sir Alex Ferguson)[62]

Having access to personal information also allows the club to draw up contractual clauses that address goals and reciprocal expectations:

"One athlete went from being a player who earned lots of money every year to finding himself with nothing, playing in the Greek championship for small change. But from a technical standpoint he was the player who was just what we needed at that time. No one knew how to handle him, but with the president's consent we decided to take the risk. ... He came from a college and a high school with one of the top US coaches, Morgan Wood, where he was used to following rules, and if North Carolina had recruited him, he knew what discipline was all about." (Simone Pianigiani)

Athletes work with the coach on technique when there is room for improvement, or much more often on tactics. On occasion there may be one athlete on a team who creates internal conflicts by disagreeing with the coach's decisions, failing to encourage others, and raising questions of fairness, making the coach's work more difficult. The managerial effort required to deal with these issues, which are often recurrent throughout the season, takes energy and focus away from the team, who are often aware of the problem. Making the same mistake with two or three players could jeopardize the entire season—especially in sports like volleyball or basketball, where teams have only 10 to 12 players. Here's what these coaches have to say on the matter:

"When there's a problem, I try to explain as best I can that that behavior is bad for the team. I use dialogue as a tool. If after a number of

conversations things don't change, then I tell the club that as far as I'm concerned [the player] is off the team, and wait for the season to end. But unfortunately that's all time for winning and growing that we've lost."
(Zare Markowski)

"I don't have to find players to make an All Star team; I have to pick players who want to be a team." (Gian Paolo Montali)[63]

It's important for every athlete to feel like an integral part of a single group, with shared values and goals. In fact, we can summarize all the criteria we collected from the coaches we interviewed in the single principle of building a superior entity: the team. Individual interests or preferences can never be put before collective identity. In some cases, excellent players have positive individual performances, but they can't get the team to play their best. All the coaches without exception expressed the conviction that the collective goal is the main job of the coach on a sports team, as the words of this coach clearly reflect:

"I think that the team is what lasts the longest, even if you leave room for great individual players within the team; you want them to play to their potential, but the team is what's most important." (Graham Taylor)[64]

In addition to being willing to work on a team, another helpful selection criterion for players is being accustomed to structured situations with clear-cut rules. The higher the caliber of the team, the more critical this aspect is. In fact, top teams participate in major competitions, which demand the maximum effort from every player and constructive contributions to the project. What's more, for sports with only a few key positions or small starting lineups, it may spell serious trouble for the coach to have one or two players who pay little attention to the club's strategy or are unaware of the balance between sporting, social, and economic results. Here's how one coach puts it:

"A player is like an artist who is asked to apply himself and have a very strong sense of discipline, of team, of technical/tactical rules. They too have to answer to the rule of 'corporate efficiency' and keep technical considerations in mind, but fundamentally they are still artists, human beings who at a very young age are subjected to all different kinds of stress." (Simone Pianigiani)

Coaches sometimes need to face a decision that is often a very difficult one: to sell or opt not to renew the contract of a star player who's been with the same club for years. There are many possible reasons for this move, for example the player in question is past their prime and can't play as well as they once did; there's a need to grow new players and to create a new project that's not anchored to the past; the club wants to generate revenue, etc. In any case, the coach who makes this choice will not be popular with the fans or the media. Often, in fact, these figurehead players stay on and serve in a management position to support the team. In whatever capacity, they are an asset to the club.

Beyond technical and behavioral factors in player selection, coaches also have to take into consideration the leaders in their portfolio of players. In fact, several coaches emphasized the importance of having a leader *not as a coach but one of the players*. However, coaches also have to take care to avoid extreme situations by not having any leaders in the locker room or having too many. In the first case, the group lacks a guide who would establish a sense of self-regulation; usually the leader (who is often the captain) is the coach's go-to person in the locker room for conveying technical messages or for reinforcing behavioral messages. But this leader isn't necessarily the best player or the champion on the team, as this coach explains:

"When I went to Barcellona to play, I was the leader because I made so many goals in every game and I played a lot. Everyone expected that from me, and I was always ready for the last ball. But my coach really wanted another player who was at the end of his career, but who could

lead the locker room and interpret the coach's words most effectively. He was a leader too, even though he wasn't as talented on the field as I was. I understand that to make a team, you need both.

"I hoped that in the transfer window I'd get a leader to head the boys on the field, or else I'd have gone out on the field myself ..." (Sasha Djordjevic)

"Leadership on the field isn't something you recognize through someone's career, or the number of games he's played. You sense it from what they say, and sometimes from what they don't say, from how they express themselves, from how they behave. Often players on a team get labeled as leaders, but in the locker room other players take the lead—players who maybe you wouldn't even expect to." (Serse Cosmi)

A coach can't talk things over with players as if they were a player too. Coaches should maintain their role and leave certain issues to be resolved in the locker room. Some novice coaches who were once great leaders on the field might initially have a hard time taking off their jerseys and switching roles; this can create awkward dynamics with the players, leading these coaches to lose their authority as technical leaders of the team. In addition, some coaches bring players with them from team to team, players who might not be terribly valuable from a technical standpoint, but who are extremely useful in the context of the locker room and the relationship with the technical management of the team. But when there are several different leaders in the locker room, the risk is that they may clash over issues that very often have nothing to do with technical matters.

Another selection process that coaches implement during the season involves deciding who will start in the game, who will stay on the bench, who will be capped and who will be sold. Coaches continually make choices as to who is in the best shape and who can be most effective on the field. These choices can prove to be critical in team management, especially in terms of communication and impact on other players.

Many coaches believe that it's best to tell the team what criteria they use to pick the starting lineup or cap players for the national team. For example, the objective may be to change formations from one game to the next depending on the opponent, or to try out a new formation, or simply to give players who see a lot of action some time to rest (turnover). The key is for the coach to explain the reason behind their choices, and to let that serve as an incentive to players by showing them where to focus their energy and what to work on in practice. Being upfront about selection criteria and openly acknowledging sacrifices are two things that coaches find useful for handling this type of situation. The following words sum up this issue, and are relevant from a motivational standpoint as well:

"The most important aspect has to do with managing people, in other words, how we deal with players and succeed in getting the best out of them. You have a team to manage and everything depends on how you behave with the players who aren't capped, because you know that sooner or later you'll need them." (Colin Todd)[65]

Beyond selecting players based on technical skills, group orientation, and a sense of discipline and leadership, a good coach is someone who can *get athletes to perform to the best of their abilities.* This can happen from a technical or tactical standpoint, the first by teaching skills and moves and the second by exploiting the athlete's attributes to the fullest. As one coach told us:

"The coach's job is to teach the player how to grow. If I always give you the answer, you stop looking for it, you don't apply yourself, and you always stay in the same place." (Andrea Giani)

Growing an athlete is a mechanism for realizing their potential, sparking individual motivation, increasing the coach's credibility, enhancing team spirit, and, most of all, generating value for the market and for the club. This is what two coaches had to say about potential:

"Our biggest fear should be failing to fully realize our potential." (John Kirwan)[66]

"A good coach is one who can get the most out of a player—otherwise, what kind of coach is he?"(Daniele Ricci)

Enhancing the value of players is mainly about training, designing a technical project, and having a competent staff, but also about adopting a system of play that showcases individual talent and ultimately enhances the value of the whole team. A culture based on growing player value contributes to a stronger market position for the club, but more importantly it creates a positive attitude among individual athletes who decide to embark on a given project.

"I have a system for the guys on this unit. No matter what your skills are, there's a place for you in this system. I will never say to you that you have to change what you did in college or someplace else in order to play for me. We brought you here because we think you've got skills. Now it's our job to find the right spot in the system for you." (Red Auerbach)[67]

"70% of coaching is getting players properly placed where they can be most effective." (Bill Yoast)[68]

Showing players how to realize their potential means helping them grow physically, technically, and most of all in terms of personality. In fact, of all the factors that empower people to adopt a winning attitude, this is one of the most delicate and difficult. Players grow when they are part of an organizational context centered on improvement, collaboration, and solidarity, engendering trust instead of generating conflict. These words clearly describe this concept:

"I come across as a coach/value-booster. Everywhere I go they cut the budget and they want to win the championship. The problem is that I can actually do it. ... I remember once when I told a number 10 he should

become a number 3, and explained what he should do and how he should work. In a few years, he became a world champion in that position!" *(Serse Cosmi)*

Helping athletes optimize their performance is also highly contingent on the resources the club decides to invest. Many clubs are equipped to take care of athletes from a psychological and physical standpoint, collecting information and mapping out individual growth paths based on these specific needs. A commonly held opinion among people who work in these areas of the organization is that athletes are highly sensitive to what happens in their private lives, and any negative impact here can even outweigh the fallout from physical problems. Playing in an organized club also means getting attention and assistance for personal issues, not only medical treatment.

Making players as effective as possible means giving them the chance to grow by loaning them or changing their positions, or having them shadow an expert on the field with the support of the staff. The real payback for a coach oriented toward development and growth is successfully instilling in players the desire to better themselves, to practice longer, to work on areas of improvement and, above all, on technical factors that form the basis for every play. To conclude our discussion of this topic, here are some observations from coaches.

"Your statistics are tremendously useful, you live by statistics. Everyone has to improve even after practice. In Serbia, practice continued even after the team was done: no one leaves the gym unless they make three series of eight consecutive three-pointers." (Sasha Djoerdjevic)

"While you're resting, someone is sweating to beat you." (Vincent Lombardi)[69]

"My job is to make sure that every player becomes his own coach." (Gian Paolo Montali)[70]

To trigger the drive to improve, a precondition is a culture of learning, sacrifice, and constant practice. When coaches see players continue to train even during vacation, many consider this a good thing. What they don't understand are the players who go on holiday, stop training, and gain weight, oblivious to the fact that the average athletic career is a short one. Balancing veteran and novice players in light of their roles and their background helps preserve the cultural identity of a team. This culture can then be passed on more easily to newcomers. As this coach succinctly put it:

"On the pitch you need mature people, not just people with good feet." *(Marcello Lippi)*

With regard to theories on developing human capital, coaches constantly encourage learning, strive for improvement, and promote the concept of team. All the while the focus lies on building intellectual capital, which is made up of human capital (individual know-how and skills), social capital (relationships among organization members), and organizational capital (culture and work methods).[71]

Given that an athlete's growth is the combination of physical, cognitive, and emotional maturity, coaches stress that psychological factors are equally important in dealing with stress, emotions, and fears (team coaching).[72] Yet we noted that the topic of individual and team coaching, regarding how to improve the character of an athlete or a team, is left to individual experience in many cases. This contrasts with the structured approach to selecting resources and organizing physical tasks. Here's a pertinent comment from one coach:

"In soccer, psychology is too often confused with psychiatry. But I think that psychology is the most important thing there is. Unfortunately, a coach isn't a psychologist; he doesn't have the knowledge or the tools

he needs. But I like to be informed, keep up-to-date, and focus on experience in particular. I believe that the difference between teams is this [psychological] factor, more than anything else: there are highly trained groups that might lack motivation, for example, and this is due to psychological mechanisms. This is the reason they can't outperform the others." (Carlo Ancelotti)

KEY BEHAVIORS FOR SELECTING AND ENHANCING THE VALUE OF ATHLETES

Here's what coaches recommend for selecting athletes and enhancing their value:

- Gather information on the behavioral (and not only technical) traits of players before buying them.
- Assess the players' sense of discipline, willingness to work in a structured context, and readiness to understand the strategy of the club.
- Consider, encourage, and utilize the level of leadership you find among your players.
- Help athletes grow on a physical and technical level, and mature in terms of personality.
- Always give precedence to the collective over the individual: collective identity is always priority.
- Find the appropriate system of play, one that empowers athletes to play to the best of their abilities and spotlights their talents.
- Always explain your selection criteria, to communicate your guiding principles and spur nonstarters to improve.
- Make technical decisions contingent on the value of the athletes on the market.
- Adopt formal tools for analyzing potential and assessing behavioral competencies.

Despite the fact that all the coaches we interviewed recognize the importance of behavioral factors, no one mentioned any tools or formal processes for collecting relevant data to make well-informed decisions. Yet methods for analyzing behavioral competencies inherent to team orientation and team support are well known in managerial literature and practice. What's more, they represent a way to avoid the subjectivity of personal opinions or experiences interpreted by others.[73]

Summing up, we have tangible evidence of enhanced value of athletes when they are playing at the top of their form. Further proof is when the time comes to sell a player; in other words, when the market acknowledges the economic value accumulated through the efforts of the club and the coach. Naturally, this value is measured as the difference between the buying price and the selling price of a specific player—what happened in between is often to the credit (or the fault) of the coach. This is why we should consider processes such as selection, initiation, selling, and enhancing the value of athletes as closely linked to the sporting and economic dimensions of the club. In fact, these are the tools that a good coach implements to generate value, not simply buying standout players at market prices.

MANAGING RELATIONSHIPS WITH STAKEHOLDERS: THE MEDIA AND THE FANS

Every organization has a set of key actors, both internal and external, who have a decisive voice in the decisions made by the management and by the club. When managers play strategic roles, oftentimes they are inclined (sometimes even unconsciously) to find strategies for engaging these people. This orientation is associated with the *stakeholder theory*,[74] which is based on the distinction between shareholders (who own the principle production factor, i.e. capital, of an enterprise) and stakeholders (who include any individual or group who affects or is affected by the attainment of the organization's goals).[75] Examples of different categories of stakeholders include: customers, employees, suppliers, financial institutions, the community, the government, the media, competitors, special interest groups, and so on.[76] *Stakeholder theory* holds that organizations have to generate results that satisfy the interests not only of shareholders, but of a wide array of stakeholders.

The related area of *stakeholder management* calls on people who run organizations to pay attention to the legitimate interests of all key stakeholders simultaneously, both in setting up organizational structures and in making general policy and specific decisions. But this gives rise to a common criticism of *stakeholder theory*: that people of influence, however they are identified, must be involved to the same extent in all organizational procedures and decisions. Instead, a more effective approach to stakeholder management is based on careful stakeholder segmentation, where classifications can include internal or external, primary or secondary, and social or business, and additional criteria pertain to power, legitimacy, or urgency.[77] Based on the relative segmentation, every organization can decide the best way to engage every one of these actors and establish exchange relationships or partnerships at various levels.

The coach of a team is inevitably exposed to any number of external stakeholders who still play some part in the success of the sports project. Among these stakeholders, our study focuses mainly on the media and the fans, leaving out other key actors in the sports business that are equally influential, such as sports federations, referees, sponsors, etc. (Figure 4.2). Here is one example that highlights the complexity of the relationships coaches find themselves dealing with outside the boundaries of their technical project:

"Today sponsors play a very intense role in the life of the team. They're quite heavily involved, and they have their demands, and there are times when conflicts arise: sponsors quite rightly like being around the team, to come to Milanello and take pictures, watch the practices, but for us Milanello is a place for work, focus, discipline. Having people around can create a disturbance, and it's not always easy to act as a go-between." (Carlo Ancelotti)

Figure 4.2 Stakeholders in a sports team

But how much do the media (television, radio, newspapers and print media in general, Internet sites, etc.) matter to a coach? From an economic standpoint, and based on the future prospects of the sports business, media are the real customers because they pay broadcast rights, publicize places and players, and secure sponsorships. A sport that has no media coverage hardly ever has much money, so it has a hard time accumulating the resources needed for developing progressive technical management or playing an active social role among young people, athletes, and local fans. This is what two coaches have to say about the media:

"Baseball has prostituted itself. Pretty soon we'll be starting games at midnight so the people in outer space can watch on prime time. We're making a mistake by always going for more money." (Ray Kroc)[78]

"Football is a complicated game. The media try to make it a soap opera because they understand soap operas better than they do football. Most of them don't study the game. They don't really see it. I don't think most of them even really like it. They listen to other people who don't know, either, and formulate their opinions based on that. There's no depth to it. They latch on to everything that doesn't matter and forget about the game. That's not the game." (Tom Coughlin)[79]

Often the pre-game press conference is a high-pitched debate on tactics and strategies. Likewise, in the post-game press conference, the tensions from the field may still be palpable. Here is a vivid description from one coach:

"When I go to the press conference before the game, in my mind the game has already begun. And when I go to the press room after the game, the game isn't over yet." (José Mourinho)[80]

Another example is what happened to Fabio Capello when he was manager of the England national soccer team. During a pre-game training session for a friendly match against Egypt, someone planted hidden microphones all over the meeting room of the team's hotel, and eavesdropped on the meeting between Capello and the players and staff. The "spy" tried to sell the scoop to various news agencies, but no one accepted. In the meantime, the Football Association cautioned all newspapers against publishing the transcripts of the wiretap and launched an investigation. This episode is proof positive of the growing influence of the media and the news in the sports world. In fact, the media and journalists have become an *integral part of the sport system*, and are also key players during the time leading up to games, spotlighting a number of "events," from the announcement of the starting lineup and the team formations (offense and defense), to the reactions of the coach on the sidelines.

The media and journalists have become an *integral part of the sport system*.

Pre-game interviews and live comments made in the heat of the moment after the game are so highly anticipated and essential to sports events that they are regulated by specific agreements between the organization and the club that dictate duration and sequence. In some cases, news blackouts are not allowed because nothing is permitted that may take away from the event in question. After the game it's vital for the media to broadcast everything of any interest to viewers, reporters, and fans. Coaches who fully understand the value of specific public occasions meet the media as calmly and respectfully as possible for viewers and listeners, as this coach emphasizes:

"I don't shrink from the line of fire of questions during press conferences: even when we've just survived a defeat, I'd rather explain my reasoning and defend the motivations behind my decisions, even the wrong ones. This isn't presumption, it's the other side of transparency, which is why, though I'm not afraid to acknowledge the mistakes I've made, I believe it's better to make a public accounting even of the reflections that led to given choices that, in the end, didn't turn out to be particularly effective." (Marcello Lippi)

"I recognize the coach's responsibility to deal with the print media and with the radio and television interviewer. But the responsibility is not one that should compel him to reveal matters that are privy to staff and athletes. He should be cautious in his remarks and not allow his emotions after the game to accommodate the desire of the media folk. That desire is, of course, to hear some provocative remarks come out of the coach's mouth." (H.A. Dorfman)[81]

Players and coaches need to *know how to communicate with the press*, so they should practice; the press office should teach them *what* to say and more importantly *how* to say it. One thing they must always keep in mind is the impact of what they *actually* say to the media, more than the content of what they *intended* to say. According to this testimonial:

> *"And your relationship with all-star players? We've talked about the problems with Shevchenko, but to the English reporter who asks the manager whether or not he can put Ronaldinho on the team, Mourinho replies: If I answer that question I'll end up in trouble. If I say 'no' you'll say I'm stupid because I don't want this player. If I say 'yes' Ronaldinho and his brother (who is his agent) will go negotiate a new contract with Barcelona. So this is the kind of answer that I can't give!"* (José Mourinho)[82]

With regard to some comments from coaches, players themselves often read the papers as if they were fans. Instead, it's better to know how to distinguish between the news that's simply the outcome of journalists doing their job, and the real events or opinions of the club. On occasion, television stations and newspapers criticize the team and the coach can't or won't retaliate—sometimes to their own disadvantage. The media can be seen as a part of the locker room, something that is fueled by the team itself. The media can trigger bad feelings, but can also offer energy and distractions with special reports, interviews, celebrations, and so on. Here's the view of one coach:

> *"I don't ask for anything from journalists. My concern is always to take care of my team, so I never get into specifics about a player. If one of them is criticized, I always give technical explanations, starting with the assumption that a journalist can't know more than I do. My players have to know that I might be tough on the court, but off the court I always defend them. … There can be no mistake about that. When you put your own and the team's emotions on public display, you have to know what you're doing. You have to ride the wave of emotions, you always need to calm*

the waters and try to offer an interpretation of everything that happens."
(Simone Pianigiani)

There's no way around the fact that the media want news. Some news they get on the field; other news, which might be more interesting, comes from the locker room—stories about conflicts, possible punishments, and so on, that can undermine the team's peace of mind. The media build an image that can either help the team, or generate tensions and false hopes. In fact, many coaches stress the need to "know how to handle the media." In other words, it's critical to build a positive relationship with journalists and the most influential newspapers, and to learn what to say and how to say it. Here's an example of how a player can use a newspaper for personal aims:

> *"Every so often I'd read some interviews with players that focused solely on their selfishness. They made statements that called the entire team into play, such as 'I played badly because my teammates didn't serve me the ball enough.'"(Marcello Lippi)*

In some cases, players pay more attention to TV and media than they do to their jobs. One coach shared this amusing anecdote with us:

> *"Once a player said to me, 'But if I run without the ball, the TV camera won't zoom in on me!' I told him that he was in the wrong profession: he should have been an actor, not a football player." (Arrigo Sacchi)*

The media can build (and in a few cases damage or destroy) the image of a coach or a player without any real grounding in technical aspects of the job or the true traits of the person in question, but simply because they make news. Some players and coaches have leveraged their image to initiate personal projects, for example to become television commentators or launch clothing lines. Here's one telling example of how television can create a "personality":

"I've always been 'the screamer,' even when I sit still on the bench. Once a comedian saw me scream, so now if the media doesn't see me or call me by that name, it doesn't make the news. I never noticed until a player said to me, 'Coach, I thought you were more surly.'" (Serse Cosmi)

The media are always on the hunt for news, but they can also create a counterproductive image of sports. Often a certain distance between a sport and the media is a good thing. Consider Italy's two most recent soccer World Cup wins, in 2006 and 1982. Both victories came about with the coach defending the team from journalists via a famous news blackout campaign. Keeping journalists and the media at bay has no real benefit in technical or tactical terms, nor does it stop reporters from writing or speculating about news or news leaks. But this strategy does focus the energy and the attention of the team, avoiding possible conflicts, misunderstandings, or ambiguity. Also, the team has an "enemy" to fight against, someone who's looking for something to criticize, and who must be silenced with concrete action on the field.

In conclusion, it's wise to establish a constructive dialogue with the media, in particular when it comes to press statements by the coach (who often gets the most media attention) before and after a sporting event. The best approach is to come across on a human level, offering ideas, explaining tactics, methods, and mistakes, describing the work the team is doing openly and honestly, and always being respectful of opponents, the club, and the players.

Another influential stakeholder for the club is its fans. This group can be broken down into various categories (TV spectators, radio listeners, and supporters), but all of them have a passion for and an unbreakable bond with their favorite team. This bond is unique to the world of sports, unlike other business or social sectors. Fans show strong support and attachment to their teams, but at the same time they can be troublesome allies. For example, fans openly express their disagreement, influence the media and management decisions, attack coaches and players, and they rebel when they don't agree with how a project is being run or, more simply, when the results they hoped for don't materialize on the field.

"I think that retail organizations would die to have the kind of relationship with their customers as we have with our fans. But I think that they might find when they'd got it they might wonder about it. So, for example, if you increased the ticket price at Arsenal (which you could probably sell five times over), people wouldn't like it and they'd write in and complain, but they would still pay up. In retail there's a much less intimate relationship, so people are less likely to complain, because they know they have free choice to go elsewhere; in a football environment, they don't—their loyalty binds them to the club." (Keith Edelman)[83]

What relationship exists between the fans and the coach? Even though the fans buy the jerseys of their favorite players and purchase season passes after their team buys a star athlete, it's the coach who actually embodies the credibility of the sports project, and it's the coach who comes under attack for a defeat or an error during a game. Yet all along the coach represents the image of the team and a point of reference for the fans.

"To be Mourinho means to work in harmony with the players, with the club, and with the fans. We always want to play great music, but if that's not possible, you have to at least hit as many notes as you can. … I always try to get into the culture, not only of the club where I'm working, but the culture of the country as a whole. Right now it's really hard for me to learn the Milanese dialect; I do it because I like to joke around with the press." (José Mourinho)[84]

This doesn't mean that the coach has to meet with the fans or dedicate much time to them—but they must be aware of the fact that the fans are what underpins the value of the club, and the team's peace of mind. Fans represent the greatest source of enthusiasm and support, but tremendous pressure as well, as these coaches tell us:

"The street to obscurity is paved with athletes who perform great feats before friendly crowds. Greatness in major league sports is the ability to win in a stadium filled with people who are pulling for you to lose." (George Allen)[85]

"When you come to Pittsburgh you are playing 40 players and 50,000 fans." (Frenchy Fuqua)[86]

In light of this, we can see how essential it is for the coach to instill in the players proper respect and appreciation for the fans and the host community in general. Although fan relations differ from sport to sport, what we find in all sports is the central role of the coach in catalyzing opinions and prompting the players to be courteous and gracious toward their fans. Some coaches invite their players to take a lap around the field or to greet the fans with a wave at the end of the game, or have a third half, rugby style. Others see the fans as people who need to be informed, especially in terms of the pressures they put on the team:

"We have to respect the fans, who are the salt of our work, by giving 100% of ourselves, training hard, trying not to ever feel self-important. But I also tell our fans to be satisfied and proud if their players give it everything they've got on the court: let's get rid of this mindset of victory/ defeat as the only measure of performance." (Simone Pianigiani)

If the team is on a losing streak, accusations arise from the media and the fans against the coach, who often becomes the scapegoat for an unsuccessful project.

"Most of the time, fans wanted a public hanging when one of my boys made a mistake. But other people commended me for it because I was able to help so many boys over the years. I was a boy myself one time. If people had not forgiven me for some of the things I did when I was younger, I never would have made it in life." (Bobby Bowden)[87]

Explaining and communicating clearly facilitates managing this relationship. For example, here is a statement that appeared on Italian soccer team Inter's official website subsequent to José Mourinho's decision to stop allowing fans to observe training sessions:

> *"I have great respect for the fans and in fact even at Appaino last week, we opened our training session to the public. But I know, we all know, that among all the fans who came here to show their affection for the footballers, there are also many coaches and scouts from other teams, who might be our opponents during the season. So because we have to try out some tactical scenarios with dead balls for the first time, and since tomorrow we have our first friendly, I've decided to have a closed practice. And this is the only reason for my decision, and Inter fans have to know that." (José Mourinho)*[88]

In conclusion, the stakeholder theory suggests that coaches should adopt an orientation toward external parties who can influence and generate value for the sports project, with the aim of building relationships based on trust. Out of all stakeholders, we analyzed the role of the media and the fans as strategic "players" in the sports business. Although coaches clearly recognize the role and in some cases the weight of television, the same can't be said for the fans.

What's important is that the coach preps the entire team for media exposure.

Some coaches assert that their role has nothing to do with the fans, which is not supported by the findings of our research. A number of coaches see their relations with fans as mediated by the TV and the press, while only a few gave us a more subtle interpretation of the image and credibility of the coach in the eyes of stakeholders outside the club. In any case, what's important is that the coach preps the entire team for media exposure, and makes individual team members aware of the fact that they are public figures, headliners of positive or negative news cycles. A path needs to be mapped out leading to the conscious development of the primary source of value and values for a club: the fans (obviously, excluding those who are extremist or violent).

KEY BEHAVIORS FOR MANAGING RELATIONS WITH THE MEDIA AND THE FANS

Here's what coaches recommend for managing relations with the media and the fans:

- Identify key stakeholders and classify them according to importance.
- Consider the media and journalists as central players in the economy of the sports business.
- Be aware of the fact that the coach is the point of reference for the team and the media.
- Carefully evaluate press statements, because they may send ambiguous signals to the locker room.
- Focus on how a statement might be heard and not on what you want to say.
- Promote corporate training programs on communicating with the media.
- Create a positive attitude toward the media on the team, alleviating the pressure perceived by the athletes.
- The club must establish rules regarding interviews and press statements.
- Publicly express appreciation and gratitude for positive fan support.
- Ask the team to do their best at all times, because that's what the fans are looking for: commitment.
- Make no public statements and take no action that could provoke violence or any other form of unsportsmanlike conduct.
- Formulate a general strategy for identifying the key stakeholders and specific strategies engaging each group.

THE STAKEHOLDERS-ORIENTED TEAM LEADER

The profile of a team leader as manager encompasses a wide range of skills, and awareness of the importance of the role is equally pervasive. A coach should possess managerial competencies and adopt an approach oriented toward the collective and the corporate values integrating sporting results, economic results, and cultural results (Figure 4.3).

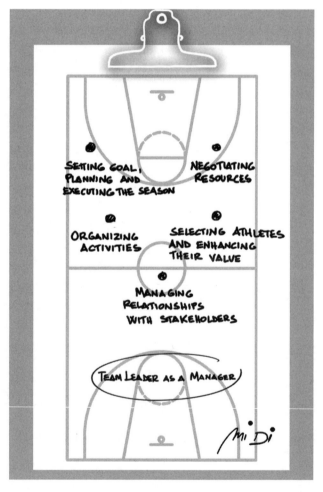

Figure 4.3 Managerial competencies that a leader should possess

All the coaches in our study agree that the coach and the players have to be supported by a club with solid ownership, competent staff, and quality resources, as the quotes below confirm:

"To win you need three things: a club, the players, and a coach." (Gian Paolo Montali)[89]

"Clearly the coach has to supervise everything and take responsibility, defend the team and protect it from senseless wastes of energy, and make the team concentrate on concrete things: the game. From the players I expect commitment and involvement, and a desire to help themselves; from the club [I expect] constant dialogue and trust, not just in words but in actions." (Ferdinando De Giorgi)

"There are only two kinds of managers: winning managers and ex-managers." (Gil Hodges)[90]

It's true that not all coaches can easily acquire these competencies, but proper training is vital. In certain cases, coaches do not think that is needed as these excerpts outline:

"I know a lot of talented people in the world of volleyball, great names, very famous too. Yet I don't recognize in any of them the ability to run the team and manage the club at the same time. I can understand that there are coaches who stop doing what they do and become team managers, and they do it well, but I don't believe that they can play both roles at the same time." (Daniele Ricci)

"The coach should take care of technical issues and group management, but not other areas that the club is responsible for—because he already has too much to do, and also because it's the club that has to guarantee continuity, since there's no telling how long the coach will remain in charge of the team." (Giuseppe Bergomi)

Theoretically speaking, the emerging need for managerial competencies for coaches—a sign of the new level of social complexity—correlates to the strategic complexity of the club. This is due to more complex goals, higher environmental pressure, scarcity of available resources, the number and needs of stakeholders, the technical level, and in some cases internationalization, etc.

"A coach has to feel like a leader, he has to be a manager, a communicator, a lot of things. It's a very complex profession." (José Mourinho)[91]

The variables that emerge from our analysis of myriad interviews with coaches lead to the realization that coaching no longer centers exclusively on running the team in the locker room and on the field. It also involves paying attention to other interlocutors, such as various roles in the club, the owners, the fans, the media, the players' market, and so forth. These aspects take on increasing importance in terms of earning credibility in the eyes of different stakeholders (the players above all), securing valuable resources for the team, filtering the pressure, and ensuring that everything the team needs is organized and managed effectively. Here's how one coach put it:

"I don't know any successful team that isn't organized, whether it's by the manager or by the players themselves on the pitch. I think that a manager has to lead, he has to be prepared to make decisions knowing that he's not going to get every one right; people look not necessarily for discipline, but a structure where they know that is what is expected of them; it's not that they're not allowed to go out of that structure, but there are consequences if they do." (Graham Taylor)[92]

Even when coaches don't have the inclination or the aptitude to handle managerial aspects of the job, they achieve better results when they work with a team manager or managing director who can fill in the gaps in terms of competencies and managerial responsibilities. One of the main findings of our study is the orientation of coaches toward engaging and partnering with others, often external stakeholders. This orientation is a distinctive factor inherent to the concept of the team leader as manager in a context that has a strong social dimension, as is the case of sports. In pairing the roles of coach and company manager, an automatic comparison emerges between a sports club and a business organization. What comes into sharp focus is the prevailing role of the social side of sports clubs, a role that can also be applied to a modern view of the firm:

- The club (firm) works in a context where there are various stakeholders, and expresses values and opinions that reflect a dominant ethic. The sustainability of the club (firm) over time depends a great deal on the ability to adopt and convey these values.
- Considering how the club (firm) produces its economic value, factors linked to the principal product are losing ground, while the reputation of the club (firm) is taking on greater emphasis and importance, along with the pact of trust established between the club (firm) and its key stakeholders.[93]

The considerations above should prompt team leaders, whatever their sphere, to adopt socially responsible managerial policies and models centered on aligning the organization's interests with those of its stakeholders, with shared values serving as the basis for action. Even though sports and business are two very different worlds, both roles share a contemporary view of social and economic performance. We believe that business managers could learn to apply the behaviors we've reviewed in this study. For executives, as for coaches of sports teams, we've identified the following characteristics/criticalities:

- *Managerial competencies for dealing with actors and resources inside and outside the organization*: What's essential for a good coach is maintaining a balance between orientation toward tasks, results, people, and external actors as sources of value. These competencies are grounded in the ability to build solid relationships with others, based on information exchange and complementarity.

- *Stakeholder orientation*: Particularly in the sports world but more and more in business as well, orientation toward key stakeholders is essential to generating value. Managers and companies have to ensure that people at every level of the organization recognize the importance of the social, cultural, and territorial dimensions of being a firm.

- *Integration of various types of results*: The more adroitly the coach deals with various actors in the club and in the surrounding environment, the more effectively the team will catalyze energy, channeling it on to the field and driving toward success. Likewise, social managers looking to the environment and the surrounding context will find the conditions for focusing their actions and decisions on managing human and financial resources. This tells us that team leaders should know how to interpret performance not only in light of economic results, but by taking a broader perspective that encompasses social responsibility as well.

Managers and companies have to ensure that people at every level of the organization recognize the importance of the social, cultural, and territorial dimensions of being a firm.

The behaviors described here represent a solid starting point for inviting coaches and executives alike to shore up their strengths, whether training for the field of play or the office desk.

"We are all good at something, and yet all of us do not cultivate our strengths. Forget about weaknesses. Why waste time on weaknesses when we have strengths that we can build on?" (Ken Carter)[94]

THE TEAM LEADER AS MANAGER: KEY MESSAGES

1 A manager, generally speaking, is a person who is responsible for setting goals for a project or a firm, organizing available resources (material and human, tangible and intangible), making decisions that are consistent with the strategic orientation of the organization, and vouching for results.

2 The team leader as manager is an emerging figure. This title refers to a coach who has a voice in strategic decisions or takes direct responsibility for activities that impact the project and the team, in addition to handling technical aspects of the job. The team leader as manager deals with technique and mission, tactics and market, and at the same time vouches for the quality of the project, answering to players, fans, owners, media, and key stakeholders.

3 The coach plays a key role in the sports business in terms of generating value.

4 Team leaders as managers do the following:
   - Acquire new competencies to manage a more complex organization, in light of the higher level of technical abilities of the players; greater expectations of athletes, fans, and owners; more intense environmental pressure; and more numerous key stakeholders—often with conflicting interests—who affect the club's decisions.
   - Take on new roles: goal-setting, planning and executing the season, negotiating resources with owners, organizing staff activities, recruiting athletes and enabling them to fully realize their potential, and handling relations with external stakeholders, in particular the media and the fans.

- Delegate activities that are constructive for the technical project to competent, specialized staff members, dedicating time to coordinate and manage these people so they can perform effectively and provide high-quality services.
- Become go-to people not only for the owners, but also for other important stakeholders outside the club.

5 Business executives can do the following:

- Borrow the emphasis on the social side of business from the sports world, which slots into a modern view of management and the firm.
- Draw inspiration from sports coaches in managing people and resources inside and outside the organization, adopting a stakeholder orientation, and integrating various types of results.
- Adopt the behaviors of team leaders in sports more easily by taking a comprehensive analytical perspective and leveraging a skill set that includes persuading, negotiating, building, and managing multiple relationships, communicating, dealing with collaborators, and resolving conflicts.

NOTES

1 Rosner, S. and Shropshire, K. (2004) *The Business of Sports*, Sudbury, MA: Jones & Bartlett Publishers; Masteralexis, L.P., Barr, C. and Hums, M. (2008) *Principles and Practice of Sport Management*, Sudbury, MA: Jones & Bartlett Publishers.
2 Mullin, B., Hardy, S. and Sutton, W. (2007) *Sport Marketing*, 3rd edn, Champaign, IL: Human Kinetics.
3 Zweig, E. and McDonell, C. (2010) *Big Book of Sport Quotes*, Buffalo, NY: Firefly Books.
4 Lepak, D. and Snell, S. (1999) "The Strategic Management of Human

Capital: Determinants and Implications of Different Relationships," *Academy of Management Review*, 24, 1, pp. 1–18.

5   Latham, G.P. and Locke, E.A. (1975) "Increasing Productivity with Decreasing Time Limits: A Field Replication of Parkinson's Law," *Journal of Applied Psychology*, 60, pp. 524–6; Locke, E.A., Latham, G.P., Smith, K.J. and Wood, R.E. (1990) *A Theory of Goal-setting & Task Performance*, Englewood Cliffs: Prentice Hall, p. 544; Locke, E.A. and Latham, G.P. (2009) "Has Goal-setting Gone Wild, or Have its Attackers Abandoned Good Scholarship?," *Academy of Management Perspectives*, 23, 1, pp. 17–23.

6   Locke et al., op. cit.

7   Knight, D., Durham, C.C. and Locke, E.A. (2001) "The Relationship of Team Goals, Incentives, and Efficacy to Strategic Risk, Tactical Implementation, and Performance," *Academy of Management Journal*, 44, pp. 326–38.

8   Carty, J. and Wooden, J. (2005) *Coach Wooden's Pyramid of Success*, Ventura, CA: Regal Books.

9   Zweig and McDonell, op. cit.

10   Ibid.

11   McCallie, J.P. (2012) *Choice not Chance*, Hoboken, NJ: Wiley & Sons.

12   Zanardo, L. and Nitro, G. (2009) *Lo sport sale in cattedra l'azienda scende in campo*, Milano, Italy: Apogeo, p. 133.

13   Di Lenna, A. (2008) *Time out management: Citazioni dal mondo dello sport per manager appassionati e vincenti*, Milano, Italy: Il Sole 24 Ore, p. 65.

14   Brady, C., Bolchover, D. and Sturgess, B. (2008) "Managing in the Talent Economy: The Football Model for Business," *California Management Review*, 50, 4 (Summer), p. 91.

15   Zweig and McDonell, op. cit.

16   Ibid.

17   Amhurst, J. (2005) *The Special One: the Wit and Wisdom of José Mourinho*, London, UK: Virgin Books.

18   Palladino, E. (2011) *Lombardi and Landry*, New York, NY: Skyhorse Publishing.

19   Zweig and McDonell, op. cit.

20 Carty and Wooden, op. cit.

21 Bowden, B. and Schlabach, M. (2011) *Called to Coach*, New York, NY: Howard Books.

22 Zweig and McDonell, op. cit.

23 Amhurst, op. cit.

24 Yoast, B. and Sullivan, S. (2005) *Remember this Titan*, Lanham, MD: Taylor Trade.

25 Di Lenna, op. cit., p. 16.

26 Carty and Wooden, op. cit.

27 Neubert, M.J. (1998) "The Value of Feedback and Goal-setting over Goal-setting Alone and Potential Moderators of This Effect: A Meta-Analysis," *Human Performance*, 11, 4, pp. 321–35.

28 Harrity, M. (2012) *Coaching Wisdom*, South Portland, ON: Sellers Publishing.

29 Schweitzer, M.E., Ordóñez, L. and Douma, B. (2004) "Goal-setting as a Motivator of Unethical Behavior," *Academy of Management Journal*, 47, 3, pp. 422–32.

30 Carty and Wooden, op. cit.

31 Ordóñez, L., Schweitzer, M.E., Galinsky, A.D. and Bazerman, M.H. (2009) "Goals Gone Wild: How Goals Systematically Harm Individuals and Organizations," *Academy of Management Perspectives*, 23, 1, pp. 6–16.

32 Druckman, D. (ed.) (1977) *Negotiations: Social-psychological Perspectives*, Beverly Hills, CA: Sage Publications.

33 Bazerman, M.H. and Lewicki, R.J. (eds) (1983) *Negotiating in Organizations*, Beverly Hills, CA: Sage Publications.

34 Sebenius, J.K. (2001) "Six Habits of Merely Effective Negotiators," *Harvard Business Review*, 79, p. 87.

35 Baron, R.A. (1989) "Personality and Organizational Conflict: Effects of the Type a Behavior and Self-Monitoring," *Organizational Behavior and Human Decision Processes*, 44, pp. 281–96.

36 Raiffa, H. (1982) *The Art and Science of Negotiation*, Cambridge, MA: Harvard University Press.

37 Pruitt, D.G. (1983) "Strategic Choice in Negotiation," *American Behavioral Scientist*, 27, 2 (Nov–Dec), p. 167.

38 Conger, J.A. (1998) "The Necessary Art of Persuasion," *Harvard Business Review*, 76, p. 84.

39 Theobald, T. and Cooper, C. (2005) *Business and the Beautiful Game: How You Can Apply the Skills and Passion of Football to be a Winner in Business*, London, UK: Kogan Page Publishers, p. 126.

40 Riley, P. (1993) *The Winner Within*, New York, NY: Berkeley Books

41 Williams, G.A. and Miller, R.B. (2002) "Change the Way You Persuade," *Harvard Business Review*, 80, p. 64.

42 Amhurst, op. cit.

43 Zweig and McDonell, op. cit.

44 Siang, S. and Sitkin, S.B. (2006) "Coach K on Leadership: An Interview with Mike Krzyzewski," *Leader to Leader*, S1 (Fall), pp. 34–39.

45 Bowden and Schlabach, op. cit.

46 Theobald and Cooper, op. cit.

47 Ibid., pp. 152–3.

48 Zweig and McDonell, op. cit.

49 Cavaliere, C., Mulazzi, P. and Paterni, R. (2009) *Rugby: dal campo all'azienda. Oltre il semplice fare squadra*, Milano, Italy: Guerini e Associati, p. 93.

50 Burke, C.S., Stagl, K.C., Klein, C., Goodwin, G.F., Salas, E. and Halpin, S.M. (2006) "What Type of Leadership Behaviors Are Functional in Teams? A Meta-Analysis," *The Leadership Quarterly*, 17, pp. 288–307.

51 Dansereau, F. (1995) "A Dyadic Approach to Leadership: Creating and Nurturing this Approach under Fire," *The Leadership Quarterly*, 6, pp. 479–90.

52 Gerhart, B., Hollenbeck, J.R. and Noe, R. (2005) *Human Resource Management*, New York, NY: McGraw-Hill.

53 Huselid, M.A., Becker, B.E. and Beatty, R.W. (2005) *The Workforce Scorecard: Managing Human Capital to Execute Strategy*, Boston, MA: Harvard Business School Press.

54 Boyatzis, R.E. (1982) *The Competent Manager: A Model for Effective Performance*, New York, NY: Wiley; Spencer, L.M and Spencer, S.M. (1993) *Competence at Work: Models for Superior Performance*, New York, NY: Wiley.

55 Kuehl, K., Kuehl, J. and Tefertiller, C. (2005) *Mental Toughness*, Chicago, IL: Ivan R. Dee.

56 McCallie, op. cit.

57 Holtz, L. (2006) *Wins, Losses and Lessons*, New York, NY: itbooks.

58 McCallie, op. cit.

59 Zweig and McDonell, op. cit.

60 Zweig and McDonell, op. cit.

61 Jamison, S. and Wooden, J. (2004) *My Personal Best: Life Lessons from an All-American Journey*, New York, NY: McGraw-Hill.

62 De Rond, M. (2012) *There is an I in Team*, Boston, MA: Harvard Business Review Press.

63 Di Lenna, op. cit., p. 46.

64 Theobald and Cooper, op. cit.

65 Bolchover, D. and Brady, C. (2006) *The 90-Minute Manager: Lessons from the Sharp End of Management*, New York, NY: Pearson Prentice Hall Business.

66 Cavaliere et al., op. cit., p. 103.

67 Russell, B. and Steinberg, A. (2009) *Red and Me*, New York, NY: Harper.

68 Yoast and Sullivan, op. cit.

69 Di Lenna, op. cit., p. 135.

70 Ibid., p. 29.

71 Youndt, M.A., Subramaniam, M. and Snell S.A. (2004) "Intellectual Capital Profiles: An Examination of Investments and Returns," *Journal of Management Studies*, 41, 2, pp. 335–61.

72 Hackman J.R. and Wageman R. (2005) "A Theory of Team Coaching," *Academy of Management Revie*, 30, 2, pp. 269–87.

73 Lado, A.A. and Wilson, M.C. (1994) "Human Resource Systems and Sustained Competitive Advantage: A Competency-Based Perspective," *Academy of Management Review*, 19, 4, pp. 699–727.

74 Freeman, R.E. (1984) *Strategic Management: A Stakeholder Approach*, Boston, MA: Pitman.

75 Carroll, A.B. (1991) "The Pyramid of Corporate Social Responsibility: Toward the Moral Management of Organizational Stakeholders," *Business Horizons*, 34, pp. 39–48; Freeman, R.E. (1994) "The Politics of Stakeholder Theory," *Business Ethics Quarterly*, 4, 4, pp. 409–21.

76 Freeman, R.E., Harrison, J.S. and Wicks, A.C. (2007) *Managing for Stakeholders; Survival Reputation and Success*, New Haven, CT: Yale University Press.

77 Mitchell, R.K., Agle, B.R. and Wood, D.J. (1997) "Toward a Theory of Stakeholder Identification and Salience: Defining the Principle of Who or What Really Counts," *Academy of Management Review*, 22, 4, pp. 853–86.

78 Zweig and McDonell, op. cit.

79 Callahan, T. (2008) *The GM: A Football Life, a Final Season, and a Last Laugh*, New York, NY: Three Rivers Press.

80 Tossani, M. (2008) *L'altro mago: Mourinho dopo Herrera*, Arezz, Italy: Limina.

81 Dorfman, H.A. (2003) *Coaching the Mental Game*, Lanham, MD: Taylor Trade Publishing.

82 Ibid., p. 101.

83 Theobald and Cooper, op. cit., p. 107.

84 Tossani, op. cit., pp. 87, 93.

85 Zweig and McDonell, op. cit.

86 Ibid.

87 Bowden and Schlabach, op. cit.

88 Ibid., p. 10.

89 Di Lenna, op. cit.

90 Zweig and McDonell, op. cit.

91 Ibid.

92 Theobald and Cooper, op. cit., p. 68.

93 Rifkin, J. (2004) *The European Dream: How Europe's Vision of the Future is Quietly Eclipsing the American Dream*, New York, NY: Jeremy P. Tarcher.

94 Holtz, op. cit.

CHAPTER 5

THE TEAM LEADER AS COACH

TEAM COACHING

In this chapter we'll explore the relationship between the coach and the team in a sports context, specifically focusing on the coach's role in motivating team members.

A key component of team leadership is *team coaching*—that is, "direct interaction with a team intended to help make coordinated and task-appropriate use of their collective resources in accomplishing the team's work."[1]

Three different forms of team coaching impact team performance.

Three different forms of team coaching impact team performance (see Figure 5.1):

- *Motivational coaching*, which serves to enhance the individual and collective efforts of team members and the team as a whole.
- *Consultative coaching*, which aims to find the most appropriate strategies and procedures for performing team tasks and achieving team goals.

Figure 5.1 Types of team coaching

- *Educational coaching*, which is used to improve the skills and competencies of team members.

Ideally, team leaders excel at all three types of coaching. But every leader has a natural inclination toward one kind over another, and shows a different level of proficiency for each one. Correspondingly, some sports coaches have built their careers on an image of excellence either as motivators, as particularly gifted strategists in terms of tactics or planning, or as teachers who mold and grow their players.

The three forms of coaching serve different—albeit interdependent—functions. Specifically, educational coaching and consultative coaching can be powerful drivers of motivation. The first improves players' abilities to perform their tasks and, in doing so, enhances their self-esteem and confidence in themselves and their teammates.

This boosts motivation at both the individual and team levels: all the athletes realize that on a personal and group level they have (or will acquire) the skills and competencies they need to reach their goals. So, educational coaching motivates because it reduces uncertainty in individual and collective abilities (self-efficacy theory). A strong conviction of self-efficacy is a potent antidote to failure. This conviction pushes people to persevere, even in the face of defeat, to take on bigger challenges and to drive themselves beyond their limits:

"If the players realize they're working well, they won't lose heart, and they persist in the face of defeat, and they train with renewed enthusiasm." (Stefano Pioli)

Task-focused coaches typically put a strong emphasis on educational coaching: they concentrate on developing players' skills and competencies (tactical, technical, and athletic), and on helping players grow and learn. These coaches see their role as teaching players how to do their jobs as best they can to achieve team goals. Here are some examples of this approach:

"My job is to coach, which means to help the boys improve." (Roberto Donadoni)

"I base my philosophy on a work culture. Working on the pitch is the only way to grow and create a team." (Cesare Prandelli)

"I foster the players' growth by creating plays that hone their ability to make judgments. If I never present players with problems, they'll have a hard time resolving them." *(Arrigo Sacchi)*

Similarly, consultative coaching spurs team motivation by alleviating doubts, fears, insecurities, and ambiguities with regard to goals and the best way to achieve them. This is done by conveying clear and credible strategies, precise programs and plans for implementing these strategies, and effective work methods. All this is consistent with the path-goal theory and the goal-setting theory, which emphasize an essential component of motivation: the leader's ability to set and manage goals, and to map out the path for attaining them. The degree to which consultative coaching can increase motivation depends on how effectively this approach conveys to team members a dual conviction:

- Team goals are legitimate and credible. The leaders and their staff need to raise the bar on goals and ambitions of individual team members, for example by resorting to transformational leadership:

  "As I see it, motivation is the ability to touch people's hearts, to open them up and make them see goals that had been unimaginable before." *(Gianni De Biasi)*

  "Every player has to have a dream, and it's up to the leader to find out what it is, to work on it, to help it grow, observing it from a distance. Because the key is the dream. The secret that pushes people to achieve things they never thought that they would do, or more importantly that they could do. And when one dream is done, another must follow. The ability to coach dreams, this is one of the characteristics that a good coach and a good leader has to have." *(Gian Paolo Montali)[2]*

- The appropriate strategies, plans, and resources are in place to reach these goals. This means that the team leader needs to invest in detailed, meticulous planning to show that everything possible has been done to create the conditions that enable the players to realize the team's projects.

"I believe in extremely precise, minute-by-minute, tightly structured practices. Making judgments under severe stress is the most difficult thing there is. The more preparation you have prior to the conflict, the more you can do in a clinical situation, the better off you will be. […] Say it is the last 20 seconds of a game and we're losing. We have already practiced six plays that we can apply in that situation. That way, we know what to do, and we can calmly execute the plays. We'll have no doubts in our minds, we will have more poise, and we can concentrate without falling prey to desperation." (Bill Walsh)[3]

In some cases consultative coaching is so essential that some coaches go so far as to consider leadership as a "system of play." For these coaches, what counts more than their own leadership, or the leadership of a player, is getting the group to wholeheartedly embrace the tactical "creed" and the work methods put forward by the coach and the staff:

"On my teams, the leader was the system of play, which has the advantage of never getting injured or getting out of shape." (Arrigo Sacchi)

Consultative coaching boosts motivation because it engenders the team's perception of collective self-efficacy. This form of coaching is also normally associated with highly task-focused coaches.

THE HEART OF TEAM COACHING: MANAGING INTERDEPENDENCIES AND PROMOTING SOCIAL SUPPORT

A team leader seeks to improve team performance not only by forging competencies, motivations, and behaviors of team members individually, but more importantly by managing the *interdependencies* that arise among them. This fundamental concept has critical ramifications for choices relating to team composition and team management:

"A group isn't like a car; it's like a living body, an organism. Even a car is something more than a simple set of parts. But if one part gets broken, I can replace it with an identical spare part. That's not how it is with a group. Putting in a new player alters the entire team configuration, from a tactical standpoint as well as psychological and emotional one. A sentence is like a team, too. The true meaning of a sentence is something more than just the sum of its parts. Simply by moving a comma the whole thing takes on another meaning." (Marcello Lippi)[4]

"Any good coach or manager has got to be responsible for phasing out people through the organization. When you do it, you often end up as the most unpopular person in the organization. Yet it has to be done continually. There will be some suffering, and there is no way to avoid it. The real danger is if the decision aimed at improving the team leads to so much bitterness that the fallout causes other players to take sides. When the team becomes divided, the decision has done more harm than good." (Bill Walsh)[5]

Management literature identifies various forms of interdependence (Figure 5.2):

- *Goal interdependence* among team members, which we naturally find when there are team goals, can also exist when there are different individual goals that are mutually compatible.
- *Reward interdependence*, which on a team can be:
  - Positive when there are group rewards such as collective bonuses for hitting a target.
  - Negative when reward systems are based on rankings, so that only top performers on the team get rewards. In this case, the better your teammates perform, the less chance you have to win a reward.

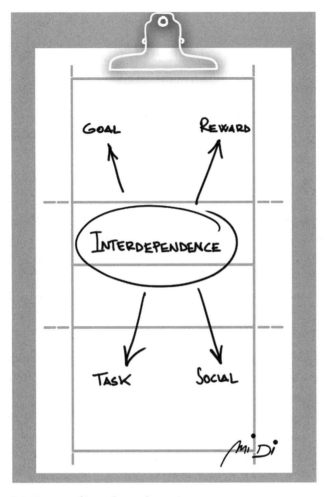

Figure 5.2 Forms of interdependence in teams

- Neither positive nor negative when the reward for a team member is completely independent and unrelated to teammates' rewards.
- *Task interdependence*, that is, the degree to which the activity undertaken by every individual impacts—and is impacted by— the activity performed by a teammate in terms of reaching team

outcomes. An example of very high interdependence is a medical team performing surgery.

- *Social interdependence*, which reflects how team members relate to their teammates. This interdependency can be positive (cooperation), negative (competition, antagonism), or neither (individualism).[6] In team sports, athletes who have an individualistic attitude try to optimize their own performance; players who have a competitive bent strive to outperform their teammates. Instead, those with a cooperative inclination are interested in maximizing team performance. Consequently, they try their best to help their teammates do their best too. Generally, research shows that the tendency to cooperate improves team results, so the team leader should encourage this kind of positive social interdependence.[7]

To sum up, we can interpret team interdependence in two different ways:[8]

- *Structural interdependence*, which encompasses how the team's work is organized, evaluated, and compensated. This incorporates goal, task, and reward interdependence.
- *Psychological interdependence,* which covers the predispositions and perceptions of team members in terms of how they relate to their teammates (social interdependence).

Generally speaking, a good team leader should use goal, task, and reward interdependence to increase social interdependence.

Structural interdependence doesn't necessarily require leadership skills. In fact, coordinating processes and individual contributions to operational procedures simply calls for solid managerial skills, including organizing work, assigning roles, and planning activities. From a motivational standpoint, what carries far more weight is the team leader's ability to shape *discretional* and *contextual* (extra-role) behaviors of team members toward their teammates. In other words, what lies at the heart of motivational team coaching is the leader's ability to enhance the cooperative aspect of social interdependence among team members. In doing so, the leader activates and reinforces the desire of team members to support their colleagues and adopt behaviors that shore up individual contributions to the realization of team goals.

What lies at the heart of motivational team coaching is the leader's ability to enhance the cooperative aspect of social interdependence among team members.

These are some examples of psychological interdependence and how a team leader can stimulate it:

"When we watch tape, it's not just watching how you shoot or defend. If I see a sequence where a player shows this magnificent face that's strong, I'll stop and say something about it. This past summer in Madrid, I stopped the tape as Kevin Durant, a great young player who I wanted to emerge, was coming down the court. He looks magnificent; he's just so strong. So I asked his teammate, Russell Westbrook, 'When Kevin looks like that, how do you feel?' And he says, 'Coach, when he looks like that, I feel like we're going to win.' So I turned to Kevin and said, 'Kevin, I want you to understand the power you have. Even before you shoot or defend, you can create an atmosphere where the people around you feel like they can win. How good is that, man?'" (Mike Krzyszewski)[9]

"When we played the Davis Cup Final against Argentina, David Ferrer, our best player, the first day of singles lost by a landslide to David Nalbandian. From his statements after the match, I realized that he was very depressed, he'd lost his confidence. So I decided to replace him with Fernando Verdasco. Two days later, when Verdasco played his single, Ferrer was the first to motivate him and try to cheer him on even though Verdasco was playing in Ferrer's place. At one point, at a tough moment in the match (his opponent was up two sets to one) I told Verdasco: 'Turn around and look at David. See how he's cheering for you? Think of how he'd love to be in your place right now! Play for the team, not for yourself!' From then on he reacted. He turned the match around and he won." (Emilio Sánchez)

The model in Figure 5.3 summarizes the dual level of influence that a team leader needs to exercise over team members to improve team performance:

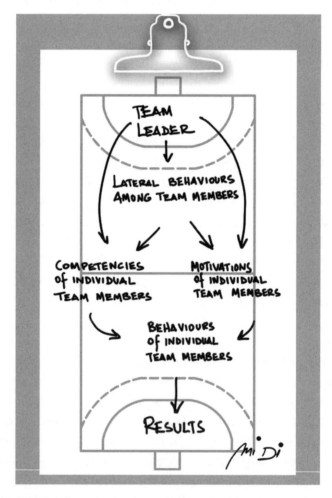

Figure 5.3 The direct and indirect influence of the team leader on team results

- On one hand, coaches have to manage their personal relationships with each team member in a way that reinforces the competencies and motivation needed to best enact individual behaviors that serve to achieve team goals.
- On the other, coaches need to create the conditions for all team members to be able and willing to engage in behaviors that support their teammates, building up their competencies and strengthening their motivation.

The key message in this model is that the team leader can and should impact team performance by acting both directly and indirectly (by shaping lateral relationships among team members) on individual competencies, motivations, behaviors, and results.

A key role of the team leader involves channeling and encouraging constructive lateral influence among colleagues, which is useful in accomplishing team goals. Here's an example of lateral influence fostering teammates' skills development and motivation:

"In our academy we always encourage our tennis players to play doubles too. That way, they have to make an effort to understand their partner, which also helps them develop skills in self-assessment (Where and how can I improve?) and in analyzing opponents (How can I beat them?), and they can learn from their partners. All this creates the conditions for improving and increasing the chances of becoming successful athletes. What's more, all of our kids travel as a group; they all watch each other's matches, and are taught to celebrate the victories of their teammates. We think that if they help each other out, they can all become stronger, and turn a potentially negative feeling like envy, which drains so much energy and prevents players from succeeding, into the drive to emulate, which encourages learning and continuous improvement." (Emilio Sánchez)

In fact, lateral influence can be positive, generating social support behaviors, or negative, taking the form of antagonistic and conflictual behaviors.

Successful teams are typically characterized by positive lateral influence fostering cohesion and a collaborative spirit, which in turn stimulate learning, continuous improvement and, ultimately, task accomplishment:

"Teams, even the best of them, make small mistakes, but they make many of these mistakes over and over again that can compromise a season. To understand the reasons behind losses and to make continuous incremental improvements on factors that are only apparently marginal, it's important to work in a positive context. All the most successful teams call themselves a 'family.' That means that you can have a row, but the next day you're all fighting together again on the same side because there's love. Without all this it's hard to build an environment that grows and improves, while winning as well." (John Kirwan)

Such a team atmosphere is usually created by stimulating four main social support behaviors:[10]

- Helping teammates reach individual goals with either person- or task-focused support. The first aims at enhancing self-esteem and supporting colleagues who are dealing with personal issues, in particular by showing friendship and expressing emotions. The second focuses on assisting colleagues in solving professional problems, mainly though support in carrying out work-related tasks—for example, giving information or practical advice for improving how certain activities are done.
- Cooperating with colleagues, voluntarily offering resources, time, and energy.
- Being courteous to teammates, showing consideration, listening, being open to dialogue, and willing to accept other points of view, taking note of the effects that personal actions can have on colleagues.

- Motivating teammates by complementing them on their success, encouraging them when they're struggling, expressing confidence in their skills, and transmitting positive energy.

A team leader's ability to foster these behaviors among team members can lead to better outcomes,[11] because team members who get social support from their teammates enjoy greater job satisfaction. In addition, they're more committed, and **The greater the social interdependence in the group, the more positive influences there will be.** expend more effort in carrying out their tasks. In many cases, the teammates' influence is even stronger than the leader's influence in generating these positive results. The greater the social interdependence in the group, the more positive influences there will be.

Because they are discretionary, the quantity and quality of social support behaviors within the context of a team depend in part on the natural propensities of team members,[12] and in part on their willingness and ability to enact such behaviors. This means that the role of the team leader is vital both when building and running the team. To do the first successfully, the leader chooses altruistic and collaborative team members; for the second, the leader should help develop motivation, knowledge, and skills that team members need to engage in social support behaviors. In fact, it's not enough for team members to want to help their teammates; they also have to know how to go about it. The necessary knowledge and skills, summarized in Figure 5.4, can be nurtured by the team leader primarily through appropriate educational coaching.

Now we'll focus our attention on motivational coaching: the actions that the team leader can take to foster willingness among team members to adopt positive social support behaviors.

In team contexts where there is both cooperative and competitive interdependence, one of the biggest challenges for a coach lies in reconciling legitimate individual goals with team goals. This is challenging if we consider that team members often have conflicting

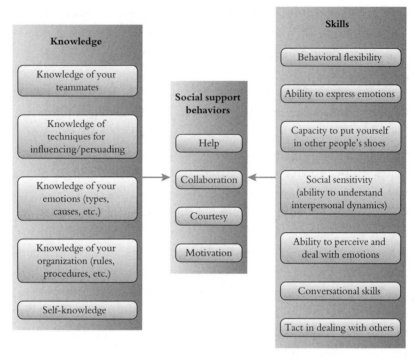

Figure 5.4 Skills and competencies that facilitate social support behaviors on a team
Source: adapted from Dudley and Cortina (2008)

individual goals (for example, every player's personal aim is to get as much game time as possible). So an effective team leader understands individual aspirations, sets motivating individual objectives that are compatible with team goals, and then convinces players to sacrifice some of their own objectives for the good of the group when necessary (at least partially or temporarily). In addition to team goals, there must be compatible and personalized individual objectives: young athletes could aim to better personal records of the number of games or minutes played, or veterans could focus on mentoring rookies, or strikers could try to score more goals in a soccer match.

HOW TO MANAGE TEAM COACHING: LEADERSHIP STYLE, LEADER FOCUS, AND COMMUNICATION PROCESSES

Team coaching processes can be implemented in a wide variety of ways, with various decision-making and communication styles, or with a focus on tasks or people.

Directive and democratic decision-making styles

A clear distinction can be drawn between coaches with a directive leadership style and those who prefer a more participative style, who consider rule-making detrimental and encourage involvement and empowerment instead. The following quote reflects the first approach:

> "There are different ways to manage a group, but the coach is the one who has to lead it. Within a group there may be some people who are more respected than others, people whose words carry more weight, also as far as eliciting motivation ... but the person in charge is the coach. ... The leader has to be the coach, he's the one who lays down the law. ... The important thing is that players do as I say." (Luigi Delneri)

And here are descriptions of the second leadership style:

> "First and foremost you have to give players responsibilities, share the program with them and set goals together. ... How? There is any number of ways—one might be to have players participate in running training sessions or games. ... I'm a kind of mediator, I try to get people to come up with ideas, I analyze them, and together we decide what actions to take." (Carlo Ancelotti)

"Winning teams are more like open forums in which everyone partici-pates in the decision-making process, coaches and players alike, until the decision is made. Others must know who is in command, but a head coach must behave democratically." (Bill Walsh)[13]

"What happens when you empower is you create ownership. The outcome of that empowerment is the ability to share ideas and contribute ideas across the board. The other thing that happens if you get that going is, if the leader leaves or is no longer there, that team has a greater chance of still going forward because it wasn't just the leader. The values, the way you did it, belongs to the team. If a leader has done a great job with his team, then that team can function without the leader at a certain level— whether that leader is on leave or just leaves. This gives an unbelievable base to whatever the new leadership is." (Mike Krzyzewski)[14]

Both styles can have a constructive impact on motivation, although they follow very different paths. The directive style can motivate by reducing uncertainty. The democratic style can motivate by making work more meaningful and by fostering a more satisfying personal relationship between players and coach.

Task/people orientation

Some coaches have a tendency to be *task-focused*. They believe that the team's success derives primarily from players performing their tasks to the best of their abilities, being clear on what they have to do, how they have to do it, and why. These coaches therefore focus on *educational coaching* and *consultative coaching*:

"I believe that a coach has to teach techniques and tactics." (Paolo Indiani)

Coaches who focus mainly on people emphasize motivational coaching, pay personalized attention to athletes on the team, and place value on individual relationships. They promote team cohesion and foster emotional bonds, based on the belief that the working atmosphere, team spirit, and the quality of interpersonal relationships are the basic building blocks of team success:

"The way I see soccer is based mainly on my relationship with the players. I believe that by creating a clear, straightforward relationship of mutual respect, there's a better chance of getting the athletes to give it their all." (Luciano Spalletti)

"I always start with the man, not the soccer player. I try to find out what makes him tick even though it's not easy. Understanding what a man is made of helps enormously to position him within the group." (Gianni De Biasi)

All coaches should possess the proper skills to manage both functions as effectively as possible. But each coach has a stronger inclination toward one or the other.

Managing communication

Leadership is essentially exercised through communication processes, both verbal and nonverbal, that convey goals, expectations, beliefs, and assessments to the team:

"You need to know how to communicate well, both verbally and nonverbally. For example, I used to use 'tactile' communication too: patting a player on the head when he's coming off the pitch, if he's been substituted or sent off, is an important, gratifying physical gesture. By communication I also mean face time with the player, with the person; there's so much to get to know. Then there's communication with the team as a whole. This has to be direct and clear; you have to look the players in the eyes, positioning yourself where everyone can easily see

you. Before a game I used to make a short speech, 12 to 13 minutes long. I demanded to be understood, not interpreted, even if I had to repeat the same concept a thousand times to be sure that it was perfectly internalized. I used to prepare every pre-game meeting carefully, and I wrote down everything I'd say, everything on one sheet of paper, with key messages for each player and for the team as a whole." (Sandro Gamba)

Team communication processes lie at the very heart of the coach's role. From a motivational viewpoint, communication is often critical—especially so in reducing uncertainty. The coach has to reassure players and avoid raising doubts, and to enhance confidence, conviction, and self-esteem. Reducing uncertainty about individual and team abilities motivates both individual athletes and an entire team, fostering self-confidence (*self-efficacy theory*[15]). The following statements reflect this concept:

"The coach doesn't have to be a father or a big brother who gives you a pat on the back, but a strong, confident leader who gives the group the feeling that he can lead them toward their goals. It follows that being popular or unpopular isn't very important." (Marcello Lippi)

"What's essential is the coach's ability to communicate his confidence in his athletes, to give them the impression that they can do something wonderful, and to focus on this rather than on the mistakes they might make. For example, in a 4×100 meter relay race, there's always the chance that a runner will fall down, or some accident will happen along the way, but it's important to focus on the positive things you have to do. There's always the fear of making a mistake—you have to live with that, especially if you're fully prepared. A good coach knows this, and he should alleviate the pressure anyway. He can do this by using nonverbal communication with gestures, or with a reassuring, calming tone of voice; this transmits certainty, positivity, and confidence. A lot can be communicated by how you look the athletes in the eyes when you talk to them, in a way that has to convey the desire to win and the belief in their chances to

do so. The final advice you give just before the match is fundamental: the coach should never remind athletes not to make their habitual mistakes! Or else this becomes a self-fulfilling prophecy." (Andrea Colombo)

"If you convey confidence and certainty before a match, you can help a player. It's important to transmit a sense of security." (Arrigo Sacchi)

Coaches can also lessen uncertainty by keeping it short and simple, so these two concepts are crucial for team communication:

"I try not to talk a lot, and to communicate key concepts as simply as possible." (Giancarlo Camolese)

"I prefer group discussions. I try to use a confident tone of voice, with words that leave an impression. A coach shouldn't talk too long: it's better to talk a little and often. When you go off on tangents with long speeches, the players quickly stop paying attention." (Carlo Ancelotti)

Clear and *transparent* communication also minimizes ambiguity and uncertainty. As the path-goal theory affirms, reducing uncertainty with regard to goals, strategies, roles, and expected behaviors can impact team motivation in a positive way. Many coaches believe it's appropriate to *justify decisions*, explaining their reasoning to facilitate acceptance by the team:

"I always offer a technical explanation to the players who stay on the bench, because if they understand the motivations behind my choice, they see it as an action that benefits the team, not as a personal affront." (Claudio Gentile)

"When you make certain choices, you try to dialogue with the players and get them on board as to the reasons behind those choices. I always illustrate the technical/tactical assessment that prompted my decision, and I'm willing to give any explanation players may need." (Luigi De Canio)

"It's essential to explain your choices and make the reasoning behind them understood." (Gianni De Biasi)

"The coach owes it to the players to be straight with them." (Silvio Baldini)

Coaches must understand the circumstances and the types of messages that may call for *individual communication* with a single athlete, or *collective communication* with the entire team:

"The relationship with individual players centers on specific technical issues, personal matters, or problems relating to behavior. The relationship with the group covers the collective technical/tactical spheres, or behavior that relates to the group as a whole." (Luigi De Canio)

"If something is damaging to everyone, such as a statement to the press or specific conduct on the field, I always talk to the whole group. If there's a personal problem, or something that has to do with an individual player and myself, I handle it one-on-one." (Giancarlo Camolese)

Another key competency pertains to the proper timing of team communication. Often the choice of timing takes into account the impact the communication may have on morale or motivation at an individual or group level:

"The day of the match I only talk to the team for ten minutes, summarizing everything we did during the previous week on the blackboard. After that I don't say anything else to the players. If you keep repeating the same things you've already said till the last minute, you give a sense of insecurity and a lack of confidence." (Marcello Lippi)

Coaches tend to avoid communication when emotions are running high. At times like these, the risk is that the capacity to resolve *conflicts*[16] and face problems in a rational, constructive way is compromised, and the climate created in the team will be polluted:

"I avoid talking to the team after the match, except in exceptional circumstances. The reason is that the coach is still far too invested emotionally, and the players are under too much stress. You have to know how to go about it, how to measure out your comments, choosing the right way and the right time." (Serse Cosmi)

Coaches tend to avoid communication when emotions are running high.

"You have to know how to choose the right moment to make a critical comment, because sometimes you risk doing more harm than good. After the match I never make any comments, negative or positive. That's a time when the coach and the players are tired, emotionally too, so they're more prone to have negative reactions. So I put everything off until Tuesday or Wednesday." (Luigi Delneri)

"I always avoid talking to the players after a match, because you're not thinking clearly and you could say things that are out of line." (Giancarlo Camolese)

The *timing* of communications has to be based on the level of attention that the coach can expect from the team:

"I usually give a detailed profile of our opposing team on the matchday morning. So it's only a few hours before the match that I demand the utmost attention to details." (Delio Rossi)

Nonverbal communication is also vitally important. In fact—particularly from a motivational standpoint—athletes are often more influenced by what coaches *do* rather than what they *say:*

"How I gesticulate is a way of communicating. I think that once they get used to it, the players are more sensitive to the coach's body language rather than the verbal language." (Serse Cosmi)

Beyond handling communication with *followers*, team leaders also have to shape *lateral* communication among team members:

"Leadership is a shared responsibility among the team. There are many leadership opportunities and we try to encourage people to find moments to lead no matter how small, such as encouraging another or having a quiet word with a teammate about his tone of voice." (Jack Clark)[17]

"Conviction and involvement are what it takes to make the team leaders help the coach to spread his ideas amongst the other teammates and get them involved too." (Gianluca Vialli)

Sharing information with a team lays the groundwork for finding the best answers to problems and complex decisions. Team leaders should encourage information-sharing and manage this process in a planned, structured way. They should hone team members' ability to share *unique* information (available to only one team member) and to exchange information *throughout the team* with openness and transparency. This can be done by organizing discussion groups (actively designing, planning, and running them) while encouraging a spirit of collaboration among team members. To activate this process, coaches need to implement a participative leadership style and manage feedback effectively.[18]

THE MOTIVATIONAL TOOLKIT FOR SPORTS COACHES

The coaches we interviewed placed strong emphasis on team motivation. In fact, they often consider it even more critical to team performance than the technical, tactical, and athletic capabilities of players:

"It's motivation that makes the difference." (Stefano Pioli)

"Everything depends on the players' motivation." (Arrigo Sacchi)

For some, motivation is essential mainly because it enables both individual athletes and the team as a whole to enrich their personal and collective stock of skills and competencies through continual learning and improvement:

"If you have a winning team, change it ... the moment you get the feeling that the players no longer have a desire to improve." (Arrigo Sacchi)

"Leadership is the ability to make those around you better and more productive. All team members are expected to act as leaders." (Jack Clark)[19]

This explains why, of all the functions of a coach, motivating the team takes top priority. Motivation can be created in various ways. Based on our research, here are the key functions coaches perform within the context of team motivational coaching:

- Collecting and selecting information
- Providing feedback to the team
- Establishing rules
- Managing rewards and punishments
- Giving personalized attention
- Providing role models
- Managing workloads in light of results
- Designing training tasks that are absorbing and fun
- Encouraging competition among athletes
- Encouraging socialization among players.

These are summarized in Figure 5.5.

Figure 5.5 The motivational functions of a team leader/coach

Collecting and selecting information

A priority function of team leaders is gathering, analyzing, and interpreting the information they need to make decisions.[20] Acquisition and selection of information indirectly impacts team motivation by providing team leaders and staff with input for making decisions and directing their actions with regard to all other motivational functions. The information function is often complemented by extremely in-depth analysis sourced from statistics, video footage, etc.:

"Advances in technology have helped a great deal, because countless images shot from various angles enable us to make extremely precise analyses. We 'dissect' the video footage of key plays and then we thrash them out. This means taking a technical and tactical perspective, but it also has motivational repercussions because the player understands what his responsibilities are and where he can improve." (Claudio Ranieri)

In a business context, the quality of results is often determined by subjective, debatable assessments. This subjectivity exposes the team to the risk that team members and the coach may come up with divergent interpretations of results. Consequently, they might disagree on the seriousness of the situation, the urgency of the need for corrective measures, and the intervention that would be most effective. In the world of business, it's often harder to determine what generated a given result or to accurately measure the quality of the activities performed by team members. The main explanation for this is that there is a lower level of supervision of the team's "production processes." In sports, a coach spends a great deal of time with the players, and is physically present at practices and matches. Images and statistics are available that allow the coach to conduct in-depth analyses into the causes behind a win or a loss. Conversely, in the business world, the information that a team leader can usually access (visual, verbal, data-based, etc.) is less copious and often less detailed. Since it's difficult to attribute specific responsibilities to specific members of a business team, this makes it much more complicated to identify what corrective measures should be adopted, and to whom they should be applied.

Collecting and evaluating information can also provide important insight into the team's motivational state. To ascertain this, nearly all the coaches we interviewed pick up on visible signs, which equate to the players' behaviors and attitudes when executing their assigned tasks:

"You go into the locker room and start looking all the players straight in the eyes while they're changing: in some of their faces you read concentration, others are impenetrable. Then you look again while their taping up their ankles, and you realize that some of them are wrapping the tape too tightly, or not tightly enough." (Walter Zenga)

"During the final training session I observe the behavior of the players who won't get into the game, to see if they work just as hard or if they seem demotivated and feel excluded. The fact that a player gives it his all is an important sign." (Claudio Gentile)

The ability to note and interpret these signs—especially the attention, concentration, and motivation of the players—is often considered a critical competency for a coach that comes from sensitivity and experience:

"Experience has given me the ability to perceive things that can't be explained. … Often we coaches aren't psychologists, we're psychics!" (Claudio Ranieri)

"It's a question of sensations: with your eyes you always communicate something. When I explain things, I can see if someone really doesn't understand by the way he looks at me." (Serse Cosmi)

Coaches can regularly check behavioral signs from the team by creating recurrent rituals that can serve as "thermometers" to measure the group's level of motivation:

"The behavior of the boys during the trip to the stadium lets me put my finger on the pulse of the team. Before the game begins we hold hands and shout 'All for one and one for all'—even the way the players shout tells you whether they are properly focused." (Luigi Delneri)

The capacity to perceive signs and acquire the information needed to run the team also depends on the quantity and quality of the interactions between the coach and the athletes. Many coaches we interviewed talked about how important it is for them to spend a lot of time in the locker room with the players, so as to have ample opportunity "to pick up on the right signals."

Coaches who use a participative, democratic leadership style prefer two-way communications. They're convinced that to make the best decisions they need to elicit input from all the players, asking for suggestions even from the ones who don't freely voice their opinions. The coach has to be willing and able to listen, and also have the humility to accept ideas and advice. Coaches who use a participative leadership style garner information that helps decision-making by sounding out the team directly and overtly:

The capacity to perceive signs and acquire the information needed to run the team also depends on the quantity and quality of the interactions between the coach and the athletes.

> *"It's important to get information from every practice. … I always ask if they think the work was worthwhile, or if they feel too tired or fatigued."* (Carlo Ancelotti)

Information analysis is crucial in managing feedback to the team. When this process is handled effectively it can also make a considerable contribution to motivation. This brings us to the next point.

Providing feedback to the team

Managing feedback is a vital step in leadership processes. In sports, a key function of the coach is to give players feedback on their performance: after every game, coaches spend hours studying video footage to prepare for the next day's team debriefing; analyzing the performance of players helps them play to their full potential; and during training, too, good coaches always give constant and immediate feedback.

This communication process is a mainstay of educational coaching. Feedback motivates players by increasing the perception of individual and collective self-efficacy and also reduces uncertainty about expectations regarding task performance and evaluation. A motivational boost can even come from shifting the focus of goals and feedback from winning to improving:

> *"It doesn't matter whether we win, it matters whether we improved. Getting better is the best feeling in the world, and it can help build the confidence of the players. No one can instill confidence in you. Whatever confidence you get depends on how well you have prepared and how much you put into it. Have you deserved the right to be confident? No one really is going to tear you down if you believe you put everything you have into this." (Jack Clark)[21]*

With regard to managing this delicate process, the coaches we interviewed expressed diametrically opposed positions. Some place the emphasis on positive feedback as a motivational tool, thanks to the enhanced self-esteem and self-confidence that results. This is consistent with *self-efficacy theory:*[22]

> *"I always tend to emphasize what my player did well, and so when we look over the previous game, I always point out the plays that worked, rather than the flaws. All this enables the team to gain greater confidence as far as what they're working on." (Luigi De Canio)*

Other coaches give priority to *negative feedback*, because they want to elicit learning by identifying and correcting the errors made by players:

> *"I work hard on the negative. I don't believe much in positivity, because I think that's the normal state of things. So the important thing is to tell them where they went wrong, otherwise they'll never improve." (Luigi Delneri)*

However, feedback based on correcting errors can generate negative consequences for players' motivation, self-esteem, and confidence. In fact, the risk is that whoever made a mistake might have a negative reaction such as a loss in self-confidence if the mistake is pointed out publicly. One coach described the strategy he adopted to alleviate this risk:

"When I show video footage I use other games. Often I don't show the boys their own games for a reason: you can correct an error without putting the person who made it on the spot. It's not nice to say to someone, 'Look, you made a mistake.' I'd rather take the video, pause it during the replays of errors and say 'So-and-so on that other team did something he shouldn't have. He should have done this.' On the team, we have players who are smart enough to understand that I'm talking to them. But I don't like to point fingers. Most importantly, you can't pillory people who make mistakes, otherwise in the next game they might be frightened when they go out on the pitch." (Delio Rossi)

In the business world, experts have found[23] that the tendency of the leader to focus on the negative instead of the positive leads team members to work with less intensity, complain about trivial problems, and resist attempts by the leader to influence them. On the contrary, leaders who have positive attitudes increase the inclination of individual team members to help their teammates.

Another way of dealing with feedback is using it as a tool for *balancing emotional states* of the players. Here, the primary aim is pursuing motivational goals such as (at one extreme) preventing or counteracting a sense of complacency or overconfidence that comes from success, or (at the other extreme) avoiding a loss of confidence in self-efficacy after a failure:

"When I was a player, Giovanni Trapattoni would shout at us after we won, but after we lost he'd point out all things we'd done right." (Walter Zenga)

Clearly, the effectiveness of communication processes between a leader and their teams for motivational purposes depends a great deal on the coach's ability to analyze information and manage the resulting feedback. During the course of the season, coaches find themselves facing myriad situations; each one exposes the team to risks, and calls for different behaviors and management strategies by the coach. To simplify matters, we can identify eight typical situations arising from the combination of three elements:

- The quality of the activities performed by the athletes during training, when preparing for matches, which can be good (the team trained well) or bad (the team trained badly).
- The quality of the activities performed by the athletes during matches; here too we can draw a simple distinction between good or bad.
- The outcome of a match can also be interpreted as positive or negative, which again we simply represent as a win or a loss— although naturally in many sports there may be a draw. But it's reasonable to assume that we can even interpret a draw as positive or negative on a case-by-case basis.

A framework of possible situations is outlined in Table 5.1.

Table 5.1 Framework of possible situations faced by a team

		The team wins	**The team loses**
The team trains well	The team plays well		
	The team plays badly		
The team trains badly	The team plays well		
	The team plays badly		

How can coaches successfully manage the motivational level of the group? For the most part, this depends on their ability to accurately diagnose specific situations, to evaluate the extent to which the athletes agree with this diagnosis, to get a clear idea of the actual risks that could potentially be linked to the situation in question, and to come up with an approach that is consistent and convincing for dealing with the situation. Good team leaders have to know how to plan and manage continual learning for themselves and for the team, learning from mistakes by comparing plans with actual results:

"'Don't think it, ink it!' is the best way to learn and to be able to verify what worked and what went wrong. I still have all the notes I drew up to present to the players for every game." (Sandro Gamba)

Table 5.2 shows a simplified example of some typical situations that may arise in team management. For each one, the table highlights the recommended motivational communication approach.

These considerations highlight once again how vital it is for coaches to be able to take on a situational perspective. In other words, team leaders have to gauge their behaviors, in particular how they communicate with the team, according to their analysis and understanding of the circumstances.

Establishing rules

One of the most common topics that coaches brought up in our interviews pertains to establishing and sharing *rules,* and relative punishments when these rules are broken. Rules are major motivators for a team because they serve both to convey a perception of *fairness* among team members, and to reduce uncertainty with regard to goals and expected behaviors:

Table 5.2 Motivational communication by the coach in various situations

	The team wins	The team loses
The team plays well	*Risks* • Over-confidence • Self-complacency • Lapse in concentration or commitment • Lethargy. *The proper approach* "Good job, I'm really satisfied. Did you see what we can do? If we keep it up we can do great things. But remember, if we don't maintain the same level of commitment, concentration, and focus, we won't always have a reason to celebrate."	*Risks* • Loss of morale • Team attributes the loss to external factors beyond the players' control, resulting in low incentive to improve. *The proper approach* "We came close. We have to iron out the details that tipped the balance against us. If we correct our mistakes and improve on those points, next time we'll win."
The team plays badly	*Risks* • The team becomes convinced that they can win, even if they don't do their best • Loss of focus and drop in pressure. *The proper approach* "I'm not satisfied at all. We won, but that doesn't mean anything. We were lucky, but we won't always be. If we don't work hard to do better, we won't get anywhere."	*Risks* • Loss of morale • Loss of self-esteem and confidence in self and in the team. *The proper approach* "I know we can do a lot better than that. I know because in other situations we've shown that we can play much better. I'll do everything I can to do better, and I'm asking you to do the same. I guarantee that we'll succeed."

"Rules are needed to show us where to go and how to get there. They're a frame of reference, especially for times when things aren't going well in terms of results. Rules give the team a sense of order and people a sense of security." (Ettore Messina)[24]

Setting down rules is a way to clarify, share, and institutionalize group norms. Rules spell out the collective expectations of behaviors, both linked to tasks and context, of team members.

Group norms are vital because they enhance team cohesion and improve performance, especially in teams with high task interdependence and intense interaction among members.

Group norms are vital because they enhance team cohesion and improve performance.

Rules can also impact motivation, because to some extent the behavior of individuals on a team is influenced by the expectations of their teammates and the team leader. These expectations are standards that delineate appropriate and inappropriate behaviors and, as such, are closely linked to defining and applying rewards and punishments if team members respect or break the rules. The team leader should maximize the number and the charisma of people on the team who can pressure their teammates to respect the rules. If the majority of team members (especially the people who enjoy the most influence and respect) actively work to see this happen, everyone is liable to live up to the expected standards of behavior and conform to the rest of the team.

On a team, the behavior of teammates can have a powerful influence on motivation of individual members. In fact, athletes tend to make less of an effort if they realize that their teammates aren't doing their best (a phenomenon called *social loafing*).[25] With team sports, the risk of a drop in motivation can be avoided by applying norms for competition, such as role involvement, supportive behavior, and consistent commitment.[26] One of the goals of a good team leader involves establishing and disseminating these norms, with the aim of preventing—or at the very least counteracting—the risk of social loafing.

Summing up, then, the team leader can make a major contribution to setting down and sharing guidelines for the behavior of team members. For example, we find more communication, coordination, and commitment to finding constructive solutions to problems on teams in which leaders promote norms for collaborative conflict resolution.[27]

Team leaders must decide *what* the norms should regulate, and *how* they should be determined and enforced. In team sports there are four basic types of norms:[28]

- Attendance, punctuality, concentration, and commitment expected during training.
- Attendance, punctuality, concentration, and commitment expected during matches/competitions.
- Maintaining social contacts (e.g. phone conversations) and keeping in shape during the off-season.
- Attendance, quantity, and quality of interactions when socializing with teammates off the pitch (e.g. dinners).

What the rules actually involve and how they are defined and applied may vary from one coach to another. As regards the former, in most cases rules refer to standards of behavior that apply during practices and games, and when dealing with external parties (typically statements to the media):

"My expectations apply to what happens on the pitch during training or games. Beyond that, as I see it, it's better to be fairly flexible." (Giancarlo Camolese)

Some coaches extend the rules to apply to the general lifestyle of team members. For example, one coach told us about meeting a player at a restaurant late one night—behavior that earned the player a punishment.

As regards applying rules "across the board," in most cases:

"People will only respect the rules if they apply to everyone." (Mino Favini)

But in some situations there are exceptions. In this case, however, coaches should spell out the situation clearly from the start, explaining and justifying their motivations. As one coach said on the first day of pre-game training:

"You're all equal except for one. For Ronaldo the same rules can't apply." (Gigi Simoni, cited by Giuseppe Bergomi)

We also find different opinions as far as the process of rule-setting. Some coaches opt for the directive approach:

"It's up to the coach to lay down the rules and see that everyone respects them." (Silvio Baldini)

In most cases, instead, coaches prefer to get the team involved:

"It's better for the group to come up with the standards of behavior, because the group is much more strict than the coach in enforcing the rules." (Giuseppe Bergomi)

"When I first came to Juventus the rules of the group were already in place, the players had established them over the years. So I could work on the important things on the pitch, instead of playing the police dog, constantly reprimanding or punishing the players." (Claudio Ranieri)

Beyond making it easier to enforce the rules, getting the group involved in defining them is a good way to make members responsible, creating a moral obligation for players toward themselves and their teammates:

> *"If the group sets down the rules, then everyone has to answer for himself as far as applying what they've agreed on. So players don't see this agreement as something I've dictated. There's more acceptance of possible punishments; it's a way to make the player responsible, he has to gain an awareness of his role in the group. The player who breaks the rules has to realize he's letting himself and his teammates down." (Luigi De Canio)*

Generally speaking, rules are set down at the beginning of the year so that they are accepted and shared by the group from the outset. But these rules can be changed if the players give plausible motivations. Sanctions for rule-breaking depend on the seriousness of the infraction:

> *"Rules are essential for the life of the group. They have to be clear, and they always need to be enforced. But I don't want to play the sheriff with a loaded rifle who keeps the players under control at gunpoint as if they were outlaws. It's the group who has the obligation to enforce the rules, with the captain intervening when something goes wrong. Then for more serious problems or for special permission I take charge directly. After that, the club deals with any unresolved issues." (Carlo Ancelotti)*

Managing rewards and punishments

Where there are rules, there are sanctions for infringements. By properly handling rewards and punishments, the coach can encourage individual team members to feel responsible toward others. To reinforce this reciprocal sense of responsibility within the team—an example of social interdependence—one option is to punish the whole group, even the "innocent" teammates, for the infraction of one member:

"The group knows that when one person makes a mistake, everyone pays. This is an extra incentive for avoiding mistakes, and reinforces reciprocal respect. The entire group has to know who is responsible for the punishment. That way, everyone is responsible for everyone else."
(Luigi Delneri)

"I used to use team punishments even if one person made a mistake: for example, I'd make the whole team do really tough sprints while I left the player who hadn't been paying attention sit and watch, to make him face his responsibilities toward his teammates. By doing so, in the end the team put pressure on the individual athlete who was in the wrong."
(Sandro Gamba)

Another coach had this to say about collective rewards and punishments:

"Never used them! I'm against them. I believe in other ways to regain motivation. Instead of punishing the athletes I used to put together a training session that would break their backs … but it wasn't a punishment, it was getting them motivated again. You can't get motivation back with rewards or punishments. I'll give an example. If the president of a team says to the team, 'If you win a home game you'll get a reward of 50, if you win away I'll give you 100,' he's creating the expectation that away games are harder … so there's more fear and anxiety! It's a self-fulfilling prophecy. And you can be sure that we'll lose the away game!" (Dan Peterson)

In keeping with expectancy theory, when managing rewards and punishments coaches often take into account the motivational driver that can be triggered as a result. For example, the coach can move a player up from the reserves to the starting team for a big match, rather than for a less important or less challenging competition. This is a way for the coach to leverage both the value of the reward for the player who moves up, as well as the weight of the punishment for the starter who is being substituted.

Giving personalized attention

Motivating team members is also driven by the coach's willingness and ability to listen, analyze, and understand the needs of every single component of the team, and to adopt individualized initiatives:

"I try to find the right talking points for each player to encourage him to get the best from himself and for himself." (Luigi De Canio)

"Within the group, there are people who need a wake-up call in private, people who need to be told off in front of others, and people who need to be handled with kid gloves. Because the group is made up of lots of people who are all different, who need different treatment." (Luigi Delneri)

Usually, coaches who are more people-oriented are the ones who provide more personalized attention:

"What can also work is calling every player by his nickname, or however he wants to be called. This creates a less formal, more intimate atmosphere, while maintaining respect for roles." (Sandro Gamba)

Personalized attention can be particularly motivating in light of self-efficacy theory, which is based on the assumption that people are more motivated when they are less uncertain of their abilities. Setting individual goals and designing personal development plans for team members help reach this objective:

"At the start of the season, I gave each player a form to fill in with his personal goals and the team goals, what he wanted to improve on and how, his strengths, his weaknesses and how he intended to be useful to his teammates. Then I drew up a personal improvement plan. Periodically we verified progress on the plan, honestly assessing if, how, and how much the player was actually activating the plan in his daily behavior. The plan was based mostly on what he had written himself, so the player

*felt responsible for achieving it, and he would have a hard time coming up
with excuses when he behaved in a way that wasn't helping him realize
the plan. This was also a sign of listening and a message of planning for
the players." (Gianluca Vialli)*

At an individual level, encouragement and other signs of appreciation
by the team leader can also reduce this uncertainty among individual
players. In other words, players need positive reinforcement:

*"If a player believes in his potential, he can give it his all during every
practice and every game. Especially if he's not afraid when he has to make
a tough play." (Roberto Donadoni)*

In this sense, individualized attention plays a critical role. With certain people at certain times (such as athletes who are having a crisis
of self-esteem), the coach may opt to go beyond verbal persuasion
and purposely—even artificially—set up a scenario that gives the
player an injection of self-confidence. For example, a soccer coach
might get a player who hasn't scored in a long time to take a penalty kick, or ask the defense to let him score during practice.

The coach can demonstrate their trust in players and build up players' self-esteem and self-confidence by assigning them responsibilities.

The coach can demonstrate their trust
in players and build up players' self-esteem
and self-confidence by assigning them
responsibilities. This makes players feel
valued. A typical example is deciding who
will receive the captain's armband: this is a
highly symbolic message, conveying the respect of the coach and the
team, who regard this player as worthy of distinction.

Other key motivational drivers include sensitivity in listening and in dialoguing, because these behaviors by team leaders
demonstrate thoughtfulness and involvement with team members
individually. Listening is a way to let athletes know that they're being
heard, they're important, and they're appreciated. This can elevate

motivation, in particular because listening shows individualized attention toward each player and helps enhance the quality of the leader–member exchange:

"I tell my players: if you have a problem off the pitch and you want to talk to me about it because you think I can help you solve it, here I am." (Delio Rossi)

But the other side of the coin, as far as personalized attention goes, is the risk that differentiated relationships develop between the leader and team members.

In fact, when the *quality* of the relationships between the team leader and various team members is heterogeneous, this can trigger negative reactions within the group by generating the perception of unequal and unfair treatment that could ultimately lead to destructive group dynamics. For example, when team members feel that a teammate is given unjustifiable preferential treatment, they tend to communicate less with that person, treating them with disdain and distrust.[29] Perceptions of favoritism undermine the leader's reputation for fairness,[30] leaving the impression that they lack impartiality. These perceptions may also give rise to envy and dissonance in the group, creating a hostile work environment rife with tension and conflict that, in turn, has a negative effect on team motivation.[31] These repercussions are especially severe in groups with high levels of interdependence, and in those with very similar demographics among members. Some degree of heterogeneity in leader/member relationships is more acceptable and justifiable when team members range widely in terms of age, experience, background, and seniority.

Summing up, the leader's ability to relate to team members in a differentiated and individualized way can generate positive repercussions on one hand (because leaders can adapt their behaviors to the specific needs of a diversified group of collaborators) but negative consequences on the other (such as creating envy and tension among group members, and eroding the team leader's credibility[32]).

Sub-groups may also form, based on the differing quality of relationships with the leader (the "protected" as opposed to the "neglected").[33]

How can team leaders deal with this apparent incongruity? They can differentiate how they distribute resources among their collaborators. In terms of time and information resources, for instance, differentiation can be justified by the different levels of experience, skills, and motivation of the people on the team. If the leader dedicates more time and attention to a new recruit, a young person, or someone who's having a hard time in their personal or professional life, team members can see the logic behind that behavior and accept it. By the same token, the team leader also needs to show the same respect for every person on the team. This is a way to reconcile the principles of fairness and equality. Fairness implies that rewards and resources allotted to a team member have to be proportional to the contribution that person can (and actually does) make to the group. Equality holds that everyone on the team should be treated alike.

Differentiation in leader/member relationships is far more likely to occur on large teams, where it's practically impossible for the leader to maintain identical relationships with all the team members. In these cases, the winning strategy for the team leader is often to build solid relationships with a core of charismatic team members who then act as informal leaders, exerting their influence on the rest of the group, and serving as liaisons between the leader and the rest of the team.[34]

Ultimately, some level of differentiation in relationships between the leader and team members is probably inevitable. The impact that this can have on team processes and results may be positive or negative, essentially depending on the perceptions that team members have about the fairness of their leader. To avoid negative repercussions, it's critical to prevent the team from perceiving differentiation as unfair, unwarranted, or arbitrary. The key here is the leader's ability to get team members to accept differentiation among various roles, along with the resulting disparity in the allocation of some resources, rewards, and punishments. The whole team must realize that these differences are indispensible because every team member offers specialized and interdependent contributions that have to be coordinated.[35] To ensure that the team acknowledges the need for differentiation, specific differentiated roles need to be defined for each team member.

Providing role models

In order to improve motivation, two things are necessary regarding the roles assigned to team members. The first is task significance. This contributes to work motivation by enabling employees to think that their work is meaningful,[36] in particular when combined with role uniqueness:

> *"It's important to give all the players a role, and make them feel like they count, and that their contribution to the team is important." (Dan Peterson)*

> *"You must develop within the organization and the player an appreciation for the role each athlete plays on the team. You talk to each player and let each one know that, at some point, he will be in a position to win or lose the game. It may be one play in an entire career for a certain player or many plays each game for another. But the point is that everyone's job is essential. Everyone has specific roles and specific responsibilities. And each player has to be prepared both mentally and physically to the utmost to play that role." (Bill Walsh)[37]*

The second is clarity. Assigning well-defined, specific individual roles is a way to clarify the potential and expected contribution that each team member should make toward reaching collective goals:

> *"The symphony will be sublime, but on one condition alone: that every single team member reads well the score he is given. Providing a score is a determining factor, it's the principal duty of a good director. It has to be written clearly and meticulously, and roles and responsibilities have to*

be explicit. Whether the people who play in the orchestra are friends or enemies doesn't matter." (Gian Paolo Montali)[38]

Coaches also stress the need to give their players models for behavior that will motivate them to do given tasks in a specific way. These role models might be other players or the coach. Often coaches affirm the importance of "setting a good example yourself," especially in creating team spirit and motivating players. What coaches *do* counts more than what they *say*:

"What counts is the example of the coach, as far as punctuality, fairness, and lots of little things that taken together become important." (Mino Favini)

"A team expects a lot from the coach. The example the coach sets is important as far as dedication to work, passion, and professional behavior. Always being on time, always standing by the team no matter what, especially when times get tough. I'll give you an example. Once I was coaching a team 100 kilometers from my house and very often, when we went to play away games, on the way back the team bus passed three kilometers from my house. I always went with the team to the end of the journey, without ever getting off early and going home directly. This didn't make us win or lose any games, but it did create a positive attitude, a professional relationship, and confidence in the coach." (Mario Beretta)

A common belief among coaches is that it's critical to have a leader in the locker room or on the field who serves as an assistant or a delegate of the coach—someone who can act as liaison between the coach and the team. The role of this leader, who is often appointed team captain, primarily consists of conveying the coach's ideas, convictions, and behavioral models to the team, and in turn informing the coach of the team's needs, problems, and doubts. The captain has to be a leader recognized by the group thanks to the example they set. This role is particularly crucial when it comes to diffusing player discontent and attenuating the risk of divisions in the group:

"If you have a captain who gets to practice a half-hour early, this sets an example that prompts the younger players to do the same—and it's worth more than constant nagging by the coach, who becomes a pain in the neck. An example counts more than words." (Luciano Spalletti)

Ideally, the group chooses the captain, since this person has to serve as a role model that others are inspired to follow. In fact, the captain has to be legitimate in the eyes of the team. Normally, the person who plays this role spontaneously comes to the fore.

In sum, role-modeling is a vital process in coaching.[39] Providing athletes on a team with a role model (either in the first person or though others) is an effective way to motivate them, as affirmed by the *goal-setting theory*.[40] If players have a model to follow, it reduces role uncertainty and clearly shows which objectives take priority, what activities are most important, and how to behave and perform certain tasks. On the contrary, role ambiguity engenders uncertainty and dampens motivation, undermining people's confidence in their ability to perform their tasks effectively. Coaches can minimize role ambiguity by assigning formal or informal roles to their athletes that specify the meaning, position, and contribution expected of each player in relation to the team. Also, coaches can identify exemplary role models for players to emulate.

In the context of team sports, nonstarters experience greater role ambiguity than starters.[41] Due to this fact, coaches should dedicate time to nonstarters to build their motivation, to let them know they count, and to lessen their role ambiguity.

Managing workloads on the basis of results

Sports coaches can impact the motivational level of the team by handling wins and losses differently. For example, after winning a match, coaches tend to intensify the workload during practices to tap into the ensuing energy, enthusiasm, euphoria, and surge in motivation. After a loss, however, coaches very often run easier training sessions so as to avoid excessively depleting athletes' physical and emotional reserves.

Many coaches believe that they can influence the team's degree of motivation by adjusting the training workload to match the athletes' physical and mental energy levels. Coaches can modify the amount of effort they demand from the team over time, taking into consideration the team's performance and their consequent willingness to work:

> *"At times it's detrimental and counterproductive to keep players on the pitch longer than usual if they're coming off a bad performance. Making a group work when they don't want to creates endless problems. When we win, then that's the time to push them during the week; there's more enthusiasm and spirit of sacrifice." (Carlo Ancelotti)*

> *"When I lose, I usually work less. That's because I think that after a loss, there's a drop in energy, so increasing the workload can be detrimental. It means spending too much energy, both at a physical and psychological level. By the same token, when I win I can intensify the workload because players are in the right state of mind." (Luigi Delneri)*

Designing tasks that are absorbing and fun

How tasks are designed—especially in training sessions—can influence the amount of effort that players are willing to expend in performing related activities. In many sports, training often equates to doing tiring, repetitive, monotonous exercises. In order to motivate athletes to work their hardest, many coaches feel they need to invest resources and creative thinking to come up with entertaining and interesting ways to carry out training tasks and activities:

> *"Sometimes I sit at my desk, even for three hours, to try to figure out new training exercises. It's another way to motivate players." (Paolo Indiani)*

"Players have always appreciated the fact that I look for new ways to avoid the same routine. If the warm-up is fun, it's easier to begin the training session with the right attitude to do your best. So the warm-up is done like a game. Here's an example: a player with shaving cream on his hand has to try to touch his teammates, who naturally run away." *(Silvio Baldini)*

"We work hard during practice, but we also set aside a lot of playing time. Very often I use theme-based scrimmages, setting different objectives each time." (Massimo Ficcadenti)

A good coach needs a generous portion of creativity to enhance motivation. As for inspiration, it's often helpful to look beyond your own field:

A good coach needs a generous portion of creativity to enhance motivation.

"I've always believed you can learn a lot from other sports. For example, I used to watch swimming training to see how to motivate athletes who have to do the same, boring work. I watched athletics training, which involves similar problems, and they try to find solutions by using a wide variety of exercises. Sport has to be fun for the people doing it, and it's important to understand how to help athletes train hard while having fun. From soccer, instead, I've learned a lot about finding space, a vital factor in basketball, my sport. I also liked to study athletic training for goalkeepers, which is the most complete training because physically they use their whole body, and mentally they always have to pay attention and concentrate." (Sandro Gamba)

So good team leaders should invest time and resources in carefully designing the tasks they assign to team members. On this topic, research in the business context explores how psychological states and performance of workers are impacted by work characteristics,[42] breaking them down into three main classes:

- *Motivational characteristics*, which can make a job more or less interesting—examples include autonomy, level of responsibility, variety in the types of tasks people are assigned and the skills and competencies they need to accomplish them, and the overall meaning (i.e. the capacity to influence the lives of other people). Work can also differ in terms of specialization, complexity, creativity, etc.
- *Social characteristics*, such as interdependence and interaction with colleagues and people outside the organization. These features enable people to learn, face more challenging tasks, and develop friendly relationships.
- *Contextual characteristics*, such as a pleasant, comfortable work environment.

These characteristics are summarized in Figure 5.6.

Summing up, the team leader has to try to design work for team members by leveraging various factors that can influence their motivation and performance.

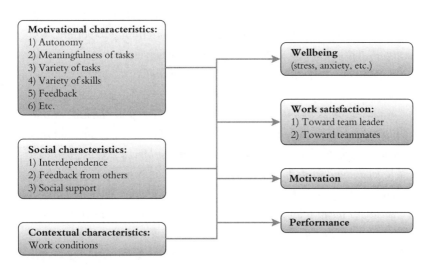

Figure 5.6 Work features and their impact on performance
Source: adapted from Humphrey et al. (2007)

Encouraging competition among players

Coaches can also affect team motivation by encouraging members to compete against one another. On sports teams, players are competing for scarce resources (for example a starting position). So coaches can decide whether to build up or tone down competitive (or cooperative) tendencies among athletes, how to do so and to what degree:

"Healthy competition among athletes who play the same role is essential to maintaining a constant tension toward improving one's performance to have a place on the team. This is a very positive virtuous circle. What's more, the fact that one athlete plays less than another one is relatively less important, since the priority is winning the games you play in, rather than playing in a lot of games and losing. You need to make it clear that it's better to play in 5 winning games than in 35 losses! The ability to reconcile individual and collective goals springs from this. Being part of a winning team has to be everyone's top 'individual' goal." (Mario Beretta)

"No one should ever rest entirely easy, players have to be spurred on to do their best, and often the coach's words aren't enough. Seeing that there's someone else who can take your place is certainly important. On my ideal team, there's a core of five or six key players, but there has to be competition among the other twelve." (Paolo Indiani)

"A player comes in with another player and is constantly looking at that other player as the barometer of how successful he is and he might transfer or never achieve the level that he could have achieved because he never felt good about himself because he always felt he wasn't good enough no matter what you said to him because of what that other kid was doing in his class. I mean those are the dynamics that go on in the workplace and on teams all the time and sometimes you can control them and sometimes you can't. So you have to be very careful about how you bring people along and the competition that they see within their own class or within the team or within the business." (Mike Krzyzewski)[43]

Finding the best balance between cooperation and competition among team members is not an easy task. Especially with star players the coach can play a key role:

> "I need to be the best player's best friend. Being the best player is a lonely position. Even though you get accolades, no matter how good a team you have, there is always some level of jealousy. Always. Because you're competitive. A little bit of it is not bad. But I want to make sure that I'm connected with that guy because in a tense moment he also might produce better knowing that he's not out there alone." (Mike Krzyzewski)[44]

Encouraging socialization among players

On a team, individual motivation can be strongly shaped by the ability to foster a sense of belonging and pride in being part of a team—the feeling of being involved in an "us" that's bigger, stronger, and more exciting than a "me." These emotional states are contingent on the quality of the relationships that teammates have with one another. Several coaches emphasize that the quality of relationships among athletes is the responsibility (and indeed a key function) of the coach:

> "On the Olympic team I had this alpha dog in Kobe Bryant and I had another alpha dog in LeBron James. One had accomplished a lot, and the other wanted to accomplish what that other guy had accomplished already. I tried to have them interact. So I said to Kobe, 'You need to be good with LeBron,' and I said to LeBron, 'You need to be good with Kobe.' Well, LeBron has a really good sense of humor, he's an entertainer. So, when we would be in a team meeting, LeBron would imitate Kobe—he would take his warm-up pants and pull them up to here and go through a whole routine. And the team is laughing and Kobe is laughing because one of the best things about imitating you is that it means I accept you, I like you. Those two stars became, at least during

that time, not competitors but just real good teammates. It set the tone for everyone else." (Mike Krzyzewski)[45]

Socialization depends largely on how team time is spent. Just because players are often together for hours on end, it doesn't necessarily follow that they spontaneously build solid, positive interpersonal relationships:

"We spend a lot of time together, so it's essential to create a positive environment, without any hard feelings or animosity. Also, by respecting shared rules in the locker room and on the pitch, we can smooth over any sharp edges." (Gian Piero Gasperini)

The intensity of interactions can be extremely variable:

"Once there used to be a group, and the group used to spend time together, playing cards, or someone playing the guitar and singing. Today everyone comes in with their mobiles, computers, and videogames: everyone's in their own little world, and minds their own business. There's no together-ness anymore." (Walter Zenga)

"I remember that in the early '80s, there wasn't anything high-tech, so we used to spend time together. Now all the players go to their own rooms with their mobiles, PlayStations, DVDs ... so forming a group is more complicated." (Giuseppe Bergomi)

With professional sports, when the team goes to the training camp, either pre-season or during the championship, this is a vital time for creating team spirit and building or maintaining interpersonal relationships. Little things such as which players should share a room, for example, are carefully analyzed to maximize the potential for socialization in whichever the direction the coach sees fit. The coach can and must actively shape the quantity and quality of social relationships that are established among players, deciding how to act to encourage or discourage them:

"When we're at our training camp, I'm around but I'm very discreet and I let the boys make a bit of a racket in their rooms. Because being together helps build community and mutual understanding. So after a while I go to my room, but I would never dream of checking who's sleeping and who's still up." (Claudio Gentile)

"You build a spirit of community with dinners and get-togethers outside of work, and that's when you get to know one another; you discuss the goals you want to achieve together. By having experiences together beyond what happens on the field, you can come together and get on the same wavelength. The differences become unimportant and you see the results on the field." (Luigi Delneri)

"Spending time together off the field is also important: getting together for dinners, appetizers, lunches. … It's essential to promote them and make sure they're always enjoyable and that the athletes want to do it again, even on their own. You only achieve this if these occasions are a chance for everyone for personal growth and fun, and for reinforcing relationships in the team, and with the staff and the coach." (Mario Beretta)

Even the way physical spaces are designed can be important in fostering or hindering interactions among team members:

"It's very helpful for players to always change in one common locker room—they shouldn't split up, because locker room time is personal and extremely important. Once I coached a team and on the training field there were two separate locker rooms. That can happen, because teams today are much bigger than they were when some sports facilities were built. As a result, two separate groups emerged, because every player always changed in the same place, out of habit. This created a lot of problems in terms of team unity. That's why I always ask for a locker

room that's big enough for everyone to use, not just to change in, but also to talk face-to-face." (Mario Beretta)

According to some coaches, socialization isn't necessarily about creating friendly relations:

"We're not a family, membership is conditional." (Jack Clark)[46]

What seems to count the most is building mutual esteem and respect:

"The better people know one another, the more their differences emerge. And diversity provokes conflict, animosity, and envy, which inevitably spill over into the professional sphere. The real enemy of organizations is time; if we really want to attack it we can't waste it by trying to form a group. It would take too much time and there's no guarantee that you'll actually succeed in the end. The groups that become teams are the ones who naturally play together like a real team, without being asked or forced; they begin to realize that the teammate next to them is the best possible player in that position. This obsessive work—striving to build professional esteem among players—is what turns the group into a team. You can transition from a group to a team only when among players there is esteem—the only thing that counts in work relationships." (Gian Paolo Montali)[47]

HOW TEAM MOTIVATION PROCESSES WORK

In addition to the indirect impact of consultative coaching and educational coaching, our study identifies a toolkit of instruments and specific behaviors that team leaders in the sports world use for motivational coaching. We outline the relative functions in the previous section. To understand the processes these functions leverage to stimulate motivation, we can refer to the main theories on motivation detailed in Chapter 2.

A good coach motivates the team by increasing perceived individual and collective self-efficacy, setting higher goals, and helping the team see those goals as attainable

Professional sports coaches primarily motivate their teams indirectly through consultative coaching and educational coaching. Specifically, coaches increase the perceived individual and collective self-efficacy of the team, which allows them to set more ambitious goals and reinforce the conviction that these goals can actually be achieved (transformational leadership). The following example clearly shows this motivational function, and represents a concrete manifestation of the key concepts of the goal-setting theory and the path-goal theory:

> **Professional sports coaches primarily motivate their teams indirectly through consultative coaching and educational coaching.**

> *"I had to give the impression of a high level of professionalism right from the start. For our training sessions we had a gym built that covered 600 square meters. Actually, we would only use 15–20% of that space, but the structure gave a strong sense of organization, work, and commitment. This was important because Juventus hadn't won anything for ten years and lacked self-esteem, and the team had to start believing in themselves again." (Marcello Lippi)*

First and foremost, the team leader creates motivation by nurturing in the athletes the conviction that goals are realistic and achievable, making individual and collective goals more and more challenging over time. To do so, coaches often break goals down into a series of sequential sub-goals that progressively raise the bar on the expected level of performance. For example, a team might start out with the goal of staying in the league it plays in; the next goal might be outperforming teams that are higher up in the rankings. Next the team aims to earn more points than the previous year, and then breaking the club's all-time record for points, and so on.

Consultative and educational coaching are also the main drivers of personal and collective self-esteem of team members (self-efficacy theory). However, self-efficacy can also be encouraged through certain functions of motivational coaching, for instance by offering individualized attention. In fact, the coach can exploit the motivational potential of an individual athlete's self-esteem:

"A coach who's a good motivator knows how to get the athlete in touch with that part of himself that knows he can do it, in touch with his dreams. An athlete might be out of touch with this part of himself, which at times aims for the highest possible goals, but he might temporarily deny it for many reasons. Fear turns into muscular tension, doubt turns into insurmountable technical difficulties, and this creates a vicious circle that's hard to break out of. In these cases, for an athlete it's essential to be told that fear is permissible. Many athletes deny fear; they're convinced they can overcome it, as if they were ashamed of it. So they repress something that's there. The first objective, then, is to help the athlete learn to accept fear, and to live with it. Then you need to help him live with the anxiety that comes from unexpected events. Many top-class athletes become almost obsessive, excessively perfectionist, in an attempt to control everything and avoid the unexpected. This isn't right. You don't overcome fear and anxiety by obsessively repeating technical drills in the utopian belief that you're eliminating errors and surprises. I always say that in sports, the winner is the person who makes fewer mistakes—not the person who doesn't make any at all. The more you train to handle the moment, the better prepared you are to react to specific situations. This engenders self-esteem and self-confidence." (Andrea Colombo)

On a team we find reciprocal interactions between members' self-confidence and their confidence in the abilities of their teammates and of the team as a whole. We can define this *collective efficacy* as "a group's shared belief in its conjoint capabilities to organize and execute the courses of action required to produce given levels of attainments." [48] In the context of team sports,[49] this belief influences (and in turn is influenced by) team performance. Motivation plays a key role in this virtuous circle of reciprocal influence, which is illustrated in Figure 5.7. In fact, the perception of collective efficacy affects what the group decides to do (in terms of challenges and goals) and how to do it (that is, what kind of commitment and effort it will take), and how long to persevere in the face of obstacles and failures. We can compare collective efficacy with the concept of a winning spirit, which means that the team sets no limits on its ambition to win, never stops believing it can do it, and never gives up.

Teams with high levels of collective efficacy are more willing to face difficult challenges and set ambitious targets, which they then work harder to achieve. These teams are also less likely to falter in their efforts when there are obstacles in their path or when they fail. It follows, then, from a motivational standpoint, that one of the priority tasks for team leaders is to create a high level of perceived collective efficacy. This in turn will enhance the perception of individual efficacy, spur motivation, and improve performance of single team members:[50]

"Confidence is contagious. So is lack of confidence." (Vince Lombardi)

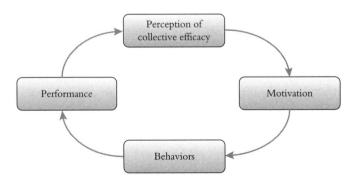

Figure 5.7 The virtuous circle of perceived collective efficacy

Team leaders can achieve all this in a variety of ways, for example by reinforcing team members' confidence in the abilities of their teammates, increasing the quantity and quality of training for team members,[51] and calling attention to the team's positive track record[52] or the positive performance of a reasonably comparable team.[53]

In a team, the perception of collective efficacy is not equal to the simple sum of the perceptions of individual efficacy of team members,[54] because collective efficacy exploits the multiplicative effect of reciprocal reinforcement mechanisms among components of the team. When your teammates are highly skilled players, you believe this empowers you to do your best. The greater the interdependence among team members,[55] the stronger the positive impact of the perception of collective efficacy on team performance.

The perception of collective efficacy can be influenced by various contextual factors. For example, a study on volleyball players shows that this perception is stronger for home games compared to away games.[56] For coaches, this means that it's important to understand which factors reduce the perception of collective efficacy and then to deal with the impact of these factors on the team, for example by prepping the team to react to the environmental conditions of a specific game in a positive way. At the start of a game or match, preparation and past performance have a positive effect on the perception of collective efficacy; as the competition progresses, the team's performance (whether positive or negative) becomes more important.[57]

With team sports, wins and losses are objective, and have deep, immediate impact on players' motivation.

Positive results obviously build self-esteem and increase collective self-efficacy. Consequently, it is important for team leaders to orchestrate early wins, especially when the team doesn't have a winning mentality or a historical record of successful performance:

"You have to have a winning mentality, and know how to transmit it to the players. For example, I've always coached teams with long losing track records: Fiorentina, Lazio, Inter, Manchester City. … With all of them,

it was important to win something right away, even relatively less important trophies like the Italian Cup, which in Italy is less important than the championship. It helps recreate a winning spirit." (Roberto Mancini)

Conversely, negative results can set in motion a downward spiral of failures, because when the team loses a game, they can lose their self-esteem and their sense of individual and collective self-efficacy. In this regard, the ability of the team leader to analyze information and manage feedback can play a vital role in motivation. An example here is when a coach accurately identifies the causes behind a loss and then comes up with convincing corrective measures and communicates them to the team.

For a team, information that can minimize uncertainty regarding self-efficacy not only includes results attained by individual athletes or the team as a whole, but also similar statistics on comparable players or teams. For motivational purposes, beyond citing outstanding past performance by their own team or by one of their athletes ("If we did it before we can do it again"), coaches can also refer to other teams and compare their team with similar success stories ("If they can do it, so can we").

On a team, fellow teammates can reduce a player's uncertainty in terms of self-efficacy by offering encouraging words and actions that shore up their self-esteem. The coach in turn can provide teammates with the same kind of support. The conviction that every player can count on highly skilled teammates for help also alleviates uncertainty. In this case, it's the perception of collective self-efficacy ("I'm part of a winning team") that positively impacts individual self-efficacy:

"Once we were about to go up against a top team with a brilliant midfielder who played in the same zone as ours. I saw that my midfielder was really nervous, so I said to him, 'Just think of how scared your opponent is; he doesn't play on a team with a "buddy system" like we have. When he gets the ball, he won't have anyone to pass it to, but you'll have help from two or three of your teammates. And when you get the ball

you'll be surrounded by five teammates, and when you go to pass you'll be spoiled for choice.'" (Arrigo Sacchi)

On a team, winning and losing have the greatest impact on motivation, which in turn impacts self-esteem, self-confidence, and belief in the team as a whole:

"It's that taste of victory that triggers higher motivation. When a player thinks back on the emotions that came with a win, the unconscious desire takes root to re-experience those emotions as soon as possible—to feel happy, satisfied, and fulfilled again." (Carlo Ancelotti)

Being a coach often involves striving to find the perfect balance in the emotional states of the players as individuals and the team as a whole in the aftermath of successes or failures. Interestingly, achieving or surpassing team goals can give rise to over-confidence, and with it comes the risk of complacency and a drop in motivation:

"Dealing with a win may be even harder than dealing with a loss, because in some cases winning generates an excess of enthusiasm and confidence. The problem is not to be satisfied, always to aim for something more." (Mario Beretta)

This is a noteworthy point because research on self-efficacy and collective efficacy conducted in a business context tends to neglect the potential negative effects of over-confidence. Obviously, at the opposite extreme, a losing streak can undermine a team's confidence and belief in its potential. In this case too, the coach's job is to reduce uncertainty:

"The coach has to make sure that the team is certain of the work on the field, the game, the roles on the pitch and off: certain of consolidated values,

being able to count on their teammates during the season in good times and bad. This provides peace of mind and confidence. Once, despite having done an amazing job, we just weren't getting results. In that case I asked the players to hold fast to the things we were certain of: outstanding athletic preparation; the plays we'd learned and practiced again and again; everyone's clear, well-defined roles; and confidence in a formidable technical staff. I shared these certainties with the players, and everyone recognized them as our touchstones. Then I asked them to believe even more. I don't think that in these cases it's right to upend everything you've done up to that point. You risk disorienting people even more." (Mario Beretta)

"After having reached an important milestone, beyond a sense of achievement and satisfaction, at times there's an excessive awareness of our abilities. We feel invincible, and risk underestimating our opponent. On the other hand, when everything isn't going right, that can generate friction ... so it's indispensible to eradicate any tension right away. ... We need to focus on what we do best, on what we know for certain—never on our uncertainties." (Carlo Ancelotti)

A good coach motivates the team by creating clear expectations that are shared with and embraced by all team members

A number of the functions described above motivate the team to the extent that they reduce team members' uncertainties regarding behaviors they are expected to adopt and the individual and collective outcomes that will result (expectancy theory). Identifying role models, establishing rules, and managing rewards and punishments are all ways to reduce uncertainties:

"We try not to have any rules on my teams. I have what I call 'standards.' Usually when you're ruled, you never agree with all the rules, you just abide by them. But if you have standards and if everyone contributes to

the way you're going to do things, you end up owning how you do things. In my experience, the best teams have standards everyone owns. With the Olympic team, I met with the individual stars. I met with Jason Kidd individually and then LeBron James, Kobe Bryant, and Dwayne Wade before we had a collective meeting. I told them, 'I'm going to have a meeting tonight, not about offense and defense, but about how we're going to live for the next six weeks. I am going to tell you two of the standards that I want. When we talk to each other, we look each other in the eye. That's one. The second one is we always tell each other the truth. If we can do those two things, trust will be developed, which will be the single most important thing for our foundation as a group.' And then I said, 'You don't have to tell me now, but I would like for you to contribute to the meeting and say at least one thing tonight. And whatever you say will become, if everyone agrees, one of our standards.' We had a great meeting in which we came up with 15 standards. Each of those guys put their hand up; they took ownership. It was no longer just their talent; now it was also the things they said. LeBron said, 'No excuses. You know we have the best talent. We're playing for the best country. So, no excuses.' And that was our first standard. Jason Kidd said, 'We shouldn't be late and we should respect one another.' ... If someone was late for the first time I probably would have taken the initiative. I would have said to a couple of the most respected players something like, 'You know, Dwayne was late—do you want me to take care of that?' They would have said that they would take care of it. And then if it happened again, I would have brought it to the whole group. I would not have been hesitant to do that if the players did not take care of it themselves." (Mike Krzyzewski)[58]

At the individual level, how motivated athletes are to work harder on certain training exercises (effort) depends on how convinced they are both that these specific exercises will help them play better (performance)—and that this improved performance during practice will result in them playing or starting in more games (reward). Naturally, the coach can also leverage the value that an athlete attributes to a given reward or punishment as a motivator. For instance, some games are more important than others, and being part of the starting lineup in a big match can be a more powerful motivator than starting in lower-profile competitions.

With regard to motivational processes that tie into the expectancy theory, we should also point out a paradox that is unique to the sports world. For coaches, unlike business managers, motivating a group faced with an impossible challenge is extremely simple. The expectancy of a low probability of success in achieving a goal (for example, winning a game against what looks like a far superior team on paper) is not demotivating for the team. On the contrary, athletes are normally highly motivated by the prospect of accomplishing such a task. What's more, they don't experience performance anxiety because the feeling that they have nothing to lose (and everything to gain) mitigates the stress linked to the risk of failing to live up to the expectations of the fans, the club, etc.

> **For coaches, unlike business managers, motivating a group faced with an impossible challenge is extremely simple.**

A good coach motivates the team by building a shared perception of justice, not equality, among team members

Some of the functions of motivational coaching outlined in our model are successful at motivation by creating the conditions for team cohesion. In fact, these functions reduce uncertainty about unjustified differential treatment, which would give rise to envy and resentment, eroding team spirit and a sense of belonging (equity theory).

What can facilitate team leaders in reducing this type of uncertainty is their ability to reconcile personalized attention with team rules, and to strike the proper balance between encouraging competition on one hand and socialization on the other. In fact, good coaches know how to give differentiated treatment to different athletes with different abilities and motivations, while at the same time conveying the perception of being fair and making impartial decisions.

So the basic challenge for team leaders in business, as well as sports, is to treat collaborators as individuals. That means interacting with each one in a personal way, while avoiding giving the impression of arbitrary, unfair treatment. The key to this apparent contradiction lies in making the team understand that there is a substantial difference between justice and equality:

> *"By 'privilege,' I don't mean gratuitous recognition, but something the player wins, something attained through exceptional performances that are consistent over time." (Ettore Messina)[59]*

Due to differences in age, technical proficiency, personality, and charisma among athletes, they can't (and usually don't) get the same treatment. Here's an anecdote describing the subterfuge that one coach resorted to in order to show the team that he treated everyone the same way, while recognizing that some team members deserved preferential treatment:

> *"The team is run by treating everyone in the same way. When you manage 25 people, you can't adopt different behaviors. Dealing with an important player is never easy, but sometimes you can apply a few little strategies, if he agrees, that let you send clear signals to the group. My best player, Luca Vialli, really helped me out. Sometimes I'd get to the training field and I would take him aside and tell him, 'Look, I'm going to get a little upset with you today,' because it was important to show the team that the coach even got angry with Vialli, because this was a powerful message for the rest of the team. Then we would go onto the pitch and after a while I'd shout: 'Vialli, what the hell do you think you're doing! Do that exercise right!' … That alliance worked like a charm." (Marcello Lippi)*

Fairness is often interpreted as offering the same possibilities to all the members of the team, giving them all equal opportunities to play a part in team processes. This has major impact on cohesion and motivation:

> *"To keep up motivation for every person in the group, you need to work with everyone in the same way."* (Luigi Delneri)

> *"The coach has to provide the same service to the entire group. You need to correct anyone's mistakes, you have to give everyone advice, without ever overlooking anyone. The people who don't play can't be left on their own, left to their fate. ... You have to prepare training sessions so that everyone is involved at the same level. Everyone has to have the same opportunities to show what they've got."* (Silvio Baldini)

> *"My commitment is not to neglect anyone. By not excluding anyone, either in terms of work or from a psychological standpoint, the players form a united front when they face competitive challenges and hard times."* (Giancarlo Camolese)

A good coach motivates the team by making team members' work more meaningful

Raising the bar for individual and collective goals plays a crucial part in motivation, in keeping with the assumptions of transformational leadership. Some functions of motivational coaching also enhance the motivation of team members through processes such as individualized attention and role-modeling, and through task significance and role uniqueness. These last two factors can contribute to providing meaning to the work that athletes do, making them feel appreciated and important. Task design can also enrich the work of team members, making it more gratifying and boosting motivation.

Team leaders should always strive to find and leverage motivational drivers that can make team members' work more meaningful.

They can increase sense of belonging, build a work environment characterized by fun and friendship, and foster responsibility:[60]

"When I played with Sampdoria, the club and the president managed to inspire a powerful sense of belonging. Our manager, Vujadin Boškov, said that many of us were so dedicated to the club that we wore Sampdoria pajamas to bed! This feeling towards the club has to be encouraged. At the start of every season, the coach should take the players, especially the new ones, to visit the club's trophy room, its stadium, its offices. He should organize for the players to meet the fans, show video clips on the history of the club. This is a way to elicit a shared identity that is actually rooted in history, in the values, and in the profound meaning of what that organization represents for the people who work there today, and who worked there in the past, and for the fans. At Juventus under Marcello Lippi, instead, the team spirit was fundamentally based on a simple motivation that the coach and the club conveyed to us: the 'duty' to win a championship again, in a team that had a tremendously successful history, but hadn't won for six years. It was about making 11 million Italian fans happy: a weighty responsibility, a difficult one, but it generated a very powerful motivational driver. Last, on the Italian national team, with Azeglio Vicini as coach, the team spirit sprung from a sense of responsibility deriving from an awareness that we represented our country; we were united in the genuine pleasure of being together, which the coach knew how to encourage effectively." (Gianluca Vialli)

A good coach motivates the team by leveraging the quality of interpersonal relationships with and among team members

The ability of the team leader to encourage socialization, to elicit healthy competition, and to give personalized attention can also enhance motivation. This is done by leveraging the motivating role of positive interpersonal relationships, which reinforce team cohesion and a sense of belonging.

CONCLUSION

The motivational toolkit presented in this chapter describes a team leader's ability to make a number of interdependent decisions that will ultimately affect team members' motivational state. Necessary preconditions for optimizing these decisions are a profound capacity for self-analysis on the part of the team leader, as well as a mental equilibrium usually stemming from an appropriate life balance, which is difficult to achieve in the typically very stressful role of the team leader:

"The key is for the coach to be able to listen, minute by minute, to question himself and understand himself, to see if he's thinking clearly or if he's tired. It's essential to test your balance. To find your own emotional equilibrium it's important that you're not too tired, that you don't listen to others too much, that you don't allow others to influence you. It's hard to think clearly all the time, especially when time is limited, for example when matches are back to back, like during the Olympics or the World Cup." (Sandro Gamba)

"When I asked Alex Ferguson the secret to his long 'bench life,' and advice on how to be a successful coach, he told me to learn to play the piano. It's a great lesson. I learned that you need to cultivate a variety of interests, because that's the only way you can handle the stress of a profession that's incredibly engaging, that absorbs you completely, and that can end up devouring you. That's the only way to keep a clear head, which you need to analyze complex situations, understand problems, and make the best decisions under pressure." (Gianluca Vialli)

THE TEAM LEADER AS COACH: KEY MESSAGES

1 Team coaching in its three interdependent forms—motivational, consultative, and educational—is a key component of team leadership. If team coaching is done properly, it can improve team performance.

2 A critical success factor of team coaching is managing the interdependencies of goals, rewards, tasks, and interpersonal relationships among team members.

3 With specific reference to motivational coaching, good team leaders are people who:
- Get the entire staff involved in team coaching processes.
- Effectively promote discretional and extra-role behaviors among team members and improve relationships among them, continuously creating the conditions that enable and encourage team members to help one another, to cooperate, and to provide mutual motivation.
- Dedicate special attention to individual and collective communication processes with and among team members, carefully assessing when and how to deliver messages, with the central aim of reducing uncertainties.
- Collect and examine all information that is potentially useful for making decisions regarding the team, paying particular attention to signs reflecting the motivational level of the team.
- Invest time and resources in defining and applying rules of behavior for team members.
- Effectively leverage collective rewards and punishments for motivational purposes.

- Possess the unique ability of showing personalized attention to every member of the team, without conveying the perception of giving anyone special treatment.
- Assign precise, unique, meaningful and differentiated roles to every single member of the team, and identify and promote role models that each person can aspire to.
- Properly manage team feedback (a fundamental process in team leadership), often using feedback as a constructive motivational tool to balance the team's emotional states.
- Carefully and continually examine the energy level of the team and manage the workload accordingly, in light of its impact on motivation.
- Constantly come up with ways to make the team's work more interesting and captivating.
- Manage to strike the optimum balance between competition and cooperation among team members.
- Constantly encourage team motivation in various ways: increasing the perception of collective efficacy; setting valid, credible goals for every member of the team that are compatible with collective goals; and clearly defining strategies, plans, and resources needed to achieve these goals.
- Always consider the potential impact that their actions and decisions regarding one team member can have on the other team members.
- Understand—and make the team understand through their behaviors—the difference between fairness and equality.
- Gauge team coaching processes, especially those regarding team motivation, to suit specific situations.
- Motivate team members by setting more and more ambitious and appealing goals.
- Never tire of learning.

NOTES

1 Hackman, J.R. and Wageman, R. (2005) "A Theory of Team Coaching," *Academy of Management Review*, 30, 2, p. 269.

2 Ibid., pp. 19–20.

3 Rapoport, R. (1993) "To Build a Winning Team: An Interview with Head Coach Bill Walsh," *Harvard Business Review*, January–February.

4 Lippi, M. (2008) *Il gioco delle idee. Pensieri e passioni a bordo campo*, Editrice San Raffaele, pp. 39–40.

5 Rapoport, op. cit.

6 Tjosvold, D., XueHuang, Y., Johnson, D.W. and Johnson. R.T. (2008) "Social Interdependence and Orientation Toward Life and Work," *Journal of Applied Social Psychology*, 38, 2, pp. 409–35.

7 Johnson, D.W., Johnson, R.T. and Krotee, M.L. (1986) "The Relation Between Social Interdependence and Psychological Health on the 1980 U.S. Olympic Ice Hockey Team," *Journal of Psychology*, 120, 3, pp. 279–91.

8 Wageman, R. (1995) "Interdependence and Group Effectiveness," *Administrative Science Quarterly*, 40, 1, pp. 145–80.

9 Sitkin, S.B. and Hackman, J.R. (2011) "Developing Team Leadership: An Interview With Coach Mike Krzyzewski," *Academy of Management Learning & Education*, 10, 3, pp. 494–501.

10 Borman, W.C., Penner, L.A., Allen, T.D. and Motowidlo, S.J. (2001) "Personality Predictors of Citizenship Performance," *International Journal of Selection and Assessment*, 9, pp. 52–69.

11 Chiaburu, D.S. and Harrison, D.A. (2008) "Do Peers Make the Place? Conceptual Synthesis and Meta-Analysis of Coworker Effects on Perceptions, Attitudes, OCBs, and Performance," *Journal of Applied Psychology*, 93, 5, pp. 1082–1103.

12 Rioux, S.M. and Penner, L.A. (2001) "The Causes of Organizational Citizenship Behavior: A Motivational Analysis," *Journal of Applied Psychology*, 86, 6, pp. 1306–14.

13 Rapoport, op. cit.

14 Siang, S. and Sitkin, S.B. (2006) "Coach K on Leadership: An Inter-view with Mike Krzyzewski," *Leader to Leader*, Fall, pp. 34–9.

15 Bandura, A. (1982) "Self-Efficacy Mechanism in Human Agency," *American Psychologist*, 37, pp. 122–47.

16 For literature on conflict management, see Dixon, A.L., Gassenheim-er, J.B. and Feldman Barr, T. (2002) "Bridging the Distance between Us: How Initial Responses to Sales Team Conflict Help Shape Core Selling Teams Outcomes," *Journal of Personal Selling & Sales Manage-ment*, 22, 4, pp. 247–57.

17 Schroth, H.A. (2011) "It's Not about Winning, it's About Getting Better," *California Management Review*, 53, 4, pp. 134–53.

18 Mesmer-Magnus, J.R. and DeChurch, L.A. (2009) "Information Sharing and Team Performance: A Meta-Analysis," *Journal of Applied Psychology*, 94, 2, pp. 535–46.

19 Schroth, op. cit.

20 See Fleishman, E.A., Mumford, M.D., Zaccaro, S.J., Levin, K.Y., Korotkin, A.L. and Hein, M.B. (1991) "Taxonomic Efforts in the Description of Leader Behavior: A Synthesis and Functional Inter-pretation," *The Leadership Quarterly*, 4, pp. 245–87; Burke, C.S., Stagl, K.C., Klein, C., Goodwin, G.F., Salas, E. and Halpin, S.M. (2006) "What Type of Leadership Behaviors Are Functional in Teams? A Meta-analysis," *The Leadership Quarterly*, 17, pp. 288–307.

21 Schroth, op. cit.

22 Bandura, op. cit.

23 Pearce, C.L. and Giacalone, R.A. (2003) "Teams Behaving Badly: Factors Associated With Anti-Citizenship Behavior in Teams," *Jour-nal of Applied Social Psychology*, 33, 1, pp. 58–75.

24 Bergami and Messina, op. cit., p. 63.

25 Høigaard, R. and Ommundsen, Y. (2005) "Perceived Social Loaf-ing and Anticipated Effort Reduction among Young Football Players—An Achievement Goal Perspective," manuscript submitted for publication.

26 Høigaard, R., Säfvenbom, R. and Tønnessen F.E. (2006) "The Re-lationship Between Group Cohesion, Group Norms, and Perceived

Social Loafing in Soccer Teams," *Small Group Research*, 37, 3, pp. 217–32.

27 Taggar, S. and Ellis, R. (2007) "The Role of Leaders in Shaping Formal Team Norms," *The Leadership Quarterly*, 18, pp. 105–20.

28 Colman, M.M. and Carron, A.V. (2001) "The Nature of Norms in Individual Teams," *Small Group Research*, 32, 2, pp. 206–22.

29 Sias, P.M. and Jablin, F.M. (1995) "Differential Superior-Subordinate Relations, Perceptions of Fairness, and Coworker Communication," *Human Communication Research*, 22, pp. 5–38.

30 van Breukelen, W., Konst, D. and van der Vlist, R. (2002) "Effects of LMX and Differential Treatment on Work Unit Commitment," *Psychological Reports*, 91, pp. 220–30.

31 Hooper, D.T. and Martin, R. (2008) "Beyond Personal Leader–Member Exchange (LMX) Quality: The Effects of Perceived LMX Variability on Employee Reactions," *The Leadership Quarterly*, 19, 1, pp. 20–30.

32 Vecchio, R. (2005) "Explorations in Employee Envy: Feeling Envious and Feeling Envied," *Cognition & Emotion*, 19, 1, pp. 69–81.

33 Sherony, K.M. and Green, S.G. (2002) "Coworker Exchange: Relationships between Coworkers, Leader-Member Exchange, and Attitudes," *Journal of Applied Psychology*, 87, 3, pp. 542–8.

34 Henderson, D.J., Liden, R.C., Glibkowski, B.C. and Chaudhry, A. (2009) "LMX Differentiation: A Multilevel Review and Examination of Its Antecedents and Outcomes," *The Leadership Quarterly*, 20, 4, pp. 517–34.

35 Liden, R.C., Erdogan, B., Wayne, S.J. and Sparrowe, R.T. (2006) "Leader-Member Exchange, Differentiation, and Task Interdependence: Implications for Individual and Group Performance," *Journal of Organizational Behavior*, 27, 6, pp. 723–46.

36 Hackman, J.R. and Oldham, G.R. (1976) "Motivation through the Design of Work: Test of a Theory," *Organizational Behavior And Human Performance*, 16, pp. 250–79.

37 Rapoport, op. cit.

38 Montali, G.P. (2008) *Scoiattoli e tacchini—Come vincere in azienda con il gioco di squadra,* Milano, Italy: Rizzoli, pp. 102–3.

39 Rich, G.A. (1998) "The Constructs of Sales Coaching: Supervisory Feedback, Role Modeling and Trust," *Journal of Personal Selling & Sales Management,* 18, 1, pp. 53–63.

40 Locke, E.A. and Latham, G.P. (1990) *A Theory of Goal Setting and Task Performance,* Englewood Cliffs, NJ: Prentice-Hall.

41 Beauchamp, M.R., Bray, S.R., Eys, M.A. and Carron, A.V. (2005) "Leadership Behaviors and Multidimensional Role Ambiguity Perceptions in Team Sports," *Small Group Research,* 36, 1, pp. 5–20.

42 Humphrey, S.E., Nahrgang, J.D. and Morgeson, F.P. (2007) "Integrating Motivational, Social and Contextual Work Design Features: A Meta-Analytic Summary and Theoretical Extension of the Work Design Literature," *Journal of Applied Psychology,* 92, 5, pp. 1332–56.

43 Siang and Sitkin, op. cit.

44 Sitkin and Hackman, op. cit.

45 Ibid.

46 Schroth, op. cit.

47 Montali, op. cit., pp. 109–11.

48 Bandura, A. (1997) *Self-efficacy: The Exercise of Control,* New York, NY: Freeman, p. 476.

49 Myers, N.D., Feltz, D.L. and Short, S.E. (2004) "Collective Efficacy and Team Performance: A Longitudinal Study of Collegiate Football Teams," *Group Dynamics: Theory, Research, and Practice,* 8, pp. 126–38.

50 Chen, G., Kirkman, B.L., Kanfer, R., Allen, D. and Rosen, B. (2007) "A Multilevel Study of Leadership, Empowerment, and Performance in Teams," *Journal of Applied Psychology,* 92, pp. 331–46.

51 Gould, D., Hodge, K., Peterson, K. and Giannini, J. (1989) "An Exploratory Examination of Strategies Used by Elite Coaches to Enhance Self-efficacy in Athletes," *Journal of Sport and Exercise Psychology,* 11, pp. 128–40.

52 Chase, M.A., Feltz, D.L. and Lirgg, C.D. (2003) "Sources of Collective and Individual Efficacy of Collegiate Athletes," *International Journal of Sport Psychology,* 1, pp. 180–91.

53 Zaccaro, S.V., Blair, C.P. and Zazanis, M. (1995) "Collective Efficacy," in Maddux, J. (ed.) *Self-Efficacy, Adaptation, and Adjustment: Theory, Research, and Application*, New York, NY: Plenum Press, pp. 305–28.

54 Feltz, D.L. and Lirgg, C.D. (1998) "Perceived Team and Player Efficacy in Hockey," *Journal of Applied Psychology*, 83, 4, pp. 557–64.

55 Gully, S.M., Incalcaterra, K.A., Joshi, A. and Beaubien, J.M. (2002) "A Meta-Analysis of Team Efficacy, Potency and Performance: Interdependence and Level of Analysis as Moderators of Observed Relationships," *Journal of Applied Psychology*, 87, pp. 817–32.

56 Bray, S.R. and Widmeyer, W.N. (2000) "Athletes' Perceptions of the Home Advantage: An Investigation of Perceived Causal Factors," *Journal of Sport Behavior*, 23, pp. 1–11.

57 Edmonds, W.A., Tenenbaum, G., Kamata, A. and Johnson, M.B. (2009) "The Role of Collective Efficacy in Adventure Racing Teams," *Small Group Research*, 40, 2, pp. 163–80.

58 Sitkin and Hackman, op. cit.

59 Bergami and Messina, op. cit., p. 53.

60 Zorn and Ruccio, op. cit.

CHAPTER 6

TEAM LEADERSHIP: A WORD FROM THE COACHES

CARLO ANCELOTTI

Carlo Ancelotti was born in Italy in 1959. A former soccer player, he began his coaching career as assistant to Arrigo Sacchi at the helm of the Italian national football team from 1992 to 1995. He then moved on to Reggiana, a team that advanced from Serie B to Serie A under his leadership. After stints coaching Parma and Juventus, he took over the bench of Milan from 2001 to 2009. In the past, he had won countless victories with this team as a player; now he earned major victories as a coach including a national championship (2003), two Champions league titles (2003 and 2007), and the Club World Cup (2007). From 2009 to 2011 Ancelotti coached Chelsea, winning the Premier League and the FA Cup in his debut season. On December 30, 2011 he signed with Paris Saint-Germain.

What is the basis for managing a team?

In the past ten years, the role of the coach in team management has gone through many changes. Up until ten years ago, a coach's job centered entirely around the players, whereas now he has to oversee relationships with the management and the administration. Clearly a coach has to be filled in on the administration of the team and act accordingly in terms of requests, building the team lineup, and commercial relations. Today sponsors play a very intense role in the life of the team, they're quite heavily involved, and they have their demands.

What about relations with the fans? And with the press?
The coach doesn't handle relations with the fans, except indirectly via the media. Actually, I consider relations with the press important, as this is a key channel of communication that can create tremendous pressure. But I think the single most critical aspect is internal communication in the team. The team isn't only made up of players who have to work well together. Teams can have 50 or 60 people: the technical staff, two coaches for the goalkeepers, the fitness coaches, the medical staff consisting of three doctors, and ten physical therapists … so a substantial number of people in the group. This, not to mention the whole administrative/club side, which the coach needs to liaise with.

In percentage terms, as far as the time you spend with the club, how much is dedicated to the players and how much to all the rest?
I dedicate 50% of my time to the team, and 30% to the technical staff and the fitness coaches. The coach isn't responsible for everything, but he has to be informed about every aspect, because in the end he's the one who makes certain decisions. He has to keep everything under control, even though it's important to delegate. I trust my collaborators completely, but I always need to know what they're doing. The relationship with the fitness coaches is closer and more constant; with the doctors it's less so, and with them I delegate 100%. The rest of the time, 20%, I spend dealing with the commercial side and the club management.

Do many conflicts arise among all these people? How do you handle them?

With the commercial side, conflict can be quite common. Sponsors, quite rightly, like to get close to the team, to go to the training center and take pictures and watch practice. But for us it's a place for work, concentration, discipline. Having people around can be a distraction, and mediating this situation isn't always easy.

As far as staff members go, my relationship with them is simpler. The staff are very important, members have to have a good relationship with the team, and the players have to respect them and see them as people who are personable, people they can trust. A player might not directly confide in the coach very much, but he may do so indirectly by talking to the fitness coach, the massage therapist, or the assistant coach. These people have to serve as filters, passing necessary information on to the coach, always in a positive and constructive way.

Do you spend much time in the locker room?

I prize sincerity highly in interpersonal relationships at any level. No one can pretend to be someone he's not for long, or adopt behaviors with the team that are inconsistent with his own way of thinking. My role is an important one, with certain rights and duties, and the same is true for the player, so the conversation has to be on the same level, as far as possible. I've met a number of coaches who relate to the lads in a paternalistic way. I simply do what I do with my players to lead the team to achieve great things, and this gives us advantages also in terms of personal satisfaction. To do this I need to stay close to the lads, to pass (not force) my ideas on to them. The challenge is just that—transmitting ideas from the coach to the players and then onto the pitch. This is the critical step.

> **"I prize sincerity highly in interpersonal relationships at any level."**

Managing relationships with the club, the management, the sponsors, and so on—how much does this impact your credibility in managing the players?

Players are very observant, they understand perfectly well when a coach has the situation under control, and he's on the same page with the other sectors and with the club. This keeps the players in line and allows them to work worry-free. Sometimes, most often with the medical staff, we don't exactly see eye to eye. When this happens, the player loses his bearings and the organization loses a bit of its credibility. Likewise, it's very detrimental when there's a conflict between the club and the coach. I always say that a coach might be the worst one around—but as long as he's there, as far as the club is concerned, he has to be the best. At the end of the year, the club can decide to let him go, but there should never be a rift between the club and the coach, or else the entire team will bear the brunt of it.

When you were at AC Milan, you tried outdoor teambuilding for the team and the staff of the club. What was the response? What was the objective and what were the results?

We were just trying to get the group to bond, and to get motivated, to get the group in synch. We did a few courses at the technical training center. We did one in Tuscany too, just with the staff, not with the players. None of these initiatives actually got a very enthusiastic response. Aside from the players, nearly everyone saw them as something forced on them. They don't see the point of nurturing the psychological side of the group, because in football, psychology is too often confused with psychiatry. But I think that psychology is the most important thing in football.

Unfortunately, a coach isn't a psychologist; he doesn't have the knowledge or the tools he needs. But I like to be informed, up-to-date, and to focus on experience in particular. I believe that the difference between teams is this psychological factor, more than anything else: there are highly trained groups that might lack motivation, for example, and this is due to psychological mechanisms. This is the reason they can't outperform the others.

Speaking of psychological mechanisms, how do you motivate a team that's in trouble, one that has to revive their energy and their conviction that victory is possible?

I think it's much easier to motivate a team when they're losing rather than winning. In critical moments, when you're down and out and everyone's coming down on you—the cycle's over, the team's old, the players aren't motivated—only two things can happen. Either everything falls apart, because there is no self-assessment and no one accepts any responsibilities, or you react. If you approach the situation with this attitude, every game becomes an important chance for a comeback, to prove everybody wrong. This is a very powerful driver.

Are there different management styles depending on the complexity or the level of the team?

No, I'm convinced that a coach maintains his style no matter what team he's coaching. I think I'm the same as I was ten years ago when I coached in the Italian Serie B: the same behavior, the same style. Only my methods have changed somewhat, because it's one thing to have seven days to train the team, it's another thing to have the whole team together just once a week, at most: this happens when you coach many star players who play with their national teams on Wednesday, for example.

Do you perceive an evolution in the role from coach to manager?

In Italy the role of coach is still linked to technical/tactical aspects. In other countries there are coaches who are managers in every sense of the word, for example Sir Alex Ferguson with Manchester United. He has total control of the club, and he gets a budget from the owners that he handles entirely on his own. This depends for the most part on the club, but I believe it's important to be "inside" the team, to go out on the pitch and into the locker room. Keeping a bit of distance between you and your players isn't a good thing, as I see it. There's no doubt that manager/coach is a more complex role, because you can't neglect the technical side just because you have to deal with management as well.

DON CASEY

Don Casey is a former professional and collegiate basketball coach. He has coached two NBA teams, the Los Angeles Clippers and the New Jersey Nets—each for a season and a half. He also worked as an assistant coach with the Chicago Bulls (1982–83) and Boston Celtics (1990–96). Prior to coaching in the NBA, Coach Casey was the head coach at Temple University (1973–82), where he led the Owls to an outstanding winning percentage of .616. Coach Casey has also served as the VP of the NBA Coaches Association and as a coach for USA Basketball.

How do you see leadership in head coaches of professional sport teams?

First of all, it should always be remembered that no one comes to the game to see the coach: people come to see the players, and the coach has to realize this. But many coaches want to have so much control. Coaches who think "it's all about me," who want to get in front of the camera—they're doomed. At Boston, we had a sign up that read "Players win games!" Coaches coach, players play. And some players have ideas, they can really help. I believe that, in a team, the players should be the leaders. In fact, we try to get the players to pick the captain, who then becomes your go-to person—the one you deliver your message to. We always like to have players who can put the pressure back on the players. On teams that are floundering, the coach needs to help shore up someone, or create someone who can emerge and take over the role.

Of course, on some teams it's the head coach who chooses the captain, but it's not always an easy decision. Some coaches appoint weekly captains, but this choice dilutes the role, making it less meaningful and relevant. Even worse, sometimes coaches appoint game captains. To me, doing this means avoiding the problem. In my experience, the best leaders are mostly quiet players who lead by example. They're not necessarily the star players, because some of them simply don't want this responsibility although they have a lot of talent. In the end, professional sport is a lot like the movie industry. Obviously the role of the head coach is similar to a director. Good actors want to work with good directors and with a good cast, because this helps them get the most out of their talent.

So who is the leader in the team? How should head coaches manage the relationship with the players?
In my career, I have learned some key things. When choosing players, one should remember that skilled players are a false positive. Coaches think, "If I had those guys, I could win." I'll tell you what, they might have more talent, but they're much bigger pains! When managing your team, you need power, you have to know the game. The question is, how do you get this player to play to his level, once you find it, consistently? Also, some rules must be applied. For example, publicly challenging the coach is something a player should never be allowed to do.

In the end, I think that the key message is that, if they want to succeed, team leaders should be listening to their people as much as they're telling them what to do. Players should feel they can contribute, and if you listen they'll tell you what they can and can't do. They want to look good, after all.

That ties in to a proverb that's big with us: "Improvise and adjust." But you have to do that on the fly, in the flow of the game. You don't get away from the script, but you let the players have some freedom, some leeway. An illustrative example of this principle is the NBA 2012 game between Los Angeles Clippers and Memphis Grizzlies. Clippers were pretty far behind. So most coaches would think, game's over, protect your best players—take them out and call it a day. But two key players of Clippers came to Vinny Del Negro, the head coach, and said, we can go after these guys, keep us in. So they scored three triples in a row, and Memphis just folded. In the next six or seven minutes, Clippers scored 26 points to their 3, and ended up winning. This was the largest comeback in the NBA playoff history in one quarter.

So those players really respect the coach now because he listened to them, believed in them, and they delivered. That would be a case of improvising and adjusting, because most of us would have put those players on the bench. But good players can sense that something special's going on, they read the body chemistry, read the other players' faces, hear what they say. For example, good players can tell if an opponent is about to lose his temper, if he's grumbling and complaining, so they'll go after that guy, and foul him again and again to try to provoke a technical foul. These games within the game are constantly being played. So I think the lesson is: listen to your players (employees, in a company) for they also have a feel or pulse for the situation. As they say in soccer: "wisdom of the crowd" can be of more benefit (at times) than the "wisdom of one."

So team members have information that is very useful to support decision-making by the team leader. And what is the role of information acquisition and management by the head coach?

In sports, the head coach and his staff collect and use a lot of information. First, on players. For example, the scouts pick up on information about every player and what he does—not only the position he plays, but his technique, his strengths and weaknesses, where he likes to shoot from, and so forth. All this player information is for the coach to digest. Then, obviously, we carefully analyze each player's performance in every game.

Second, we have information on all the opposing teams, so that serves as a kind of early warning system, so you know in advance what to expect and you can plan how to react. We have something like a textbook that tells you all the key plays. Every play has a number, so the coach just has to call out a number and the players have to know exactly what to do. Third, on officials. We get information on every call the official makes in every game. But the question is: what to do with all this information? How do you manage it? It's the coach's decision to come forth and say, "I don't want to give them all this, just the important things." You can't fill their minds with too much; if you do, they won't be spontaneous. I think it should be the same in the world of business: team leaders should collect information about their team, their competitors, the environmental factors affecting performance, and then filter that information to communicate only the relevant parts to team members.

What do you think managers in the world of business can learn from head coaches in professional sport?

I think there are several similarities.

First, team leaders must understand the psychological and physical state of team members. For example, in the NBA they play 90 games in a season. Sometimes they're tired, they don't have enough energy or attention to listen to you: then it's better to avoid long, in-depth analysis of the last game you played. Likewise, sometimes you've got to understand you cannot over-train them.

Second, for business managers and head coaches alike, it is important to learn continuously. Constant upgrading is needed. In professional sports there are a lot of clinics where you can get ideas, share best practices, and challenge your assumptions. It's a great opportunity, and managers should try to find similar opportunities. In basketball I see very few radical innovators, but many very good adaptors who perform very well by getting inspiration from their colleagues and sometimes by simply recovering ideas from the past.

"For business managers and head coaches alike, it is important to learn continuously."

Third, I think that both in sports and in business, goals must be reasonable. The goal of the day might be to run a press offense, and then you move on to the rest of the game. You break it down into segments. And team leaders should give clear deadlines. During practice, for example, you've got to get a certain play down in a certain amount of time, or you're going to keep working until you get it right. In basketball this is easier, because in this game the clock is a pressure point. It's a visual reminder that you've got to get this thing done. Players always have to keep their eye on the clock, which is a great equalizer.

Fourth, in teams, both in business and sports, a key challenge for the leader is how to create a sense of oneness without giving up the individual contribution of the star players/performers. They've got to understand that their game is not the only game—it's a game within the game instead.

So what is the key role of the team leader?

Generally speaking, players will pick up on whether you are fair and if you're trying to make them better, and not at anyone's expense. In sports, I think the key message the head coach should deliver to team members is, "I am here to help you do your best." This is especially true with star performers. In critical situations I always asked my top player, "Where do you want the ball for the last shot?" That gets the players thinking about themselves in relation to the game. It should be the same in the world of business. Managers should ask key team members, "We've got to get this thing done—what do you need?"

Another relevant role of the team leader is to make players feel that they are important. Most athletes are very fragile people; they know their days are numbered. In professional sports, the head coach, and the club in general, should do everything they can to try to eliminate any off-court trouble as much as possible, and make players feel they are not alone. Maybe you can't help them, but you can still identify who can. You've got to show them you care about them and their life—help them solve logistical problems, like rides for their kids when practices run long. We had a great medical staff that met with the wives at the beginning of the season to explain about the pressure, their health, their kids' health. The medical staff would take care of the whole family; for example, when we got flu shots, the whole family got flu shots.

Then the team president would always send a Christmas gift to their wives, just to show that we care about their life. They appreciate this. This means creating the right atmosphere, which is a relevant part of a coach's job. You can do it in many ways. At least once a month we would bring them together, maybe just for a dinner. At Boston, we always organized a Christmas party for their kids, with clowns and gift bags and everything … again, just to bring them together, but not in a forced way. It made a difference, because the other teams weren't doing anything like that. And then at the end of the year, we had a breakup dinner after the last game and everyone was invited, even the parking attendants and custodians—no speakers, just a nice dinner.

Finally, head coaches, like team leaders in general, should focus on a number of little details that can make a difference in terms of impact on the psychological climate in the team. With a weak team, for instance, coaches have to give the players the feeling that it's going to happen, they're going to break through: for example, you can try to keep your opponent from scoring more than 100 in an away game. It just sounds better when you can say you lost, say 99 to 80. By controlling these things you're really helping your team, you're not throwing them to the wolves.

What are the most important differences in terms of key success factors for head coaches and assistant coaches respectively?

The assistant coach's goal is to do everything possible to help the head coach stay the head coach by constantly putting him in the best position to succeed. The assistant coach mainly interacts with the athletes and has to neutralize the anxiety and develop the individual player. The head coach has a completely different job. He controls the minutes, makes the play calls, sets the total structure of style play, and establishes the expectations, the tone, and the work ethics. The head coach is the "big picture" person, who deals with the owner, the president, the general manager. For the head coach, it is very important to have a specific style, a personal identity which has to transfer into a clear and unique team identity. He should develop a concept of the team. The head coach can't be involved in everything—usually after around 20 games everybody gets into a rhythm, and develops an identity and a concept. When this happens, this is what we're going to do. Once we've developed our concept of the game, it can be applicable to every team. We live by it, once we've made that decision. The concept is huge.

SASHA DJORDJEVIC

Born in Serbia in 1967, Sasha Djordjevic has coached the Italian basketball teams Olimpia Milano (2006/07) and Benetton Treviso (2011/12). In 2012–13 he became assistant coach at Denver Nuggets in the NBA. During his career as a player, which ended in 2005, Djordjevic earned top-level titles with Partizan Belgrade (winning a Korać Cup, three national championships, and a Euroleague title) and the national teams of Yugoslavia and Serbia, earning a silver medal at the Atlanta Olympics in 1996. In 1992, Djordjevic debuted in Italy at Olimpia Milano, winning a Korać Cup; in 1994 he moved to Fortitudo Bologna. After a stint in the NBA in 1996 he returned to Europe and played with Barcelona, winning two championships and a Korać. Real Madrid was next, and another national championship (2000). In 2003 he was back in Italy, first playing with Scavolini Pesaro and then once again with Olimpia Milano.

What do you look at to determine whether a group is a team?

There's always a certain moment, a crucial episode, that makes a group a team. It might be a very painful defeat that leaves a mark—a particular situation in which the members of the group find themselves and realize they feel like they're something more.

What is team spirit based on?

As I see it, both on a group and an individual level, it's important to focus on the concept of ambition, which is what makes each of us members of a team. I might want to earn a lot of money, or to be known for a certain "signature move" I make, or for the points I score—or maybe I want this group to be the best of all times, or something else. There are various combinations of elements—a variety of stories behind every member of a group—and they all have to be brought into line with the same ambition. We talk about this at the start of the season, from the very first day. Sometimes some players may find it hard to be part of a group—some might be individualists and their ambition is to go play somewhere else, and you don't know that until you delve into everyone's personal situation.

One of the things that I like to do to start out with is to give each person in the group a piece of paper where they write down their thoughts and ambitions, their motivations, and what they expect from the club—not only the players, but the general manager, the doctor, and the physical therapists as well. I ask them, "What do you think the club is?" and this helps me get an immediate understanding of a player. If he only writes down a couple of lines, that means a lot of work needs to be done on team spirit. On the other hand, if he writes, "Earning the respect of the others on the court," or "My professional goal is not to lose the ball," then I have less work to do with him in the group. Then obviously I need to watch what happens next. At the end of the year I always compare the expectations, goals, and results that we've achieved to try to understand why we reached some, and why we weren't able to attain others.

How do you bring individual ambitions and group ambitions together?

First of all, you have to communicate where you want to go, and this isn't simply the coach talking to the group. Naturally, team management has to deal with the team, and help create it and run it. Every player is different, and responds differently to the words, "We have to win tonight," "We have to win this year," or "We need to do better." You have to know how to control the pressure that's created within the team effectively, especially when expectations are high.

The first thing to do is to discuss ideas, values, work practices, expectations, and goals with the president or general manager. You need to create trust within the framework of clearly delegated responsibilities in terms of the technical and sports project. Second point: relationships with journalists, the media, and the general public. They can create situations that reinforce, or damage, or in some cases help the group, and players react differently to some things that appear in the press. Third: choosing players. It's important to do this judiciously, so as to align goals and expectations. Don't choose players solely on the basis of their experience on the court. If they're good players, that's fine, but underneath that there are people. Their family and friends, their mistakes and strong points—these are the things that count the most for the good of the group, and you discover these things during the season. Fourth: coaches have to have the chance to choose the people they work with, people to share ideas with, to establish trust and rapport. You have to feel comfortable with them; your collaborators have to be your friends. There needs to be a shared philosophy as far as the game, life, proper behavior, respect. When you talk to these people, especially on a personal level, they respond with your same line of reasoning. Fifth: technique and tactics, but the game only comes if the first four conditions lay the groundwork for the team itself and how it functions.

A player is used to working hard, physically and tactically speaking. When he becomes a coach, how does he handle the repercussions?

A coach is a completely different role; there are other rules to follow. I never looked for myself in the players, but I tried to get to know them personally, to get the best out of them on the court. It's an athlete's personality that has the most impact on the group, on how they work on the court. The group also has to be willing to work, to accept ideas, criticisms, shouting, venting, smiles, tears, emotions. It's important to accept them and understand them, and go back the next day with everyone on the same wavelength. There has to be a leader in the locker room and on the court. It doesn't have to be the best player, but it's a role that no group can do without.

The leader has to be someone who strives to move forward, who acts as spokesman for the group, who earns respect by the example he sets. When I played with Barcelona I had a teammate who was 35 years old. He played for 10–12 minutes every other game, so he didn't play all the time, but he got in the game when we needed him.

Once, at a meeting after a game that we played really badly, there was a pretty bad scene: everyone was angry, the coach was shouting, journalists were circling. Three or four players wanted a revolution, to replace the coach. This player was the captain. He listened, and then with real class he managed to make his teammates see that the best thing to do was to follow the coach without challenging him, even though we didn't like what he was saying, we didn't think it was right. The important thing was to do it and to do it all together. This was the key message, and the player who got it across wasn't the best player in the group, but he was very astute …

There are coaches who tend to plan much of the on-court action, and others who place more trust in the initiative and instinct of the team. What do you think?

I don't think that either of the two ways is wrong. Personally, I believe that what you have to keep in mind is that the player is the one who goes out on the court. He has to read the situation, he has to be free to make decisions, and be ready to react and process all the information. You, the coach, have to talk to them, and in the end this means simply communicating to people: conveying to them what they have to do, what they are, what they deserve as players and as people. You need to teach the players to think like winners. For a winner, "It's hard, but it's possible." For a loser, "It's possible, but it's hard." I'd rather work with diamonds in the rough, young people I can mold, and teach what it means to win.

> **"You need to teach the players to think like winners. For a winner, 'It's hard, but it's possible.' For a loser, 'It's possible, but it's hard.'"**

Every team has its rules and schedules. How did you experience all this as a player, and how do you apply it as a coach?

As a player, being even one minute late is not OK, because this shows a serious lack of respect toward the others. Everyone—from the club to the management—has to follow the rules. If you don't respect the rules, you don't respect the others. When this happens, there's little the coach can do. He can react by leaving the player on the bench, but that way he punishes the others and hurts the whole team.

I'll give you an example. We were playing the finals of the Yugoslav championship. At that time there was a player who didn't always follow the rules. Sometimes he wouldn't show up for practice and things like that. Despite this, he was a 35 point per game player; he was a great player and all of us on the team valued him. We were playing the third game of the finals in Belgrade, and this time the coach decided not to let him play, not even a minute. We lost by 20 points. We were furious! The coach explained that it was a disciplinary measure. But it was the final and the mistake this player had made hadn't even happened the day before, but two or three months earlier. What was the point of not letting him play? The coach was right to punish him, but he should have done it two months before. The rules can't make the team suffer; the game can't be compromised.

What relationship do you have with the media?

I remember really well the semi-final and the final of the Euroleague in 1992 with Partizan Belgrade. We were an unknown team training outside of Madrid because there was an embargo in Yugoslavia. A difficult time from a human standpoint, and in terms of sports and logistics too. We were the surprise of the championship and we were unknown. At the semi-final, we went onto the court with 30 photographers ignoring us, focusing on our opponents, and only two Yugoslavian photographers for us. This gave me an incredible surge of energy, one more reason to win back the honor of the front pages of the newspapers. I transmitted this energy to all my teammates and we won by a landslide. The media are friends or enemies for an athlete or for a coach. You have to know how to take them with a pinch of salt.

JOHN KIRWAN

Sir John James Patrick Kirwan is a New Zealand rugby union footballer, and former All Black turned coach. With 35 tries in 63 tests for the All Blacks, Kirwan appears on the list of the highest try scorers in rugby union history. In 2001, Kirwan was an assistant coach with the Auckland Blues, his first professional coaching role. The following year, he moved to Italy to become the coach of the Italian national rugby team, which under his guidance recorded two victories over Wales in 2003 and Scotland in 2004. After a 2005 Six Nations campaign with no wins, he left the Italian team. In 2007, Kirwan was appointed as the coach of the Japan national rugby union team. In July 2012, he was announced as the new coach of the Auckland Blues for the 2013 and 2014 seasons.

If you had to define the concept of team, what terms would you use?

When you talk about team you often use words like "love," "courage," and "motivation"—and rightly so.

But what you need to consider is that these are all subjective concepts. Every one of us can interpret them in a different way, so resulting behaviors can be different too. If someone asked me to go onto the pitch and show you what courage is, knowing my background, I'd go out there and beat everyone up. But someone else would do it differently.

As a coach, I really insist on all these words, because if you use them superficially—if you don't get across the meaning of terms and concepts very clearly—you won't be able to create a team. What is courage for a Japanese team? Getting up when you're tired and pressing on against the adversary. What is courage in Italy? It's hard to say.

Being a team means never stopping. And it means succeeding in putting these things (love, courage, motivation) into play on the field and off, and taking responsibility for these values. What's essential is to give these words substance, or else they'll always just be empty words.

How can you share these meanings in concrete terms?

One of the goals of any team is to focus on the honesty of all the team members and the coach. Being honest means telling the truth, even when it's unpleasant, and even when the person who's made a mistake is a friend. At this point the choice is between two behaviors: a critic who goes behind the backs of a teammate—in other words, a critic who creates an environment that is negative and dishonest, a destructive critic; or a constructive critic, where there is the greatest possible transparency, honesty, and respect between the players and the coach; where things are said face-to-face and nothing is taken personally. The key here has to be *sharing* in order to *build*. Someone has to make the decisions. Players can disagree, but when that happens the responsibility falls to the coach. The important thing is to share differences of opinion and decisions with the players, and to move forward on the same path. If standards of honesty are not set when dealing with the players, there can't be a constructive environment.

It's often hard to understand where you've lost. Teams, even the best of them, make small mistakes but they make many of these mistakes over and over again that can compromise a season. To understand the reasons behind losses and to make continuous incremental improvements on factors that are only apparently marginal, it's important to work in a positive context. All the most successful teams call themselves a "family." That means that you can have a row, but the next day you're all fighting together again on the same side because there's love. Without all this it's hard to build an environment that grows and improves, while winning as well.

How do you handle this interaction to create an environment of honesty?

First of all, the coach has to be an example for everyone. Then you need to ensure that there is respect, always, in every circumstance. The players, when confronted with the truth, accept it even if it's unpleasant, and they also appreciate you more than they did before. The truth fortifies the group. Often players' spontaneous reaction is aggressive, but the next day they understand and they decide whether they'll change or not. If they don't, the consequence is the bench, or the stands. That way, in the end everyone will understand that to continue to be a part of the group, everyone needs to row in the same direction. It's a simple approach, but it's based on clear rules that apply to everyone.

If a player wants to row with the rest of the team but can't because of weakness, or fear, or lack of courage, what is the role of the coach in these situations?

The coach has to play a support role in every sense, at a technical, mental, and purely human level. After that, after trying everything, if the player can't or won't change, you have to find a solution to prevent him from creating conflicts for the team. The team comes before everything else.

"The problem that many coaches have is that they don't have the courage to tell their players what their limits are."

The problem that many coaches have is that they don't have the courage to tell their players what their limits are. Often you use the alibi that the players lack the technical skill. But actually, many players don't know where they should improve, and sometimes that's also the coach's fault, if he doesn't have enough dedication to his players to show them the right path. I have a set of parameters (technical, mental, level of commitment) that I use to understand if a player is at his limit and if he can't go beyond that to improve. Then, once he's reached the limit, if that isn't enough, you have to have the courage to make critical decisions for the good of the team, but that's life. This type of work has to be done at every practice.

In your experience, as far as the traits of players, which ones have you found that couldn't be improved on?

In general, there's nothing that can't be improved on. All players can grow in different ways, but if I had to slot them into categories, I'd say that there are four types of players.

There are world-class athletes who are easier to coach at a physical and technical level. The variables you have to work on are psychological and tactical, in terms of pivotal moments in a match.

Then there are the players who build their careers on constant commitment. These are players who often work at their maximum potential, and work hard to set an example, but they're not world-class. Sometimes their commitment isn't enough—and in these cases my job becomes a very difficult one, because it's never easy to cut someone who gives it everything he's got.

The third category is the players who don't perform as well and don't even work very hard to push their limits because they lack the skills to do so.

Last, the worst category is the players who are highly skilled and extremely talented, but they don't improve because they're lazy, or because they think they're better than they really are.

In terms of your international experience, what differences did you find coaching in Japan, Italy, and New Zealand?
To explain this, I'll use an example. If I ask my Japanese players to knock down a wall, they'll do it without any argument, they'll beat against that wall till they're bleeding—they'll follow orders, as absurd as they might seem, until that wall falls down. If I ask New Zealanders to do the same thing, they'll look for a shortcut to make it fall down sooner and avoid getting hurt—in other words, they'll try to find an alternative, the best way to do what you're asking them to do, especially if they don't think it's a logical solution. If I ask Italians, they'll tell me, "Tear down a wall? You're out of your mind!"

This means that when I coached the national Japanese team, I showed them the directions and the players would diligently follow them. In a certain sense, it was perfect for a coach. But there was a problem: they weren't using their heads. Lots of commitment and order, but little autonomy on the pitch. They follow the leader, but they don't think, and that's a problem in a sport that calls for lots of decision-making during the match. You pay for this in critical moments, when you have to use your head. So, later, you need to explain to them what their mistake was.

New Zealanders, on the other hand, are one step ahead, and they spur the coach on to keep up with them—otherwise he'll lose credibility with the group. There, a coach has to be able to demonstrate that he can improve the group, starting with the technical and tactical skills.

Italians, instead, won't start until they're convinced. The coach's role is to explain to them that if they knock down the wall, it will be for their own good.

What strategies did you adopt to increase the level of involvement of Italian players?

When I coached Italy, the players would often say to me, "But we're Italian, and this is what we are." And I would reply that we were participating in an Anglo-Saxon championship (the Six Nations). And I asked them how we would be able to beat our opponents if we didn't change our attitude, accepting their rules of play. By doing that, the players themselves were the ones to find the solution, and they convinced themselves of the path to take to knock down the metaphorical wall.

The concept is: explain and share the goal, instead of giving an order. The players have to believe in the coach and the coach has to be able to understand the culture and the needs of individual players to plan the season and to have the chance to work with players who are always motivated. For example, with the Italians, I realized that if they believe in the leader personally, they obey him rather than an idea. It's unlikely that they'll follow the right idea if it's put forward by a person they don't believe in, but you can make them do anything if you win over their hearts. That's why you need to work more on an emotional level than on a mental level.

MARCELLO LIPPI

Marcello Lippi was born in Italy in 1948, and began his soccer coaching career with Sampdoria's Junior League in 1982. After Serie A stints with Cesena, Atalanta, and Napoli, he took over the Juventus bench between 1994 to 1999 and 2001 to 2004, racking up five national championships, one Italian Cup and two Super Cups, one Champions League title, a European Super Cup, and an Intercontinental Cup. Lippi also led the Italian national soccer team to victory in the 2006 World Cup in Germany. He was named the world's best soccer manager by the International Federation of Football History and Statistics (IFFHS) both in 1996 and 1998, and world's best national coach in 2006. In 2012 he won the Chinese Super League with Guangzhou Evergrande.

What does "team spirit" mean to you?
Being a team means offering your skills to your teammates, working with single-mindedness and mutual respect. It's important that the star players realize that they can't attain anything on their own. The motto has to be: "None of us is as strong as all of us put together!"

What role does the coach play in managing the team?
It takes the players and the club, but the coach is the key person. The coach has to have conviction, solid principles, and has to get everyone on board and make everyone feel important. The coach needs to give the impression that there's a clear plan and clear collective rules. The sense of belonging and team participation are what ensure that even losses are accepted as a natural phenomenon, and aren't allowed to undermine confidence in the team. Conviction and motivation are earned not only with words, but more importantly through actions and behaviors.

What are the main mistakes to avoid when managing a team?

The key word is *authenticity.* You need to get the team to accept you with all your good qualities and bad qualities. Some coaches, when they start working with a team, make the mistake of imitating their predecessors to bolster their credibility on the team. This is exhausting, and wrong—because sooner or later this inner inconsistency comes to the surface in the person's management style, and when his true character does emerge it seems like up until then he was bluffing.

When a coach is extremely strict, this is another sign of weakness. You need to show the team that you listen to people and try to accommodate their needs. It's a way to demonstrate that you appreciate the players and what they do. It's much better to get players to collaborate than to make them follow you blindly.

How important is it to let players have a say in decisions?

It's important. If I sign top players, then I have to make them responsible—make them collaborators who participate and have a voice in final decisions. Even if the coach decides for himself in the end, he shouldn't make the players feel excluded from decision-making. There are many ways this can be done; for example, by having the best players come up with new formations for penalty kicks.

What rules do you establish with input from the team?

According to my work philosophy, what counts even more than strategies and tactics is forming a group that works well together, bonded by shared ambitions and motivations; a group that realizes that a true team is much more than the technical and athletic skills of players who wear the same jersey. When people respect and understand one another, this rapport naturally brings them into synch; when this "magic" happens there's no need to set down any rules, because rules emerge naturally.

What do you do when a player doesn't follow the rules?

There needs to be mutual respect. I sometimes read interviews with my players who would say, "I played badly because my teammates didn't serve me the ball enough." When this happened, in front of the whole team I would point out that if our opponents are better than we are and they don't allow your teammates serve you the ball enough, you need to help them out. That means you have to be willing to suffer and to work for them even harder. In cases like these it's important to deal with the problem in front of everyone, and remember the importance of team spirit.

Is it acceptable to make exceptions to the rules for certain team members? If so, when and why? How do you deal with these exceptions?

During my career I've always gone up against "prima donnas" who won't put themselves out for the team and who undermine the group. The captain and the other team leaders have to help this person understand that he has to change his behavior for the good of the group. If there's no way to bring him into line, it's better to do without him. It's true that you lose out on what he could give to the team, which clearly creates a problem, but proportionally speaking you gain even more from the others as their performance improves.

When you evaluate the performance of the team and give the players feedback, do you focus more on the positive or the negative?

If I want to reprimand a player I always start with the positive considerations first and then I go on to negative ones. First praise, then the rest. This is true with everyone, but especially with high-profile athletes. Champions need to be given criticism this way so they don't lose their self-confidence. With them, it's important always to start with compliments.

How can you encourage socialization and the creation of relationships based on respect, trust, and friendship among members of the team?

"Interchanging less talented players and top players makes it possible to keep the technical level high for the entire team, and to make everyone feel the same level of involvement and importance."

Players have to understand that the individual has everything to gain by becoming an integral part of the team. A typical problem for a coach is that every player would like to play all the time. When this happens, I tell the player: "You'd like to play more, but if you play all the time and the others never do, what happens if you ever get injured? If no one is good enough to replace you, we'll never reach our goals as a team." Intelligent players understand this reasoning. Interchanging less talented players and top players makes it possible to keep the technical level high for the entire team, and to make everyone feel the same level of involvement and importance.

And if you find yourself dealing with players who don't understand this philosophy?

You must have the more intelligent players help you get the others involved, and make them understand what it means to play on a world class team. These top players should also set an example of humility and generosity. At Juventus, for example, the "senators" helped the newcomers to fit in by demonstrating with their actions what it meant to play for that team, the right way to train, to put yourself out for the team. Criticism from teammates who serve as examples is very important, both to promote the proper spirit of collaboration and to build "healthy competition."

What do you mean by "healthy competition?"

An athlete always has to strive to demonstrate that he can do better than the others; but healthy competition isn't directed toward the others, but toward the player himself. This makes the athlete improve without pitting him against a teammate or against the coach.

How can you try to give every single member of the team personalized treatment, without letting the group notice any inequality?

You need to make everyone feel important, but the group knows very well what the hierarchies are without being told. Some coaches mainly address the younger players when they have to criticize the team. Instead, I think that criticism should be directed primarily at the best players. At Juventus, before practice, sometimes I would take Gianluca Vialli aside—he was our top player—and privately I'd tell him, "Look, today I'm going to tell you off now and again to give the younger players a wakeup call ..." I'd let him know, and I'd play the tough coach reprimanding the charismatic champion, so the young players would realize that they were part of a team where everyone was on the same level. And it worked!

Oftentimes players realize on their own when unequal treatment is acceptable. For example, Zinedine Zidane, who was one of the best players in the world from a technical standpoint, could run like a madman from the other end of the pitch, chasing down an opponent who'd stolen the ball from a teammate who wasn't technically as good, such as Antonio Conte. So Conte would think: "Damn! If Zidane goes to all this trouble to make up for my mistake, what do I have to do for him?" Athletes like Zidane will always get a bit more playing time than the others, but they earn credibility and respect on the field from everyone every day.

Most of your career you've spent coaching teams with world-class athletes. How do you handle them? What does it take?

The unique thing about champion athletes is that they want to win, and they look for other talented players, other intelligent players, because they want to win and they realize that in order to do so they need these other players. A top player also wants a strong guide, someone he can trust, someone who's sure of himself, and capable of leading a group of champions to victory. It matters very little if the coach is a nice guy. What's important is that the coach plays a role that empowers the players and the team to achieve the goals they've set for themselves.

Through the years, you've attained great credibility. But at the beginning of your career, how did you prove yourself— for example, when you arrived at Juventus for the first time?

Actually, the problem was that I'd never played or trained a powerhouse team. I didn't know the psychology. I gave a lot of thought to how to earn credibility. I came to the conclusion that, "I have to make everyone feel important, get everyone involved, and not be afraid of criticizing the star players in front of everyone."

Before the season began, I met Vialli, one of the best players. I told him, "I need you, you have to help me out. I don't know what Juve is!" He asked me, "How can I help?" I answered, "Let me treat you like the others, don't be a superstar, or you'll force me to tell you off in front of the team ..." He accepted, he wanted to feel involved. So for example from that very first meeting he came to practice dressed like everyone else, while normally he was a non-conformist and he dressed any way he liked.

Beyond working on bringing the top players around, to prove myself I thought I'd have to give the impression of a high level of professionalism right from the start. For our training sessions we had a gym built that covered 600 square meters. Actually, we would only use 15–20% of that space, but the structure gave a strong sense of organization, work, and commitment. This was important, because Juventus hadn't won anything for ten years and the team had to start believing in themselves again.

I earned trust and enhanced my credibility because of the matches we won; the players would do anything I told them to do. Often during practice I would say, "Vialli, you finish up," and I'd leave. I showed them I trusted them, that I could give them responsibilities.

You often use irony. How important is it to joke around with your players?
Joking with the players means putting yourself on their level, and being more in synch with them.

How do you explain your success as a coach? What characteristics do you think have enabled you to achieve your results?
I think my strong point is simplicity. I'm the same person I've always been, and I'm a firm believer in being sincere in my relationships with people.

ROBERTO MANCINI

Roberto Mancini was born in Italy in 1964 and made his debut in Serie A soccer with Bologna at just 16. He went on to play for Sampdoria, Lazio, and—moving to the English league—Leicester City. As a footballer he played 545 games with club teams, scoring 156 goals in Serie A and winning six Italian Cups, two Italian championships, two Italian Super Cups, two Cup Winners' Cups, and one UEFA Super Cup. In Italy as a coach he led Fiorentina, Lazio, and Inter FC from 2000 to 2009, winning three national championships, four Italian Cups, and three Italian Super Cups. He took the helm at Manchester City in 2009, and in England has won one national championship and one FA Cup.

Before becoming a coach, you were a world-class player. How important is being a former champion for a coach?

It's important because it makes players more receptive to what you're teaching them, especially at the beginning. This makes it easier to win their trust and their willingness to listen to you. But having a background as a top player also has its disadvantages. For example, you expect them to be able to do what you could do right away, to understand immediately, to learn quickly. When I first became a coach I was less patient, I wouldn't put up with mistakes, but then I realized that everyone can't instantly be or become like I was as a player. For former standout players, there's also the risk of not fully understanding what it means to sit on the bench, because they've rarely had to experience that. I'm lucky, in a way: I can relate because I spent a lot of time on the bench, especially at the beginning of my playing career. In hindsight, that experience served me well.

What's changed for you in the transition from player to coach?

A lot of things. The perspective changes completely. A player is self-ish, he has a hard time understanding the needs of the group—which for a coach is fundamental. What's more, a player can take on a number of inappropriate behaviors, but it takes a long time before he fully understands that. For example, today I realize that in a way I wasted the first three or four years of my playing career: when they didn't let me play, I worked less in training. For a coach, this is the worst thing that could happen.

You're now coaching in England after having spent your career as player and coach in Italy. What differences are you finding?

You need to understand the context and know how to adapt to it. Culturally, in the UK players live and train in a completely different way compared to Italy. For example, for them, working on tactics is torture. What's more, when training is over, they go home and don't think about work anymore, or the opponents they'll have to face. In Italy it's much harder to "disconnect." Even losses are felt differently: in the UK when you lose it's over and done with—you "turn the page"—but in Italy you don't stop thinking about why you lost that match, and how you can do better in the next one. Also, in the UK the coach is a manager who handles a lot more things and has a wider range of responsibilities: it's a harder job, even though it's more gratifying. You need to have a greater capacity to see the whole picture, to pay more attention to details, to have more patience … it's more demanding and time-consuming compared to what I experienced in Italy.

As a coach, what differences have you found between Italy and England as far as handling relations with the club?

In the UK they're less sensitive about losses—it's not as common for the club to lose faith in the coach when the team loses. In Italy, there are more people in and around the club who think they can have a say, even if they have no idea of what's really going on with the team, and their opinions are wrong or unfounded.

With Manchester City you coach players with exceptional talent and personality, but who are often labeled as "difficult." How do you reconcile these personality types with the needs of the team as a whole? What rules do you apply?

The first rule of a team is that you want to win. My initial assumption is that to win, the talent of the players is fundamental. Talented players are what I want and what I look for. My job is to enable players to realize their maximum potential at all times. Even when I select players, the first thing I consider is how much they can give to the team to make us win. I'm interested in how many problems they can solve more than how many problems they can create.

"Talented players are what I want and what I look for. My job is to enable players to realize their maximum potential at all times."

Of course, it's possible that players with great talent and personality also create problems … that's happened to me.

What do you do when that happens? For example, last season the media widely publicized the problems Manchester City came up against involving Carlos Tevez and Mario Balotelli.

You have to be practical. I've always been very clear and very direct. I demand the utmost respect toward myself and my team. At times I've also been extremely harsh in certain circumstances; I've gotten into some very heated arguments. But I never hold a grudge against anyone, that's just how I am. This helps me get over any conflict, and never to make it personal.

Let's take the Tevez incident. I've always believed in him, I've given him responsibilities from the beginning. As soon as he came to City, I made him team captain. A few days after he refused to play in a Champions League game against Bayern Munich, I invited him over to my house. I just asked him to apologize, and even though it took him a while, that was enough to get over what had happened.

And at the end of the championship, his contribution was invaluable. In circumstances like these it's vital for the coach to have the full support of the club. I had it, because Manchester City helped me a great deal, and has always been on my side. I don't know if the same thing would have happened in Italy … sometimes clubs leave coaches completely on their own.

What was your "motivational masterpiece" with the team?

In the 2011–12 season, all the psychological management of Manchester City was fundamental in terms of motivation. We were in the lead, but we weren't used to that incredible pressure, seeing as the club hadn't won a championship in over 50 years. We were terrified of winning. When Manchester United overtook us in the league table, I had to work hard on the psychological level: I had to relieve the pressure, free the players from that weight, but at the same time convey the conviction that if we played without losing our cool we had a good chance of winning. Luckily, we succeeded.

The turning point might have been when we lost an important match, when one of our best players didn't play. Three days later we had to play another major match, once again without that player. After that loss I was brutal: I told the team that without that player, they were nobodies. Of course, I didn't really believe that—I wanted to get them to react out of pride. They got really angry with me, they were hurt. But that's what I wanted. I got the reaction I was looking for. In the end, we recovered eight points in six games over a team like Manchester United … I don't think that anything like that will ever happen again.

Who are the coaches you've learned the most from?

I've had two coaches who were fundamental for me; they were totally different. The first was Vujadin Boškov. It wasn't easy to coach a team like Sampdoria back then. His genius was that he let us believe that we players made the decisions. He always pretended to go along with us, to agree with us, but then he did what he wanted to do.

This is an ability that can help a lot in managing a team, especially when the players have very strong personalities. The second was Sven-Göran Eriksson. From him I learned the importance of always thinking positive, even in difficult circumstances, when times get tough … that's how to give the team confidence.

In your opinion, how important is it as far as team leadership to be able to create legitimization—even with actors outside the team, such as the fans, the media, and club management?

In theory, it's important, although in practice, in my career I don't know nor have I ever met any coach who was able to win the trust of all the key actors outside the team. Ultimately I believe that the most important thing is to be the leader of the team. And to do that you need to achieve the goal: to win. You really have to believe in yourself, always, to think you're the best in the world. And do the same with the players: convince them that they're the best in the world. When you take over a club, it's essential to understand the context: analyze what the previous coach did, why he didn't reach his objectives, why he was replaced, and understand the situation.

Based on your experience, what are the essential skills of a good coach?

Above all, you need to be an expert in football and you have to be good at teaching.

Then you have to have a winning mentality, and know how to transmit it to the players. For example, I've always coached teams with long losing track records: Fiorentina, Lazio, Inter, City. With all of them, it was important to win something right away—even relatively less important trophies like the Italian Cup, which in Italy is less important than the championship. It helps recreate a winning spirit.

Also, a coach really has to believe in himself, especially when times get tough, when he could lose his nerve and his self-confidence.

In this sense, I've been lucky. I'm used to dealing with stress and pressure because I started playing when I was just 16—I learned early! And I've always wanted to be a coach, I knew that when my playing career was over, I'd do it, and I've always believed that I'd be able to do it well.

You also need to have a staff around you that you can trust. Mine is made up mostly of my former teammates, people who are professional, honest, and competent, who aren't afraid to speak up when they don't agree with me. Even if I'm the one who makes the final decision, I know I can count on people who openly and clearly show me if they disagree. This helps me a lot: it makes me think things over, it gives me different perspectives, it makes me question certain convictions.

And this brings me to the final point: you have to have a great capacity for self-analysis, and know how to admit to your mistakes. Taking the blame means taking responsibility, and this is always a sign of strength, not weakness.

DAN PETERSON

Dan Peterson was born in Illinois, USA, in 1936. In 1963 he emerged as a first-rate basketball coach on the US university circuit, and in 1971 he took the helm of the Chilean national team. He set out on his Italian venture in 1973 with Virtus Bologna, a team he led to win an Italian Cup and a national championship. Since 1978 he has coached Olimpia Milano, where he has racked up four national championships, two Italian Cups, one Korać Cup, and one Champions' Cup.

What does "team spirit" mean to you?

First of all, it's the pleasure of being together, of doing things together—training and playing with a willingness to make sacrifices for one another. The players create team spirit on their own, during the private moments they share in the locker room. When I used to coach, I never dared set foot in the locker room because that was the athletes' "sanctuary"—a place where they have to be able to say and do whatever they want. Only the massage therapist could go in, and I never asked him what the players said about me. The massage therapist knows everything, but I never asked him to break the spell of that place where team spirit is created and solid relationships among the players are built.

What role does the coach play in encouraging team spirit?

It's a question of rapport. The coach has to watch and take care of everyone. Even an all-star needs attention; he needs to hear you ask him how things are going; he needs motivation and contact. It's also essential to *give the players confidence in their identity*. Every athlete has to feel important, and know what role he plays on the team. For example, Franco Boselli was my "rifle," the player who would come off the bench and shoot hard; Vittorio Gallinari was my "watchman," the defender. Then there was the second string:

Mario Governa, the number ten player, never got in the game, but I took care of him, too, and once a month I told him how much I appreciated his work and how valuable I thought he was for the team.

How should you communicate with the players?

Every day during practice I talked to my players, looking them straight in the eye. I prefer pragmatism to abstractions, people to statistics. I've never agreed with all the theories on set plays. I think that a brief, effective, face-to-face speech makes a bigger impression than a thousand complex, abstract plays drawn up on a piece of paper. To explain a play you look at the paper; to make a speech you look at the people. These are the men who go out on the court. Speeches have to be simple, brief, and diversified according to the skills of each player.

> "I think that a brief, effective, face-to-face speech makes a bigger impression than a thousand complex, abstract plays drawn up on a piece of paper."

How important are rules in managing the group?

My system was based on the idea that the team didn't belong to me, the team belonged to the team. So the best rules were the ones that the team set down by themselves, not the ones the coach forced on them from the outside. The only rule that I gave the players was that they had to come up with their own rules. Establishing rules from the outside erodes relationships and *consumes* them. If you decide that everyone has to be on time, for example, when a player comes a minute late you have to penalize him. Instead, if the players handle it on their own, after someone comes late the umpteenth time, the other players themselves will make the latecomer pay for the delay. This is much more effective and productive in the relationships among the athletes and between the team and the coach. So the relationship between the players and the coach doesn't suffer and the coach can keep doing his job for years. There are lots of coaches who are forced to change teams often because their style is too centered on antagonistic confrontation and domination. After a while, no one can stand them anymore.

Many coaches claim that rules work if they apply to everyone—but they also say that certain players can't be treated like all the others. What do you think?

All players are different, and they can't all be treated in the same way. It's essential to nurture a relationship with each one, and gauge communication effectively depending on the objective that you have to achieve and the person who you're dealing with. There's no need for different rules for different players, but diversified communication processes and behavior suited to personality, timing, the situation, and the role in question. Every event involves a specific situation, and should be dealt with appropriately. This also serves to set an example for the whole team. I remember once we had to play a league game, and one player was irresponsible, and got to the bus 20 minutes late. He said, "Sorry, Peterson." I didn't answer, and I let him get on the bus. The whole trip the team was grumbling, "Peterson didn't say anything about being 20 minutes late?" I let the tension keep rising for the entire trip. Then, when we got off the bus, I told him: "You got here 20 minutes late? You'll get into the game 20 minutes late!" We won all the same, and when the game was over I had the whole team in the palm of my hand. They were thinking: "Peterson doesn't say anything, but he's willing to do everything!" And I did it without even raising my voice.

How do you deal with it when motivation founders on the team? How do you pick up the signals?

My training sessions were extremely intense, but short, and I always tried to give the team a few days' rest every so often. After two days without practicing, the players get to the court ready and raring to train, and to play ball. I also made every effort to gauge the athletes' moods continually. For example, Roberto Premier, a player who was usually a high scorer, was playing badly once during one game.

I didn't say, "You're doing a terrible job!" Instead, I said, "What's going on? Why can't you play today? Go to the locker room, I don't want you to look bad in front of all these fans …"

The message I conveyed was that I wanted to look after him, not to punish him in front of everyone. At that point, Premier regained his motivation, without getting discouraged. His fear of getting sent off the court got him going again, without hurting his pride. That's psychology. You have to know how to read the signs. There have been games where we played badly from the start. So I'd use a time out to try to turn the situation around, and in those few seconds I had to be able to shake up the mood and spark the desire, and motivate the athletes. Here again, effective communication is important.

How important are collaborators in managing a team?

It's fundamental to get everyone involved, to make them all feel like they're part of the team. The "human quotient"—interpersonal relationships with everyone—is vitally important to create a good atmosphere and make spending time together and working together a pleasant experience for everyone. When I talk to someone, and this person knows I appreciate him, that's half the battle. I became a coach of a Michigan team when I was 23. I was young and very qualified— I had two university degrees—I thought I was the top coach in the world. But as soon as they called me up to be head coach of the most high-profile team in Michigan, I started getting cold feet and feeling disorientated. I went from feeling totally self-confident to being panic-stricken. I turned to one of my teachers, a great mentality coach, and asked him what to do. I expected him to give me technical or tactical advice. Instead, he left me speechless when he wrote: "Make friends with the court custodian!" This major lesson meant that it's indispensible to make every person—from the custodian, to the secretary who organizes away games, to the cleaners—feel like they're part of the team, establishing a solid relationship based on friendship and mutual respect.

What's the best feedback to give to players? Did you focus more on positive or negative feedback?

I think you have to shout compliments and whisper corrections. You need to make corrections privately, but everyone should hear the compliments. If the players on the court hear my voice, even if they don't understand what I'm saying, they know they've done something right.

What do you think of providing players with role models?

I've had a team of special people, on a human level even more than a professional level, and in this context I needed to decide whether or not to sign on a certain player who had a very difficult, stormy past. I decided to give him a chance, because it meant *just one* potential black sheep in the midst of high caliber teammates, who could serve as models to inspire positive change and growth. Never have more than one "bad apple"—even if there are only two, they gang up against the others. Instead, a good example set by the leaders is contagious for everyone. I don't think I've ever been the model myself, but the fantastic players I've had the good fortune of working with have. All the younger players had to do was to watch their teammates on the court, who were all-star players, to see how to conduct themselves. I also think that it's better to have a broad leadership instead of just one leader who's above everyone else.

How do you motivate your teams?

Thanks to the good rapport I created, I managed to run extremely strenuous training sessions that would push even the best athletes to the limit. My prime focus was motivation, which enhances self-esteem and confidence in personal potential. Everyone knew what he was capable of doing.

Even when we went up against really tough teams, I'd say, "We've done amazing work, so we can last longer than the other team. But for the first 35 minutes we have to sweat bullets to run our opponents down. Even if they're ahead of us at that point, no worries—in the last five minutes they'll be out of steam and we won't. That's where we have to play the game!"

How do you deal with conflict between players?

My philosophy was simple: better to have everyone angry with me than angry with one another! Often my job was to act as a lightning rod to absorb the tensions among the players. That way I became the enemy for everyone to hate, and the players teamed up with one another. There should never be conflict on the court.

If you had to sum up the key characteristics of a good coach, what would they be?

You have to be able to take responsibility, even for other people's mistakes. You need to get everyone involved, and talk to everyone, and consider everyone equal. It's a good idea to set down just a few rules, to set reasonable goals, and not to put the players under too much pressure.

You have to use effective communication, and be able to say the right thing at the right time. A few simple, clear words are enough. I think it's also important to know how to use "locker room humor" and to nurture a true team spirit, in the broad sense of the term. Have a smile for everyone.

You have to be something of a psychologist, and be able to pick up on signals from the team. Last, you always need to tell the players the truth—even if it's awkward—and never make promises that you can't keep.

SIMONE PIANIGIANI

Simone Pianigiani was born in Italy in 1969, and is currently head coach of the Italian national basketball team and the Fenerbahçe Ulker in the Turkish Basketball League. He began his coaching career for the youth league of Mens Sana Siena, and in 1995 became assistant coach for the Siena team, achieving major success in the national championship, in the Final Four of the Euroleague and in the Italian Super Cup. He took over as head coach in the 2006/07 season, winning five consecutive national championships. He has also won four Italian Cups (from 2009 to 2012) and five Super Cups (from 2007 to 2012).

What's your group management style?

My initial approach at the outset of the season is essentially to take the lead, to provide players with a clear guide. They have to know that there's someone who's taking charge, and who always will, and who's not afraid to do it when times get tough.

When you have the team's total conviction, you can make exceptions and be more flexible. A part of my role is also to take complete responsibility as far as key people are concerned, both inside and outside the team. It's fundamental that players feel there's a guide who's steady and sure.

How do you interpret victories and defeats?

There are different victories and defeats. In general, we're used to working on mistakes. I think the message to give, which encompasses the meaning of sport, is to work hard every day to be better than you were the day before, to give 100% and to be as good as you can in foreseeing what challenges, problems, and needs you will have to face. At the end of every game, we don't overreact when we lose, we don't go overboard when we win. We look at what we can do better, what we did well, where we have to try harder. We know that in sports you lose—losing is a part of the game—and my team works on the concept of "decontextualizing" every single game. I'm often asked how the team keeps up their concentration after 12 consecutive wins, and I answer: "Because they don't think about the 12 wins—they think about the game ahead, they think about what they have to do every time they get on the court."

What principles do you adopt to build a team?

During the transfer market, there are scouting reports that cover every aspect of the player, and from these you can discern his professionalism, what he's done in his career. I used to think these things were much more important. Now I believe that there are players who don't perform in certain contexts because they're not inspired—but when they're put in another type of context, their intensity and their performance changes. I'm convinced that the most important thing is always a personal interview, with me and with the team management, when possible. To explain to the player why we want him, what kind of situation he'll find, how things work here, what our work ethic is, who his teammates are. To ask him: "Do you understand? Are you willing to be part of this?" Usually we paint a picture that might be harsher than what it really is.

"I think the message to give, which encompasses the meaning of sport, is to work hard every day to be better than you were the day before, to give 100% and to be as good as you can in foreseeing what challenges, problems, and needs you will have to face."

How do you handle relations with the media and with journalists?

My concern is always to take care of my team, so I never get into specifics about a player. If one of them is criticized, I always give technical explanations, emphasizing other positive aspects of the game or shifting the attention onto other things. My players have to know that I might be tough on the court, but off the court I always defend them—obviously as long as they respect the loyalty oath I ask them to take. When we lose, we lose as a team and, above all, the coach loses: if the player realizes this, you've already done half of your job of communicating with the team.

How do you handle relations with the fans?

A message has to come through, and I always repeat it to myself and to the press, even though they don't take it in very often. We have to respect the fans, who are the key element of our business, by giving 100% of ourselves, training hard, trying never to feel self-important. But I also tell our fans to be satisfied and proud if their players give it everything they've got on the court: let's get rid of this mindset of victory/defeat as the only measure of performance. Luckily, from this standpoint too, our fans have heard the message very clearly. We aren't superstars, but we'll go up against anybody—we'll give it a shot. So, even in the most dismal defeat, our fans have always stood behind us. In the end only one team wins—but a team that takes this kind of approach and philosophy, I think, can gratify a fan. If a player has only been here for two seasons but gives 100% every time, the fans like it—they identify with him, whatever nationality he might be. This is what I expect.

How are roles and responsibilities allocated to the staff?

I'm convinced that the more quality people you have, the better your job will be. So choosing collaborators is a top priority. I have an assistant who's older than me, just a few years, and he had a much more important experience as head coach. When we had the opportunity to hire him, we jumped at the chance. So my first assistant is actually a head coach. You can't handle everything on your own, yet you can't take on someone because you know him or because he's a yes man. You always have to focus on competence. We plan everything together—with the other assistant too, who's very young but extremely skilled with technological tools. We exchange opinions every time, but everyone enjoys a great deal of autonomy. In terms of responsibilities, I think the players realize the importance of the assistants based on the way the head coach treats them. What counts a lot for me is that they can run a training session on their own, and they are highly respected by the players.

I use meetings often; I talk but I don't want the players just to hear me talk: if I talk for half an hour in a meeting, I comment the video of the game for 12 minutes. Then when we go onto the court to train, for the first 45 minutes they never hear my voice, they only hear my assistants, or else they lose focus. What's more, if I criticize a player one evening, the next day my assistant might call him over, talk to him and make him see certain things, giving him positive reinforcement. It's essential to avoid a routine, to introduce variety to keep performance consistent. Players should never know what to expect.

What do you plan during the season?

At the beginning of the season I plan the type of profile that the team has to have: the technical objectives, such as how we have to play, and the milestones we have to reach along the way from a technical, physical, and emotional standpoint. I share some of these things—the ones I can—with the players. Not in terms of physical fitness, because they have to play every game with concentration, at their maximum potential. And I know that we approach certain games with a heavier workload, because we can win those games even if we're not at our best, but they mustn't realize that. I set credible technical goals, both for individual players and for the team. Obviously, at the start we put certain things in our baggage, and then we have to be able to pull them out at the right time.

What are the cornerstones of your style? The things you demand from your team?

Your "imprint" on your players has to be clear. I think that there's a lot of talk about team spirit, but what's really needed is the consistency to insist on these aspects every day. Players have to realize that they're surrounded by another team who works really hard; they have to understand how much effort goes on behind the scenes, that there are always people who work for the people who go out on the court to provide information, to handle the details.

They have to know that when there's practice on Christmas, they come for two hours, but the others stay till nighttime. So something powerful emerges. There have been many times when one of my assistants is up until two or three in the morning to finish working on the footage of the game. If we play three games in three days—which is what happens during the Italian Cup, when we make it to the finals—that's three nights with no sleep.

When there are playoffs, we play every other day, so we need to watch the video and do the editing, decide what to adjust, work out the tactics, etc. When the players come the next day to walk through the tactical situations on the court, we have to have already made tactical decisions. Every time, on the coach or the plane, my assistants and I watch the game we've just played, we evaluate it and decide what to change; we thrash it all out because the players have to know exactly what to do when they get here in the morning. There needs to be a special work group that works on team spirit every day. Everyone on the team needs to get the feeling of efficiency. Players can't have any excuses—everything has to be perfect for them, even the small things.

CESARE PRANDELLI

As a footballer, Cesare Prandelli played for Cremonese and Atalanta—but his career peaked with Juventus, where he won three national championships, one Italian Cup, one Champions' Club Cup, one Cup Winners' Cup, and one European Super Cup. As a coach, after starting out with the Atalanta's Junior League, Prandelli led a number of different teams, including Parma and Fiorentina. Since 2010 he has been coaching the Italian national football team.

What role does motivation play in managing a team?

Inciting in people a passion for what they do is an essential part of managing a team. I learned that from experience. As a child I was absolutely crazy about sports. I did anything and everything to be the first one to get to the parish recreation center by my house so I could play my favorite game. I never dreamt of becoming a champion: my dream was to get picked for any tournament in any sport, because I liked them all. By the time I was 16 I'd gotten pretty good, and I played in the junior league for Cremonese. I was a promising player, but we ran a family business, and my father was terminally ill. On one of the last days of his life, I spent a lot of time with him, and he told me something that would change my life forever: "Forget about our business, keep on pursuing your dream." I'd never forget those words. It's a very lucky thing when the people we love most are generous, and humor us in our inclinations. It's up to us to earn their respect.

How did you realize that you could become a successful coach?

I realized I could become a coach when I was still an athlete. During my last few seasons as a player, with Atalanta, I had a lot of physical problems to contend with. I didn't play much. On Saturday evenings, during pre-game training, my younger teammates started visiting me in my room. Talking to me gave them a sense of serenity; it helped them calm down. That's when I really saw how important you can be for the other players on a team, even if you don't play yourself. I think this is true for every team leader. You always have to keep in mind that the leader of the team is chosen by the team. For example, when I was a player, what sometimes happened to me was that my teammates looked up to me even more than the captain. I found this embarrassing, but it was the result of a natural process that emerges spontaneously from people: sometimes my silence was worth more than other people's words.

What does it take to be a successful coach?

I think you always have to be yourself. In our world, it's easy to slip into a role and become a victim of it—a hostage. I haven't changed a thing from when I went from coaching kids to coaching Serie A. In competitive sports, you shouldn't take yourself too seriously. Often the difference between a win and a loss can be chalked up to a goalpost or a random incident. How you work counts more than the results you get. The secret is to feel satisfied and gratified by what you do. As I see it, true success isn't so much sports success; it's having a kid you used to coach call you up after 15 years and thank you for having helped him grow. This success isn't immediate, like sports success, but it lasts a lot longer.

> "As I see it, true success isn't so much sports success; it's having a kid you used to coach call you up after 15 years and thank you for having helped him grow."

What's more, you always have to try to understand what drives the person you're working with. When I stopped playing, I started coaching junior teams for Atalanta. When I had to make my first speech to the team, I decided to say as little as possible—partly because I'm not a talkative person, but mostly because I wanted to listen to them, to get them to talk. I tried to understand why they were willing to make so many sacrifices, what goals they wanted to achieve. This is another important lesson about running a team: people really need to be listened to. And it's really important to know how to communicate, even by being quiet.

Even though it's good to be ambitious, you must never compromise your personal values. For example, a priority for me is not to compromise my relationships with people, or respect or friendship. Choices are always dictated by feeling. It's not true that you shouldn't stop at anything to reach your personal goals. I always try to go beyond professional relationships: this is a really gratifying aspect of my job, it's one of my responsibilities. Another key concept on a team is respect. If you respect whoever you're dealing with, you'll get 100% from that person, and that's what will make you a leader. You also have to know how to teach, and to do so first you need to learn.

How did you learn what you're teaching now, and who did you learn it from?

I've met many people in my life who've taught me important lessons. I remember three in particular. The first was Giuliano Amico, a young guy who spent lots of his time coaching us kids, and his only compensation was his infinite passion for sports. He died young; he was a generous person. And then there's Mino Favini, iconic manager of Atalanta's junior teams, who conveyed his great humanity, the power of his simplicity, and a desire to teach kids to become sportsmen in the true sense of the word, going far beyond the purely technical aspect. And last of all, Giampiero Boniperti, President of Juventus when I played for the team, and one of the greatest sports managers in the world: with just a few words, he could inspire tremendous motivation, and he was extremely professional.

Beyond people from the world of sports, I also learned a lot thanks to my passion for art. I like creativity; I've spent time with artists since I was a boy. I remember once I went out to dinner with some of them when a beggar came by. I was nearest, so I started digging around in my pockets for something to give him. But they stopped me and gave me a major life lesson: they took him to the bathroom, washed him up, and invited him to have dinner with us. Sharing things has a whole different flavor. There's always something to learn from artists: they open up your mind; they give you something; they're not cold, rational, or rigid. They don't live solely to achieve results or to earn money. To have good rapport with people, even on a sports team, you need to know how to look at the world from different perspectives.

Is there one ideal model for team leadership?

During my career, I've come to see that there aren't any hard and fast rules that universally apply to managing a team. The only rule is that you need to look constantly for the best approach—even when that means questioning your convictions. For example, at the beginning of my career I thought that explaining my choices was always the right thing to do. I thought that everyone had the right to know the reasons behind my decisions. Then I realized that this behavior isn't always a good idea. You always need to take circumstances into consideration. There are times when it's better to be democratic, and other times when you need to be authoritarian. Sometimes you need to listen, other times you need to speak.

What is your dream as a coach?

My dream is to see that my team respects the values of sportsmanship, that they have a clear identity and physiognomy, and that they have a strong spirit and the determination they need to realize ambitious goals.

ARRIGO SACCHI

Arrigo Sacchi embarked on his soccer coaching career in 1977. After heading the Cesena, Rimini, and Fiorentina teams in the junior league, he took on Parma and Milan. He led the Milanese red-and-blacks for the first time from 1987 to 1991, racking up victories in the national championship, and winning one Italian Super Cup, two Champions' Cups, two European Super Cups, and two Intercontinental Cups. He later returned to Milan for the 1996/97 season, after a stint as head coach of the Italian national team where he earned a runner's-up place in the 1994 World Cup. He then moved to Atlético Madrid and served as technical director for Parma and Real Madrid. The London Times nominated Arrigo Sacchi the best Italian coach of all time.

What role does motivation play for a team?

As I see it, motivation is indispensable. It's like the petrol that fuels the engine that makes everything else move. Without petrol, not even a Ferrari will go anywhere. Motivation impacts a team's physical, athletic, and cognitive abilities. Even technical competencies develop much more quickly in people who are highly motivated. Great professionalism, great enthusiasm, great passion for what you do—all this is what determines the level of motivation that a player has imprinted in his DNA. It's important to choose this kind of player because motivation is a critical success factor, even if it's hard to control.

How did you go about choosing players with these characteristics?

Michelangelo said pictures are first painted with the mind, and then with the hands. I've always believed that football is first conceived in the mind, not with the feet. So I've always sought this out in players, evaluating the person first and then the athlete. We would try to get to know players, initially talking to them. With the help of a psychologist, and by finding out what was being said about these players, we attempted to come up with a profile of their personalities. Then we had scouts analyze how they trained, and how much enthusiasm and passion they put into their work. We also took into consideration their interpersonal relationships with their coaches, with teammates, with opponents ...

Given a pool of players with this personal profile, what concrete steps did you take as a coach to nurture team motivation?

I always dialogued with my players to make them understand the importance of proper behavior—I never forced it on them. I strove to be constantly credible in the eyes of the team. This also depends a great deal on the work environment of the club in question; a coach can't do much if the club doesn't patiently follow suit.

How did you build your credibility over the years?

Through work, commitment, and by demonstrating that I was giving everything I had to in everything I did. Even when I was really tough on the team, they saw that I was just as tough on myself, and I did it only to better the team, and to better myself. Players know how to judge the quality of your work. And the better you do your job, the more your credibility grows.

Is there an episode that you consider your "motivational masterpiece?"

I would say during a World Cup match in 1994, a dramatic one, when I sidelined our best player, Roberto Baggio, for the good of the team. This meant that even the best player could be sacrificed, if necessary. No words carry as much weight as action and consistency. Pulling this player off the field during the game sent a powerful message to all the others about what I wanted them to do, and how I wanted them to do it.

Generally speaking, I talked to my players a lot. I tried to calm down the more agitated ones, to draw in the more apathetic ones to get them involved, and encourage the more nervous ones. When I coached Milan, once we were about to go up against a top team with a brilliant midfielder who played in the same zone as ours. I saw that my midfielder was really nervous, so I said to him, "Just think of how scared your opponent is; he doesn't play on a team with a 'buddy system' like we have. When he gets the ball he won't have anyone to pass it to, but you'll have help from two or three of your teammates. And when you get the ball you'll be surrounded by five teammates, and when you go to pass you'll be spoiled for choice." And what I said was credible because the facts backed me up.

Have you made any mistakes in terms of motivation?

When I went back to Milan the second time I made a huge mistake. I took on the role of some sort of Inquisitor with respect to the entire team. I didn't create the climate of collective trust that we needed at that time. I should have done what I did two years later at Parma instead; what I mean is I should have taken the stance with the players of someone who wants to do a good job, and who can only do it with the help of the team. Well, the results I got with Parma were diametrically opposed to the results with Milan.

Do the same rules have to apply for everyone on the team, or can you make exceptions for certain players?

Once a very famous player asked me why I treated him like all the others. He was one of the top players in the world. I answered that he was an intelligent man, so I knew he couldn't help but feel uncomfortable if I gave him special treatment. Creating disparity is damaging. I always tell players from the start: "We're going to have a strictly professional relationship. I'm going to give it my all, but none of you can expect any special privileges." The only thing that might vary is that players have different personalities: some need the carrot, others need the stick. But the rules have to be the same for everyone.

But isn't there a risk that even this could be seen as unfair treatment?

Good players understand this perfectly and realize that different athletes have different personal needs and personalities. These are people who have professionalism embedded in their DNA, which enables them to distinguish between inequality and behavior that's justified by the need to use a different approach with a particular personality type. It's thanks to people who understand this that great things can be achieved.

When you used to do post-game follow-ups, did you focus mainly on what the players did well, or on the mistakes they made?

I always concluded with what they did well, but I started out with what went wrong. What I always wanted to emerge was the idea that we could do better, even if we'd played a textbook match. This perfectionist mindset has always led me to be critical, even in the case of victory. I was convinced that to get players to do their utmost, yes, you need to say, "Well done." I don't agree with people who say you should never pay compliments to athletes. But, more importantly, you have to focus on areas where there's room for improvement. There are many different ways to do this. For example, I remember that before a major game during the 1994 World Cup, there was a player who was a little distracted. In front of the whole team I threatened to send him home if he kept on making the same mistakes. At other times, when a player was a bit anxious I tried to encourage him, not only with words, but with actions, explaining over and over what he had to do and what the team would do for him if the need arose.

The team must be the support system for each and every player. There are two schools of thought: the first holds that when it comes to the game, coaches are meant to be managers, not inventors. So the game is the result of the intuition of individual players. On the other hand, according to the second school of thought, which I concur with, the coach composes a sort of musical score. Everyone has to know the score before the game starts by studying it through training sessions that are custom-built and carefully planned. This minimizes the risk of unforeseen events or potential accidents, and instills confidence.

How much responsibility did you give your players? What were they responsible for?

I made everyone responsible, very much so, as far as adopting a mindset of commitment and generosity.

Did you get the team involved in making any decisions? If so, which ones?

Once, before a semi-final of a Champions' Cup, a key player was injured. I had four or five possible options for replacing him. I called in five players and asked them their opinions. Each one gave me a different answer as to what to do. At that point I realized that I had to decide for myself. It's extremely difficult to create a homogeneous team spirit, with everyone on the same page thinking along the same lines, with a single purpose and a shared goal. So the coach is the one who has to take the lead, from a personal and technical standpoint, and in choosing players. By this I mean considering both the collective skills to bring into play for every game, as well as the individual personality traits that an athlete should have: passion, discipline, and professionalism.

Is it important to create a climate of friendship among players, and between yourself and your players?

I've never managed to establish friendships. I created professionals who often didn't even spend much time together socially. The only thing I tried to prevent was sub-groups from forming, which normally emerge spontaneously. Sometimes I tried to get everyone to go out to dinner together, but it didn't work out because everyone had other things to do after practice. Everything is easier when you're dealing with intelligent people. This is what you need to look for.

In your opinion, what kind of behavior is inappropriate as far as the group is concerned?

Any behavior that tends toward self-centeredness, status-seeking, superficiality, individualism, or a couldn't-care-less attitude. I prize professionalism and perfectionism above all else. I've always sought out players who work with passion and a love of the game. One day a player told me, "We work too hard during practice—we don't have any fun!" I replied that we are entertained to the same extent that we entertain the public when they watch us. If you give a little, you get a little. In sports, chance can count, but no more than 5%. What you need more than anything is study and dedication. I've never believed those mothers who say, "My son doesn't study, but he's excellent at school."

> "I prize professionalism and perfectionism above all else. I've always sought out players who work with passion and a love of the game."

Beyond how hard the players work during training, what other signs did you look for in the team before a game to gauge their level of motivation?

They knew I was watching them and looking out for them constantly, except when they were with their families in the privacy of their own homes. But even on the bus on our way to the field, I paid attention to their behavior. For example, when I first started at Milan, I remember that on the bus before a game, on the way to the stadium, the main topic of conversation was the stock market falling. I was shocked, but I didn't say anything because up till then I had only ever coached Serie B teams, so I didn't dare comment. Then we lost the game, and that's when I got angry. Concentration and motivation are fundamental. And I'm not talking about motivation that springs from the fear of being singled out by the public as being inept, but a capacity for concentration and dedication that has to become the *modus vivendi*—the way of life, the deep-seated culture of every one of us. This was what I aimed to achieve.

Have you ever used team punishments?

I normally didn't use much punishment at all, but the way I see it, if someone makes a mistake, he's the one who has to pay for it. Why punish the others?

Many coaches say that it's important to know how to communicate effectively with the team. What do you think?

I think what's important is being consistent, pointing out salient things that serve to improve the team and the player. The hardest thing to do is to get the concept across that the more you play for the team and with the team, the more chance there is for greater success. Once a player said to me, "But if I run without the ball, the TV camera won't zoom in on me!" I told him that he was in the wrong profession: he should have been an actor, not a football player. The more intelligent a person is, the more refined his cultural background, the easier it is to convey these concepts, and counteract individualism and personal status-seeking. That's why it's important to pick players with these kinds of character traits.

How important is the club and the staff in terms of the success of the coach?

The club is essential. In many teams there's always someone who's at cross-purposes with everyone else, who just won't get on board. Instead, if the entire club is rowing in the same direction as the coach, his job will be much easier. The coach has to have staff who work together, who are sharp and efficient. I always included the staff when I had major decisions to make; I tried to create a proactive group, but one in which each person stayed in his own personal sphere without invading or overstepping into anyone else's space.

EMILIO SÁNCHEZ

Emilio Sánchez Vicario is a former tennis player from Spain. He's won several Grand Slam titles, including three in men's doubles (Roland Garros twice and the US Open once) and two in mixed doubles (Roland Garros and the US Open, both once). He won a silver medal in doubles for Spain at the 1988 Olympics in Seoul. Sánchez has tallied up 65 tournament wins throughout his career, 15 in singles and 50 in doubles (mostly with his longtime partner Sergio Casal). He was a long-standing member of Spain's Davis Cup team, which he captained for three years, leading his team to win the trophy in 2008.

Is tennis a sport that can be used as a metaphor for business managers?

In sport, from the first moment to the last, everyone works to win. In the business world, that's not always the case. In companies, often personal goals are more important than the collective goal of the organization. But I think that sport can be a valid metaphor, because it gives a universal life lesson: every relationship that we live with someone else, every goal that we have, is a game that we can always lose if we don't commit 200% of our effort and our focus to everything we do.

What are the conditions that make winning possible?

In sport, the combination of four factors (physical, technical, emotional, and motivational) is crucial to winning. The physical aspect is the simplest one, especially nowadays, when we know so much from an athletic standpoint. As far as the technical side, the game has really leveled off. Everyone knows how to do everything.

Talent and tactics are what you need to compete with top players, but the difference is your mind, emotions, and passion.

How do you train mentally?

In tennis, you prepare mentally by identifying the decisive points during a match that make you win or lose. The best players know how to recognize these key points, which become clear goals to achieve. The great players know how to give their best in game-changing moments, without getting overwhelmed by emotions.

What you can do when you train is to learn to study your opponent, so you can understand how to play those decisive moments, and practice those scenarios again and again, with pre-game repetition, which generates the self-confidence that helps you know how to handle the key moments in the match. But if during the match your emotions inhibit you, tactical preparation and self-confidence aren't enough. That's why you need to learn how to control your emotions. All players find ways to do this differently, depending on their personalities.

For example, when Andy Murray was young, he'd lose control in crucial moments—he'd get irritated and lose matches. With Ivan Lendl, his coach, he's managed to control these outbursts and channel his anger on the right track. That's what has allowed him to become an Olympic and US Open champion. You need to develop the capacity to have a structured personality that prevents outside events from having any influence. Self-esteem and self-efficacy increase when players don't perceive external threats, or when they're convinced they can control them.

Tennis is an individual sport, but it can also be played with a partner. What criteria are used in choosing a partner?

Tennis is an individual sport, but doubles bring in a team dimension. You can't simply think of yourself; you need to think about your partner also, and above all.

Choosing a partner is the key to success for a doubles team. The ideal partner is someone who compensates for your weaknesses with his strengths, and vice versa. To do this, you need to analyze your own game, and that's not a skill that all players have. That way you learn to recognize your personal style of play, and consequently the complementary characteristics of your potential partner. For example, with my partner Sergio Casal, I was a player with a consistently good serve who would take charge at critical moments. What I needed was a source of inspiration in those moments to spur me on to get the job done. And Sergio did just that. That's why we won everything.

When did you play on a doubles team that didn't work?

Once my Davis Cup captain insisted on making me play with Sergi Bruguera, someone I've never had a very good relationship with, and things didn't work out. At the time he was a great player—younger than me and higher up in the rankings—but on the court my personality crushed him and prevented him from playing well. This made us lose those famous decisive points. The great leaders in all sports are the ones who succeed in bringing together players from different generations: the experts, in the prime of their careers, and young players. Often this doesn't happen.

How did you lead the Davis Cup team as the captain?

As the captain, my ultimate goal was to make my team win on every court, both at home and away, where often we struggled. A Davis captain has some say in the decision-making process, because at home he can choose where to play, and he always decides who plays and how to play, even though in the end the players are the ones who go out on the court.

When you make these decisions, sometimes you have to know how to reconcile the needs of various actors—some even outside the team. For example, in 2008, in the semi-final with the US, I found myself in an awkward position between the president of the federation and my players. Playing at home, and as captain, I had the right to choose where the match would take place, but my decision conflicted with my president. I wanted to play in Barcelona, at sea level and on a slow surface, which suited us. The president preferred to play in Madrid, at an altitude of 800 meters, which means faster balls and conditions that favored our opponents. Of course Madrid was a more appealing location for him from a political and commercial standpoint. So I found myself having to take a stand, with the needs of my players on one hand, and the president, who had me hired, on the other. In the end, once the president's decision to play in Madrid was made official, I decided to side with the players, publicly contesting the federation's decision. This situation really pulled the group together, and enhanced the players' faith in me, and may have been the deciding factor in the final victory.

Once you beat the US, you played the final in Argentina. How did it go?

In the final in Argentina we showed up without Rafael Nadal, our best player, while they had David Nalbandian and Juan Martín del Potro, two top-ten players, and they clearly had all the odds in their favor. We all realized this, but I wanted to make my players understand the importance of the chance they had earned. At that point the greater part of the work was done. The desire to win, the need to beat the odds, and the conviction that we had gained after winning against the US drove us to victory.

From a psychological standpoint, what was the fundamental thing to do with the players?

Not all players handle the pressure of playing for their country. In some cases, if you see that they don't deal with this situation well, it's best to simply not call them, and to have players who might not be as good, but who are motivated and confident. If they give it 100% of their effort when they play, however things turn out, they won't be criticized. And a player who gives it everything he's got can make a major contribution to collective success, even if he loses a match. For example, if he tires out his opponent, fighting point by point, he forces his opponent to not play well (or not play as well) in his next match. And then you need to alleviate the pressure on the person who's playing.

It's especially important to show players opportunities. Simply to play in a Davis Cup final can be a once-in-a-lifetime opportunity in a tennis career. I stressed to my players that that had never happened to me in 14 years of playing: personal examples are always powerful! And to win it when you're playing away from home, and when you're not favored to win, with everything against you, is a chance to make history, which is a lot more than winning. That way, paradoxically, the things that look like obstacles or problems at first glance can become the most powerful motivational levers. Everyone has to be committed to this process of turning pressure into opportunity. Players shouldn't pressure one another; players' personal trainers have to work in the same direction. Even massage therapists make their contribution by preparing the players at the highest possible level.

"The things that look like obstacles or problems at first glance can become the most powerful motivational levers. Everyone has to be committed to this process of turning pressure into opportunity."

Tennis is an individual sport, but with the Davis Cup, as a coach, you had to try to build and manage relationships among players in a constructive way. How did you do it?

It's important to know how to leverage the relationships among players. David Ferrer, our best player, lost by a landslide to Nalbandian on the first day of the singles matches. From his statements after the match, I realized that he was very depressed, he'd lost his confidence. So I decided to replace him with Fernando Verdasco. Two days later, when Verdasco played his single, Ferrer was the first to motivate him and try to cheer him on, even though Verdasco was playing in Ferrer's place. At one point, at a tough moment in the match (his opponent was up two sets to one) I told Verdasco: "Turn around and look at David. See how he's cheering for you? Think of how he'd love to be in your place right now! Play for the team, not for yourself!" From then on he reacted. He turned the match around and he won.

Is it possible to influence the performance of the team through the ability to manage relationships with actors outside the team?

Of course, this is an important job for a coach. As for the final with Argentina, part of our success came from how we handled our relationships with various external actors. For example, we were always very open and obliging in interviews with the media, more so than the Argentineans. Our players met with children and signed autographs, while our opponents refused to. Even with the police who escorted us, and with the stadium employees, we were always very kind, to the point where in the end they didn't mind so much that we won—many Argentineans actually cheered for us. At least in part, hostility turned into affection, especially with the people nearest to us. All the ways we behaved were very much appreciated, creating a positive climate and the right atmosphere to enable our players to do their best.

You've created an academy that grows talented young tennis players, offering your own training model. What role does the concept of team play in this model, and how is it encouraged?

It's crucial to balance the individuality that typifies tennis with a team perspective. For example, we always encourage our tennis players to play doubles too. That way, they have to make an effort to understand their partner, which also helps them develop skills in self-assessment (Where and how can I improve?) and in analyzing opponents (How can I beat them?), and they can learn from their partners. All this creates the conditions for improving and increasing the chances of becoming successful athletes. What's more, all of our kids travel as a group; they all watch each other's matches, and are taught to celebrate the victories of their teammates. We think that if they help each other out, they can all become stronger, and turn a potentially negative feeling like envy, which drains so much energy and prevents players from succeeding, into the drive to emulate, which encourages learning and continuous improvement.

JULIO VELASCO

Originally from Argentina, Julio Velasco has coached several volleyball teams and won numerous championships in Italy. Velasco served as head coach for the Italian national men's team from 1989 to 1996, earning two World Championships, three European Championships, and five World League titles, in addition to a silver medal at the 1996 Olympics. Velasco went on to lead the Italian national women's team from 1997 to 1998, and following that took the helm for the national teams of the Czech Republic and Spain. Since 2011 he has led the Iranian national men's team.

What does it mean to be a team leader for a coach?

Being a coach, first and foremost, means managing people. This might seem obvious, but often we lose sight of certain key concepts regarding human behavior.

First of all, people aren't the roles they fill; instead they have their own unique characteristics, diverse personalities that often comprise contradictions and nurture interactions and relationships. Managing people in the sports world is simpler than in a business setting, because you work with teams that are all male or all female; this prevents potential conflicts that can arise between the sexes. Second, people form groups, a set of people who work together without a clear goal or pre-established roles and methods. In order for the group to function, it has to be united; there can't be any sub-groups. This is why the manager of the group has to encourage unity. It's better to have a group that bands together against the leader than a group with internal divisions. Third, people form a team when they accept and share a work method, when they respect roles and rules, and most importantly when things go wrong. A team that finds itself in a difficult situation, in terms of results or performance on the field, faces the challenge and overcomes it. These are circumstances in which the leader builds more than a just group; he builds something that will benefit future work.

What gives a team leader credibility?

I think that a team leader has three key characteristics. First, author-ity—in other words, how you communicate and manage the team. I don't believe that charisma alone is enough. Even when you have it, it's worthless unless you also have a deep understanding of what you're talking about. When the coach wants to be the boss without having the authority to do so, the team easily sees this and has no mercy. A thorough knowledge of contents is what it takes. You need to avoid platitudes, clichés, or general concepts gleaned from books.

Another critical factor is fairness. You need to be fair, but more importantly you need to *seem* fair. A leader can be tough, but he has to be tough with everyone. There can't be first-class and second-class team members; you can't modify your principles from one situation to another. Instead, many coaches are tough on the weak players and easy on the strong players, so none of them get any respect, and this fuels futile tensions in the team.

Lastly, a leader has to be himself; he mustn't try to imitate or to act like anyone else. He has to adopt a work method and management style that's consistent with his personality. Copying others because they've won just doesn't work; you risk making a fool of yourself. Everyone has his own personal style, which has be consistent with his background, values, and personality.

Is there one ideal model for team leadership?

No. Personnel management and team leadership styles always have to be taken in context. In the newspapers we often read about top teams, national teams, and popular sports, but there are countless coaches in the world who work with different levels of complexity.

Having one single model is comforting; it provides peace of mind; it minimizes the sense of uncertainty that we feel in the face of change. But it's wishful thinking. The world today is positivist: we want to turn everything into a science. I believe that we need to live with uncertainty, and we should do continual self-analysis; we should put ourselves out there, and strive to learn. We have to constantly question ourselves and try to verify whether the method we used to win is still the best one.

I realize that learning is vitally important. To be a good coach, a good leader, you have to have a healthy sense of curiosity about what you can learn. You need to have an open mind, which lets you see the world from different vantage points, knowing that there will always be a new angle to discover. I don't believe in a person who is successful always and everywhere. Results are always the sum of various combinations of factors that need to be identified and integrated.

Can the team leader be a role model for the team?

I've always believed in the power of passion I put into my work. It's essential to be a model for the team in terms of commitment, reliability, and professionalism. That's how you earn the respect and esteem of others, whether you win or not, and that's what makes people more willing to follow your lead.

You are a highly successful coach. What's your secret?

What's facilitated my career is the wide variety of experiences I've had, because this has enabled me to convey so many ideas to the people I've worked with. I focus a great deal on growth mechanisms. I've always been fascinated by the Socratic method of maieutics: the leader is like the philosopher who dialogues with the slave, to find a way to make people who are unaware of their own potential, or who don't recognize their own capabilities, grow. The leader has to help his team members discover their talents, to recognize and cultivate them. Some coaches think that the team has to depend on them, but I'm convinced the opposite is true: a great coach empowers the team to play well on its own, constantly striving to lead the team to achieve this goal.

GIANLUCA VIALLI

A former soccer player and coach, Gianluca Vialli is currently a television commentator. He played for Cremonese, Sampdoria, Juventus, and Chelsea, where he later took on the dual role of player-manager. He also managed Watford. As a player he's won 20 trophies, and is the only player in the world to win both gold and silver medals in all three major European competitions (Champions League, UEFA Cup, and Cup Winners' Cup). He also scored 286 goals in more than 500 games. Vialli is a sports consultant for Sky Italia, where he works as football analyst.

What are the main responsibilities of a coach?

A manager does 50% of his job when he chooses and signs his players in the summer. In fact, success depends a great deal on how the team is built. You need to find talented and skilful athletes who are also intelligent, professional, and highly motivated. It's essential to clearly define the club's goals and share them with all the members of the team, making sure they are all convinced those goals are achievable. In my opinion it is also better to openly communicate to fans and press the target for the season, as when everybody's expectations coincide it's easier to get the necessary support.

The next step is to motivate the team to achieve these goals. It's crucial to choose a philosophy toward the game that best serves to reach your goals, and to get the players to share this philosophy. The key is to put forward innovative ideas in a credible way. For example, when I played for Juventus, after just a few games our coach Marcello Lippi revolutionized the team's tactical formation, playing three strikers at the same time. He succeeded in convincing us that this formation was a good one because he justified the decision based on the attributes of the strikers. He proposed an idea

"It's crucial to choose a philosophy toward the game that best serves to reach your goals, and to get the players to share this philosophy."

that was simple, but revolutionary at the time—in other words, in a football team, the quality and effectiveness of the defensive game depends first and foremost on what the strikers do and how they move. The idea was counterintuitive, but logical; it pushed us to outrun the others and help one another out more on the pitch. And it worked great!

The last of a coach's responsibilities is day-to-day team management. This primarily involves showing the players how to overcome (or bypass!) obstacles that week after week make it complicated to reach their objectives. Last, the club's organization and the coach's skills have to create an atmosphere in which players feel they're in a position to do their best, and more importantly to improve from a professional point of view.

What lies at the basis of a coach's credibility?

It's the synthesis of three components: charisma, consistency, and dialogue. Charisma is the capacity to demonstrate your competence without lording it over anyone, putting yourself on the same level as the players. Consistency has a dual meaning. First, you need to demonstrate with actions what you say with words: you should never make promises to the players that you can't keep. For example, it's wrong to say things like, "With me, the fittest players will always be the ones who play." Because, in actual fact, the coach decides on the lineup by taking into account other variables as well, such as the strengths and weaknesses of the opposing team. Consistency also means that the ideas you propose to the players must be aligned with team goals. You need common sense and pragmatism. Finally, credibility takes for granted the ability to get the players involved. As I see it, this always implies dialogue: the ability to understand how the players think, what their personal preferences are, their support for the sport project.

Without this understanding, it's very unlikely that athletes will do what the coach asks with true conviction. Conviction and involvement are what it takes to make the team leaders help the coach to spread his ideas amongst the other teammates, and get them involved too. A coach builds and reinforces credibility in his work group day after day, practice after practice, match after match. But when the team "meets" a new coach, the willingness of the group to follow the new work philosophy with conviction depends on the coach's prior track record.

How do you encourage team members to participate in decision-making and to share their opinions?

When I started coaching, I really wanted to show my players that I'd thoroughly prepared for the game ahead of time, and that when it was over, I had understood everything that had happened. So I talked a lot, and when I asked for feedback I rarely got any. I found this situation annoying, because there was no dialogue, and I felt like the team wasn't participating, they weren't following me. Once I asked José Mourinho what to do. He answered very simply: "Try to be the last one to speak." And it works!

You've played on a number of teams throughout your career. Which ones did you find had the most team spirit, and why?

You can and should try to build team spirit in various ways. When I played with Sampdoria, the club and the president managed to inspire a powerful sense of belonging. Our manager, Vujadin Boškov, said that many of us were so dedicated to the club that we wore Sampdoria pajamas to bed! This feeling toward the club has to be encouraged. At the start of every season, the coach should take the players, especially the new ones, to visit the club's trophy room, its stadium, its offices. He should organize for the players to meet the fans, show video clips on the history of the club. This is a way to elicit a shared identity that is actually rooted in history, in the values, and in the profound meaning of what that organization represents for the people who work there today, and who worked there in the past, and for the fans.

At Sampdoria we were a group of young players who shared a dream: to win the first national championship in the history of a club with a long tradition, but that had never won a championship. We wanted to become the first and only ones in history, and we succeeded! At Juventus under Lippi, by contrast, the team spirit was fundamentally based on a simple motivation that the coach and the club conveyed to us: the "duty" to win a championship again in a team that had a tremendously successful history, but hadn't won for six years. It was about making 11 million Italian fans happy: a weighty responsibility, a difficult one, but it generated a very powerful motivational driver.

Last, on the Italian national team, with Azeglio Vicini as coach, the team spirit sprung from a sense of responsibility deriving from an awareness that we represented our country; we were united in the genuine pleasure of being together, which the coach knew how to encourage effectively.

How do you deal with every member of the team individually without giving the group the impression of using unfair or preferential treatment?

In a team, there have to be rules that are the same for everyone; but you need to interact with every single player differently, because every person is different. For example, I always played to the best of my ability when I had coaches who trusted me and gave me responsibilities—but this isn't the thing to do with everyone, because many players don't want to be given responsibility.

As a coach, I've always tried to establish a personal relationship with every athlete. In concrete terms, at the start of the season, I gave each player a form to fill in with his personal goals and the team goals, what he wanted to improve on and how, his strengths, his weaknesses, and how he intended to be useful to his teammates. Then I drew up a personal improvement plan. Periodically we verified progress on the plan, honestly assessing if, how, and how much the player was actually activating the plan in his daily behavior. The plan was based mostly on what he had written himself, so the player felt responsible for achieving it, and he would have a hard time coming up with excuses when he behaved in a way that wasn't helping him realize the plan. This was also a sign of listening and a message of planning for the players.

In your career you had quite an unusual experience,
because with Chelsea you were manager and player.
What lessons did you learn from that experience?

I found myself acting as coach as well as player quite suddenly. In 15 days I had to learn how to be a coach. Actually, I wasn't ready, and the team needed to get quick results, so I opted for the simplest solution: I duplicated the same teaching my former coaches had given me. I think that in situations like this one, when you change while work is "in progress," it's important to establish your legitimacy by making some new and personal contribution, but at the same time by providing continuity in some respects. For example, I didn't change the team leader, but I modified the tactical formation and brought in a new fitness coach, who would help us both in supporting the new formation, which was physically more demanding, and in minimizing the chance of injuries. These were two credible arguments.

Normally, it's hard to handle the transition from player to coach/player for two basic reasons. The first is that your role changes radically, and often neither you nor the players are ready for this change. I went from being a nice guy and a teammate to being the boss, who often has to make difficult, unpopular decisions. It's a transition that doesn't involve simply assigning responsibility; instead it can only happen with a profound change in how you interpret your role. The second reason is that it's hard to do two jobs well, especially very different, high-level jobs; you pay a high price in terms of the physical and nervous energy you expend. You can only succeed if you're actively supported by competent staff, a well-organized club, and a strong sense of your own abilities.

Being a player-manager is very similar, I guess, to acting in and directing a movie at the same time.

Your professional career has taken you to both Italy and England. This puts you in a privileged position to compare these two different socio-cultural contexts. What conclusions have you drawn?

Until 15 years ago, the differences were immeasurable, but they've lessened to some extent in recent years. In Italy, football is treated like a job from the time players are children. Success and results are the most important things. Young players are often taught that the end justifies the means: victory at all costs is what to strive for. In England, on the other hand, first and foremost football is considered a game, and children learn the important values of the game. English footballers feel it's a moral duty to give their utmost, and often they play more with their hearts than with their heads.

In your opinion, what are the key characteristics of a successful coach?

First of all, you need to know how to pick the right people. Beyond technical and athletic skills, players have to have rare but precious human qualities such as honesty, altruism, and capacity to face challenges—the desire for self-improvement. As coach at Watford, I made a mistake in choosing some players: we signed one particular player to make him into a leader, but after just two weeks it became clear that none of his teammates could stand him. It's very difficult to rectify errors made in building the team when it comes to team management.

Second, you can't be too rigid and inflexible. You also have to know how to get people involved. You can do this by making decisions yourself, or doing so democratically, depending on many factors, but it's indispensible to have the players' staunch support so they give it their all. The coach has to have a clear understanding of who decides what, who plays the key roles in the club, and he

"The coach has to have a clear understanding of who decides what, who plays the key roles in the club, and he has to try to have a direct relationship with these people." has to try to have a direct relationship with these people, who in most cases are the presidents. The coach should avoid having intermediaries who provide partial information, creating pointless pressure for the team, or conveying inappropriate messages to the media. What's more, a successful coach always knows when it's time to leave one position and embrace another. The timing as far as professional choices is key.

Last of all, you need to know how to "disconnect." Giovanni Trapattoni, the football coach with one of the best track records of all time, says that there are two kinds of coaches: the ones who've been fired, and the ones who are about to be fired. I say there's a third kind, and that's Alex Ferguson, who's been coaching Manchester United for more than 25 years. How does he do it? When I asked him the secret to his long "bench life," and advice on how to be a successful coach, he told me to learn to play the piano. I learned that you need to cultivate a variety of interests, because that's the only way you can handle the stress of a profession that's incredibly engaging, that absorbs you completely, and that can end up devouring you. It's a great lesson.

WHO'S WHO OF
SPORTS COACHES

The biographies of the coaches cited in Chapter 6 are included at the beginning of each interview.

Dick Allen

A former American Major League Baseball player, he played first and third base and outfield in the Major League, and ranked among the sport's top offensive players of the 1960s and early 1970s.

George Allen

An American football coach in the NFL and the United States Football League. Allen had the third best winning percentage in the NFL (.681), exceeded only by Vince Lombardi (.736) and John Madden (.731). He also never coached a team to a losing season. He was inducted to the Pro Football Hall of Fame in 2002.

Arnold "Red" Auerbach

An American basketball coach who headed the Washington Capitols, the Tri-Cities Blackhawks, and the Boston Celtics. As a coach, he won 938 games, a record upon his retirement, and nine

NBA championships (surpassed only by Phil Jackson). As general manager and team president of the Celtics, he won an additional seven NBA titles.

Silvio Baldini
An Italian soccer coach in the Serie A. He led Chievo Verona, Empoli, Lecce, Palermo, Parma, and Catania.

Mario Beretta
An Italian soccer coach in the Serie A. He headed Chievo Verona, Parma (qualifying for the UEFA Cup), Siena, Lecce, and Cesena.

Giuseppe Bergomi
A retired Italian soccer player who won the FIFA World Cup in 1982 and spent his entire career at Inter. He coached youth teams at Atalanta FC (Italian Football Serie A).

Bobby Bowden
A retired American college football coach who holds the NCAA record for most career and bowl wins. He coached the Florida State Seminoles from 1976 to 2009.

Paul "Bear" Bryant
An American college football player and coach. During his 25-year tenure as Alabama's head coach, he amassed six national championships and 13 conference championships.

Giancarlo Camolese
A former Italian soccer player, he has coached several Serie A teams, including Torino, Reggina, and Livorno.

Ken Carter
An American business owner, education activist, and former high school basketball coach. The story of his 1999 season is the basis

for the 2005 film *Coach Carter*. He continues to coach sports teams, except basketball. He coached the Slamball team Rumble, which he led to their first-ever Slamball Cup victory in the 2001/02 season.

Jack Clark

A former rugby player for University of California, Berkeley, and the US National Team. As head coach of the Cal Golden Bears, he won 22 national titles. Clark served as head coach of the US national team from 1993 to 1999, general manager for the national team from 1993 to 2003, and head coach for the Collegiate All-America team from 1985 to 1992.

Andrea Colombo

An Italian sprinter, he was a member of the national athletics team from 1993 to 2004, and finalist at the 2000 Sydney Olympics with the Italian 4×100 relay team. He has a university degree in psychology, and is an expert in applied sport psychology and mental training for athletes.

Serse Cosmi

An Italian soccer coach, he coached Perugia (qualifying for the UEFA Cup), Udinese, Brescia, Livorno, Lecce, Genoa, and Siena.

Hugh "Duffy" Daugherty

An American football player and coach. He served as head coach at Michigan State University from 1954 to 1972, where he compiled a career record of 109–69–5, winning two National Championships.

Gianni De Biasi

An Italian soccer coach and former player, he served as head coach for the Albanian national team, Udinese, Torino, Brescia, Modena, and Levante UD in Spain.

Luigi De Canio

An Italian soccer coach and former player. He has coached teams such as Lecce, Siena, Reggina, Napoli, Udinese, Pescara, and Genoa in Italy and Queens Park Rangers in England.

Ferdinando De Giorgi

A former Italian volleyball player who won World Champion titles in 1990, 1994, and 1998. He began his career as player–coach in 2000 at Cuneo, and stopped playing and continued coaching in 2002. With Lube Macerata he won the championship in his first season, a CEV Cup, two Italian Cups, and the Italian Super Cup. In the 2012/13 season he became coach at Fakel Nov Urengoi in Russia.

Luigi Delneri

An Italian soccer coach who has worked at Chievo Verona, FC Porto (Portugal), Roma, Palermo, Atalanta, Sampdoria, Juventus, and Genoa. In 2009, while at Sampdoria, he qualified for the Champions League.

Roberto Donadoni

A former Italian soccer player who with AC Milan won six national championships, three Champions Cups, two Intercontinental Cups, two European Super Cups, and four Italian Super Cups. He also played and coached the Italian national team, and in the Italian Serie A he coached Livorno, Napoli, Cagliari, and Parma.

Harvey A. Dorfman

An American mental skills coach who worked in education and psychology as a teacher, counselor, coach, and consultant. He earned World Series Championship rings by serving as a mental skills coach for the 1989 Oakland A's and the 1997 Florida Marlins.

Keith Edelman

An English businessman and the managing director of Arsenal Football Club from 2000 to 2008.

Mino Favini

Considered one of the greatest Italian soccer coaches of all time in the youth leagues. He coached for more than 20 years at Como and more than ten at Atalanta.

Sir Alex Ferguson

A Scottish soccer manager and former player who has managed Manchester United since 1986. His tenure has seen the club go through an era of success and dominance both in England and Europe, giving Ferguson a reputation as one of the most admired and respected managers in the history of the game.

Massimo Ficcadenti

A former Italian soccer player who has coached Reggina, Cesena, and Cagliari in Serie A.

John "Frenchy" Fuqua

A former American football running back in the NFL from 1969 to 1976. Over the course of his career, Fuqua played in 100 games, rushing for 3031 yards, and scoring 24 touchdowns.

Sandro Gamba

A former basketball player who won ten Italian national championships. He began coaching in 1965; in 1979 he took the helm of the Italian national team, winning a silver medal at the 1980 Moscow Olympics. In seven European Championships he won a gold medal in 1983, a bronze in 1985, and a silver in 1991. Since 2006 he's been a member of the Basketball Hall of Fame.

Gian Piero Gasperini

An Italian soccer coach who's led the Serie A teams Genoa, Inter, and Palermo. In 2008 he won Italy's prestigious "Silver Bench Award" as an outstanding coach.

Claudio Gentile

An Italian soccer coach and former player in the national team, winning the FIFA World Cup in 1982. He coached the Italian national under-21 football team, which won the 2004 UEFA European Under-21 Football Championship, and the Under-23 team, which won a bronze at the Athens Olympics in 2004.

Andrea Giani

A former Italian volleyball player and currently a coach. He played on the Italian national team that won three World and four European Championships. In 2007 he made his coaching debut, leading Modena to win a Challenge Cup. In the 2009/10 season, he coached M. Roma, where he won the A2 Italian Cup. In 2008 he was inducted into the Volleyball Hall of Fame.

Pasquale Gravina

A former Italian volleyball player who won six National League titles. He was a gold medalist in the 1994 and 1998 Volleyball World Championships, and also won gold in the 1993, 1995, and 1999 Volleyball European Championships, plus three Volleyball World Leagues. He won a silver medal at the 1996 Atlanta Olympics and a bronze at the 2000 Sydney Olympics.

Dan Henning

A former American football player and coach. He played quarterback at The College of William & Mary and professional football in 1966 for the American Football League's San Diego Chargers.

Gil Hodges

An American Major League Baseball first baseman and manager. He led the New York Mets to the 1969 World Series title, one of the greatest upsets in Series history.

Lou Holtz

A retired American football coach who has set records for being the only football coach to lead six different teams to bowl games, and four different programs to the final top 20 rankings. Holtz also coached the NFL New York Jets during the 1976 season.

Paul Howard

An American Major League Baseball executive who served as general manager of three teams and, perhaps most famously, as president of the New York Yankees under George Steinbrenner during the 1970s.

Paolo Indiani

An Italian soccer coach with more than 30 years' experience, he's headed several Italian minor league clubs, winning four championships.

Phil Jackson

A retired American basketball coach and former player, his reputation was established as head coach of the Chicago Bulls from 1989 to 1998, winning six NBA titles. His next team, the Los Angeles Lakers, won five NBA titles from 2000 to 2010.

Mike Krzyzewski

He has served as the head coach for men's basketball at Duke University. He has led the Blue Devils to four NCAA Championships, 11 Final Fours, 12 Atlantic Coast Conference (ACC) regular season titles, and 13 ACC Tournament championships. He is also the coach of the US men's national basketball team, which he led to two gold medals at the 2008 Beijing Olympics and 2012 London Olympics.

He was elected to the Naismith Memorial Basketball Hall of Fame in 2001.

Tony La Russa

A former Major League Baseball manager and infielder, best known for his tenures as manager of the Chicago White Sox, Oakland Athletics, and St Louis Cardinals. La Russa led teams to six league championships and three World Series titles, and ranks third in all-time major league wins by a manager.

Abe Lemons

An American college basketball coach and one of the most successful head coaches in Oklahoma history.

Vince Lombardi

An American football coach who is best known as the head coach of the Green Bay Packers during the 1960s, where he led the team to three straight league championships and five total in seven years, including winning the first two Super Bowls following the 1966 and 1967 NFL seasons. The National Football League's Super Bowl trophy is named in his honor. He was inducted into the NFL's Pro Football Hall of Fame in 1971.

Zare Markowski

A former basketball player and currently a coach. He has coached Air Avellino, Sassari, Reggio Emilia, Bologna, Milano, and Biancoblù Bologna in Italy, and Limoges Élite in France. His background includes experience and success with KK Skopje, the national Yugoslavian youth team, and the national Macedonian team – in addition to Fidefinanz Bellinzona and Lugano in Switzerland (where he won three national championships), and Darücafaka S.K. in Turkey.

Joanne P. McCallie

Head coach of the Duke University women's basketball team. McCallie is known as "Coach P" because of her maiden name. She became the first Division I head coach to win a conference title in four different leagues, and also the first Division I coach to be named conference Coach of the Year in four different conferences.

Steve McClaren

An English soccer manager and former player. His managerial career began at Middlesbrough in the Premier League, who won the League Cup in 2004 and were runners up in the 2006 UEFA Cup final. McClaren then served as manager of England from August 2006 to December 2007.

Ettore Messina

An Italian basketball coach. He has won four Euroleague championships as a head coach. He was named one of the 50 Greatest Euroleague Contributors. In 2012 he served as a consultant for the NBA's Los Angeles Lakers. In the 2012/13 season he serves as coach at CSKA Moscow.

Sam Mitchell

A retired American basketball player and former NBA head coach with the New Jersey Nets. He coached the Toronto Raptors from 2004 to 2008, and in 2007 was named the NBA Coach of the Year.

Gian Paolo Montali

An Italian volleyball coach who has won several championships and has led the Italian national team to win two European Championships (in 2003 and 2005), and the silver medal at the 2004 Olympic Games in Athens.

José Mourinho

A Portuguese soccer manager who has coached Porto, Chelsea, Inter, and Real Madrid. He's the fourth coach to have won league titles in at least four different countries (Portugal, England, Italy, and Spain). He also won the Italian league and cup, and the UEFA Champions League with Inter in 2010.

C.M. Newton

A retired American basketball player, coach, and administrator. He was inducted into the Naismith Memorial Basketball Hall of Fame as a Contributor in 2000.

Bill Parcells

An American football coach for the New York Giants, New England Patriots, New York Jets, and Dallas Cowboys. He won two Super Bowls with the New York Giants. He was also the general manager of the New York Jets and the executive VP of football operations with the Miami Dolphins.

Stefano Pioli

A former Italian soccer player with Juventus and Fiorentina, and coach of the Italian Serie A teams Parma, Chievo, Palermo, and Bologna.

Claudio Ranieri

A former Italian soccer player who has coached Napoli, Fiorentina, Parma, Roma, Juventus, and Inter in Italy, Chelsea in England, Monaco in France, and Valencia and Atlético Madrid in Spain. With Valencia he won the King's Cup and the European Super Cup.

Carlo Recalcati

An Italian basketball coach and former player. He coached the Italian national basketball team from 2001 to 2009, leading them to take the silver medal at the 2004 Olympic Games in Athens and the Bronze Medal at EuroBasket 2003.

Daniele Ricci

A former volleyball player who is currently a coach. In his career he won numerous titles with Ravenna: national league titles, the Italian Cup, the European Super Cup, the CEV Cup, and the World Championship, in addition to the national championship and Greek Cup in 2001 with Olympiakos. He also coached Panathinaikos.

Pat Riley

An American basketball executive and former NBA coach and player. He is team president of the Miami Heat. Widely regarded as one of the greatest NBA coaches of all time, Riley has served as the head coach of five championship teams and an assistant coach to another team. He was named NBA Coach of the Year three times (1989/90, 1992/93, and 1996/97, as head coach of the Los Angeles Lakers, the New York Knicks, and the Miami Heat respectively).

Delio Rossi

A former Italian soccer player who has coached various Series A teams: Lecce, Atalanta, Lazio, Palermo, Fiorentina, and Sampdoria. He won an Italian Cup with Lazio.

Dean Smith

A retired American head coach of men's college basketball. Called a "coaching legend" by the Basketball Hall of Fame, he's best known for his successful 36-year coaching tenure at the University of North Carolina.

Luciano Spalletti

A former Italian soccer player who has coached several Serie A teams – Empoli, Sampdoria, Udinese, and Roma – leading the latter to win two Italian Cups and an Italian Super Cup. He coaches the Zenit San

Pietroburgo in Russia, and has won two championships, a Russian Cup, and a Russian Super Cup.

Jerry Tarkanian

Also known as "Tark the Shark," he is a retired college basketball coach and one of the few to lead three different schools to 20-win seasons, each time in his first year.

Graham Taylor

Best known as the manager of the England national soccer team from 1990 to 1993, he has also been the manager of Watford, a club he took from the fourth division to the first in just five years, and then – two decades later – from the bottom of the second division to the Premier League in two seasons.

Colin Todd

An English soccer manager and former player. He has served as manager of several English league clubs – Middlesbrough, Bolton Wanderers, Swindon Town, Derby County, Bradford City, and Darlington – as well as the Danish Superliga side Randers FC. He led Bolton Wanderers to win the Division 1 title with 98 points and 100 goals.

Jean Todt

A French racing car driver. After a successful career as a rally co-driver, he made his reputation in motor sport management: first with Peugeot Talbot Sport and then with Scuderia Ferrari, before being appointed chief executive officer of Ferrari from 2004 to 2008. Since 2009 he has served as president of the Fédération Internationale de l'Automobile (FIA). During his stint at Ferrari, the Scuderia won a total of 13 Formula One World Championship titles (drivers and manufacturers).

Bill Walsh

A former head coach of the San Francisco 49ers and the Stanford Cardinals American football teams. Walsh achieved a 102–63–1 record with the 49ers, winning ten of 14 post-season games along with six division titles, three NFC Championship titles, and three Super Bowls. He was named the NFL Coach of the Year in 1981 and 1984. In 1993, he was elected to the Pro Football Hall of Fame.

John Wooden

An American basketball player and coach. Nicknamed the "Wizard of Westwood," he won ten NCAA national championships in a 12-year period (seven in a row) as head coach at UCLA. He was named national Coach of the Year six times.

Bill Yoast

An American high school football coach best known for being featured in the 2000 film *Remember the Titans*. His 1971 season at T.C. Williams High School served as the inspiration for the movie. The team enjoyed a dominant season, taking the state title and earning a second-place national ranking.

Alberto Zaccheroni

An Italian soccer coach who won the Asian Cup with the Japanese national team in 2011. He is best known for managing a number of top clubs in the Italian Serie A, and won a national championship with AC Milan in 1999. He also coached Udinese, Lazio, Inter, Torino, and Juventus.

Walter Zenga

A former Italian soccer player, he played goalkeeper for Inter and the Italian national team. He was elected Goalkeeper of the Year three consecutive times by IFFHS and UEFA. As a coach, he's led the New England Revolution in the US; National Bucarest, Steaua Bucarest, and Dinamo Bucarest in Romania (winning a national championship); Crvena Zvezda in Serbia (winning a national championship and a Serbian Cup); Gaziantepspor in Turkey; Al-Ain in the United Arab Emirates; Catania and Palermo in the Italian Serie A; and Al-Nasr at Dubai.

INDEX